T0311608

SERIES ON
ECONOMIC DEVELOPMENT
AND GROWTH VOL. 1

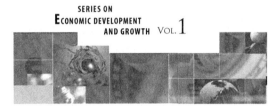

GLOBALISATION AND
ECONOMIC GROWTH
IN CHINA

Series on Economic Development and Growth   (ISSN: 1793-3668)

SERIES ON
ECONOMIC DEVELOPMENT
AND GROWTH   VOL. 1

GLOBALISATION AND
ECONOMIC GROWTH
IN CHINA

Edited by

Yang Yao
Beijing University, China

Linda Yueh
University of Oxford & London School of Economics and Political Science, UK

 **World Scientific**

NEW JERSEY · LONDON · SINGAPORE · BEIJING · SHANGHAI · HONG KONG · TAIPEI · CHENNAI

Published by

World Scientific Publishing Co. Pte. Ltd.

5 Toh Tuck Link, Singapore 596224

USA office: 27 Warren Street, Suite 401-402, Hackensack, NJ 07601

UK office: 57 Shelton Street, Covent Garden, London WC2H 9HE

Library of Congress Cataloging-in-Publication Data
Globalisation and economic growth in China / edited by Yang Yao &
Linda Yueh.
p. cm. -- (Series on economic development and growth, 1793-3668 ; vol. 1)
Includes bibliographical references and index.
ISBN-13 978-981-256-855-7
ISBN-10 981-256-855-7
1. China--Economic conditions--21st century--Congresses. 2. Globalization--China--
Congresses. 3. China--Economic policy--Congresses. I. Yao, Yang. II. Yueh, Linda Y.
(Linda Yi-Chuang)

HC427.95 .L74 2005
330.951--dc22

2006048637

British Library Cataloguing-in-Publication Data
A catalogue record for this book is available from the British Library.

First published 2006 (Hardcover)
Reprinted 2016 (in paperback edition)
ISBN 978-981-3203-29-7

Printed in Singapore

ACKNOWLEDGEMENTS

CENTRE *for* ECONOMIC
PERFORMANCE

Many of the papers from the volume were from the first annual LSE-PKU conference held at Beijing University in August 2005. The output therefore reflects in large part the fruitful collaboration between the China Center for Economic Research (CCER) at Beijing University and the London School of Economics, particularly the Globalisation Programme at the Centre for Economic Performance (CEP). The book benefited greatly from the editorial work of Gillian Lodge, and the support of the CCER, CEP and the LSE Partnership Programmes Office.

Finally, we are pleased to be the first volume of the Series on Economic Development and Growth published by World Scientific, and would like to thank the publishers, particularly Max Phua, Chean Chian Cheong and Yvonne Tan Hui Ling.

CONTENTS

Part III: Conclusions and Implications

CHAPTER 1

INTRODUCTION

Yang Yao & Linda Yueh

In the 27 years since market-oriented reforms were introduced, China has grown remarkably well and has emerged onto the world stage as a major economic presence, particularly since accession to the World Trade Organisation (WTO) in 2001. China's influence on the regional and world economy is notable, as are the effects of further integration with the international economic order on China's growth prospects and the direction of its development.

The book brings together a collection of papers on the topic of China's economic growth prospects and reforms in the context of globalisation. The question of the sustainability of China's continuing economic reform and the necessary reforms to sustain that growth are among the questions explored in this volume. Also, the considerable effects of integration into the global economy and its implications for the conduct of Chinese economic policies, including its exchange rate regime and trade policy, are examined. The influence of China on the regional and world economy is the final area of coverage. China's competitiveness in exports has begun to challenge the market share of developing and developed economies and its role in intra-regional trade and monetary cooperation will be explored.

The first section of the book focuses on internal elements of China's reform path. The section starts with a chapter by leading economist, Justin Yifu Lin, who provides a cogent analysis of economic growth in China. He analyses why it was possible for China to maintain a high growth rate alongside falling energy consumption during a deflationary period. He also discusses the prospect for China's long-term growth,

1

including the effects of WTO accession and global integration in stimulating economic growth.

The next chapter by Ping Chen analyses transition in China as compared with the former Soviet Union and Eastern Europe as an interplay between state and market. He argues that market forces alone are insufficient to support marketisation, and China's experience suggests that decentralised experimentation with reforms and an active role of the state are necessary for a stable transition.

The final chapter in this section focuses on a key area of internal reform that has significance for global integration and indeed the effects of globalisation for China. Ligang Song and Yang Yao find, using firm-level data from China, that privatisation has had a significant and positive impact on firm profitability, but no effect on unit cost and labour productivity. Increasing private share ownership was found to have a positive effect on profitability but only under the condition that the amount of private share ownership passes a certain threshold. They conclude that when there is no external share ownership, it takes time for a reformed state-owned enterprise to overcome the inertia inherited from the command period. For *gaizhi* (enterprise restructuring) to be effective in improving firms' performance, they argue that it has to be connected with a certain degree of privatisation.

The second part of the book comprises five chapters on external sector reforms in China and an analysis of the wider impact of China's increased openness. The topics covered include exchange rate reform, structure and policies; the impact of China's international trade; and monetary issues in the Asian region. Eswar Prasad, Thomas Rumbaugh, and Qing Wang review the issues involved in moving towards greater exchange rate flexibility and capital account liberalisation in China. They argue that a more flexible exchange rate regime would allow China to operate a more independent monetary policy, providing a useful buffer against domestic and external shocks. At the same time, weaknesses in China's financial system suggest that capital account liberalisation poses significant risks and should be a lower priority in the short term. This chapter concludes that greater exchange rate flexibility is in China's own interest and that, along with a more stable and robust financial system, it should be regarded as a prerequisite for undertaking a substantial liberalisation of the capital account.

The next two papers concern international trade. Linda Yueh examines the widespread perception that China's competitive strength has had a harmful impact on other countries, particularly its export-led Asian neighbours. She finds that since China undertook its "open door" policy in the early 1990s, China has transformed itself into one of the most open economies in the world with an export-to-GDP ratio of 30% and one that accounts for an impressive 6% of the global manufacturing export market. It is a market share that rivals the old and new Asian "tiger" economies, which are known for their export-oriented growth strategy. She finds that China's growth in global market share has been accompanied by a growth in market share by all of the developing Asian nations except for Hong Kong, whose analysis is complicated by its rejoining China during this period. She finds that there is also evidence of a rise in intra-industry trade in the region, which suggests closer trade links through production chains in Asia. She concludes that China may well be a centre for attracting foreign direct investment (FDI) in the region, and its competitiveness has not inflicted harm on its neighbours.

The next paper by Christer Ljungwall and Örjan Sjöberg examines the effects of globalisation in Pacific Asia, which has resulted in rapidly growing international flows of goods, portfolio capital, and direct investments. At the same time, several countries have shifted from a command to market economy. Against this background, they analyse the popular model used to depict the process of economic integration and development in Pacific Asia, the "flying geese" pattern of shifting comparative advantage. They find that China will start to realign the flying geese pattern of regional economic integration along a different path than that which has prevailed during most of the post-war period. The drivers of this shift will be dependent not only on comparative advantage but also global trends in globalisation, political factors and development of markets in Asia.

The final two chapters in this section relate to trade policy and regional monetary agreements, placing China in the wider context. The first is by Razeen Sally, who looks at China's trade policy developments compared with related trends in India and southeast Asia. First, the chapter sets China, India and southeast Asia in the context of economic globalisation and policy reforms around the world. Then, he examines their trade policy frameworks, including linking recent reforms to domestic economic policies, and to foreign policy and trade diplomacy. The central argument is that trade policy matters more than trade negotiations. There has been a significant degree of trade and investment liberalisation, but this has happened unilaterally for the most part, rather than through trade negotiations, whether in the WTO or via free trade agreements (FTAs). Trade negotiations have distinct and perhaps increasing limitations, and their effects should not be exaggerated. There is strong evidence, therefore, to rely on the unilateral engine of free trade with China setting the late 20th/early 21st century example, much as Britain did in the second half of the 19th century. This is expected to have powerful emulatory effects elsewhere, particularly in Asia. He concludes that a combined 'China-and-India' effect, with India accelerating liberalisation in response to China, will send even stronger liberalisation signals throughout the region.

The next paper by He Fan, Zhang Bin and Zhang Ming examines monetary cooperation in Asia and the role of China. After the Asian financial crisis, the pace of regional monetary cooperation in Asia has picked up. They argue that entering the new century, Asian economies are facing new external risks. Without coordinated efforts these risks can easily develop into financial crises. The chapter puts forth the argument that the Chiang Mai Initiative (CMI) is a stepping-stone for launching full-fledged Asian monetary cooperation, but has problems and defects. The authors suggest that the multilateralisation of the CMI can both enhance its function as a liquidity provider and pave the way for a future regional common monetary arrangement. Exchange rate coordination should also be added to the agenda but the proposals examined in this paper are not realistic in the sense that individual countries are not willing to give up the autonomy of domestic policy formation.

Multilateralisation of the CMI can help to bridge the gap and eliminate some obstacles. The authors conclude with an analysis of the role of China in Asian monetary cooperation and its attitude toward the multilateralisation of the CMI.

The final chapter of the book is by Justin Yifu Lin and the two editors of the volume. In this piece, the authors assess China's economic reforms in the context of globalisation. They argue that the reforms undertaken in China must be consistent with its gradualist approach to transition and a slower pace of liberalisation due to its developing country status. The chapter then analyses major aspects of external reforms in China, including trade and exchange rates, followed by an analysis of China's wider economic impact. The chapter concludes with a view on how China has been affected by and benefited from globalisation, and also how it has changed the global economy in terms of trade, capital flows, global commodities markets, and influenced global incremental growth.

This book addresses a number of pressing questions for both academics and policymakers. As China becomes increasingly important in the global economy, the question of the sustainability of its growth is relevant worldwide. This collection of papers reflects research on key questions relating to China's development and growing influence.

PART I

GROWTH AND INTERNAL REFORMS

CHAPTER 2

IS CHINA'S GROWTH REAL AND SUSTAINABLE?

Justin Yifu Lin

China Center for Economic Research, Beijing University

Abstract: Since the reforms of 1978, China's overall economic performance has been remarkable. Average annual GDP growth rate reached 9.4% between 1978 and 2004. However, in the last few years, the robustness of China's economic growth has been questioned, with deflation particularly evident at the end of 1997. In spite of the Chinese government's many efforts, this deflation persisted until 2003. Deflation in an economy is normally accompanied by stagnation of the economy or slower than average rate of GDP growth. However, China's GDP growth rate still reached 7.8% during the deflationary period between 1998 and 2002. The growth rates achieved were the greatest by any economy over this period globally. Moreover, energy consumption dropped in 1998 and 1999. This abnormality prompted some economists to question the reliability of China's statistics. In this paper, the author analyses why it was possible for China to maintain high growth rates alongside a reduction in energy consumption during the deflationary period. We also suggest a way for China to absorb excess capacity and move away from deflation. The author will also discuss the prospects for China's long-term growth.

1. Introduction

Since the reforms of 1978, China's overall economic performance has been remarkable. The average annual growth rate of Gross Domestic Product (GDP) reached 9.4% in the period 1978-2004[1]. However, as shown in Figure 1, the economy has experienced several growth and inflation cycles since the beginning of these reforms.

---

[1] Unless specified, the statistical figures in the paper are taken directly or are calculated from figures in the various issues of *China Statistical Yearbook*.

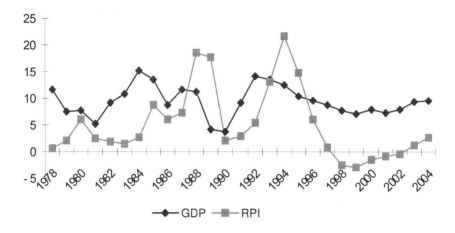

Figure 1. Annual Growth Rates of GDP and Retail Price from 1978 to 2004
Source: Various Issues of *China Statistical Yearbook.*

Before 1993, the boom in growth was primarily as a result of an increase of investment following the government's relaxation of investment and credit controls. A rush in investment would generally result in the expansion of credit and money supply in the economy, which in turn should result in inflationary pressures. Following the implementation of a retrenchment program to control inflation, the economic growth rate would be expected to subsequently drop (Lin *et al.*, 1996).

The Chinese government adopted a retrenchment program in 1994 to control investment and stop overheating. As shown in Figure 1, economic growth rate began a gradual slowdown in 1995 though it was maintained at a relatively high level. At the end of 1997, the Chinese economy started to show signs of deflation. In 1998, the Chinese government under the leadership of the then new Premier Zhu Rongji altered its economic policy by adopting a package of expansionary fiscal policies to both stimulate economic growth and to pull the economy out of the deflation it was experiencing.

However, these policy changes did not achieve the economic outcome that might have been expected. Deflation persisted. The retail price index dropped 2.6 percentage points in 1998, 3.0 percentage points in 1999, 1.5 percentage points in 2000, 0.8 percentage points in 2001, and 1.3 percentage points in 2002. Furthermore, inflation did not return to positive territory until 2003.

Deflation in an economy is normally accompanied by economic stagnation or slow growth in GDP[2]. However, China's GDP growth rate reached 7.8 % in 1998 and maintained these relatively high levels in the years following. Specifically, Chinese GDP growth rates stood at 7.1% in 1999, 8.0% in 2000, 7.5% in 2001, and 8.0% in 2002. While these rates were all lower than the average annual growth rate of 9.8% in the previous period of 1978-97, they were the highest growth rates posted by any economy globally during those five years.

Alongside these high growth rates was a reduction in energy consumption in 1997, 1998 and again in 1999. A high economic growth rate is in general associated with increased economic activity, which in turn is associated with higher than average energy consumption. However, in those three years, annual energy consumption fell by 0.8%, 4.1%, and 1.6% per annum respectively. The incongruency of Chinese growth rates with existing international experiences during deflationary periods and the inconsistency between high growth rates and falling energy consumption made some economists question the reliability of China's growth statistics (Rawski 2002, Zhou *et al.*, 2002). According to Rawski, the estimate of GDP growth rate in China during the deflationary period should have been at most 3% instead of the 7-8% as claimed by the Chinese government.

In this paper I analyse how and why it was possible for China to maintain dynamic growth during the deflationary period from 1998 to 2002 and discuss the policy options available to the Chinese government for escaping from this period of deflation. I also assess China's potential for maintaining dynamic growth in the coming decades.

---

[2] See Bordo and Redish (2001) for an interesting historical study on the effect of deflation on output.

2. Investment Rush and Chinese Deflation

Deflation is the economic phenomenon characterised by a continuous decline in the general price level in the economy. Theoretically, deflation is either caused by an overall drop in demand in the economy, or a sharp increase in supply.

The decline in demand might be as a result of changes in household wealth following the collapse in the financial or real estate markets. The reduction in the aggregate level of national wealth would eventually lead to a decline in domestic consumption. At the same time, the level of bad loans may increase while credit contracts and investment demand decreases. As is well known, the 1929 stock-market crash in the US and the consequent deflation that persisted throughout the Depression were a result of the stock market bubble bursting and the consequent breakdown of the financial system. These led to a sharp decline in consumption and investment demand.

The Japanese deflation from 1991 onwards is also a result of the retraction of the stock market and real estate market. These market crashes reduced the likelihood of investment, with the overall effect being a decrease in labour income and worsening consumption. With the decline in consumption and investment, GDP growth rates would be expected to be minimal or even negative unless the government actively intervenes by increasing fiscal expenditure sufficiently to offset the decline in demand[3].

Economists in the world (and in China) tend to emphasize the demand side factors in their analyses of deflation (Bordo and Redish, 2001; Yi 2000). Whether these demand side factors can explain China's deflation can only be assessed through empirical analysis.

---

[3] Theoretically, the demand drop could also result from credit contraction, which leads to an increase in real interest rates and a decline in investment and current consumption. The decline in investment and possible massive bankruptcies along with a reduction in consumption may lead, in turn, to enterprises operating below capacity.

We examine the stock market, real estate market and other possible demand side factors and show that none of them could be responsible for the cause of China's deflation (Lin, 2000).

We have already mentioned that the declines in the stock and real estate markets triggered both the Great Depression in the US and the more recent deflationary period in Japan. However, as the Chinese stock and real estate markets work under a special institutional environment and are still relatively insignificant in relation to the aggregate size of the Chinese economy, their effects in terms of total demand should not be overestimated.

Figure 2. Shanghai Stock Index 1990-2002

Although the level of debt and bad loans in China's banking system are high, there is no inevitability that this would lead to a financial crisis provided that the public still maintain confidence in the banking system. This is quite different from the situation in other East Asian countries. In May 1997 the Chinese stock market experienced a shock; the 'Shanghai Stock Index' fell by one-third; transactions decreased significantly and many shareholders suffered severe losses (Figure 2). However, since the Chinese stock market was only created in the early 1990s, its impact was still quite insignificant relative to the national economy as a whole. The percentage of household financial assets held in the form of stocks and shares were very low. As shown in Table 1, the share was only 7.7% in 1997. In addition to the low exposure households had to stock markets, stock and other securities' prices moved in opposite directions in the markets further reducing the impact of stock market movements. In 1997, 11.9% of households' financial assets were held in the form of government bonds, which was far higher than the share of stock assets. The drop in stock-market prices led to an increase in the price of alternative securities. This resulted in partially offsetting the adverse effects of the initial dip in share prices.

Table 1. The Structure of Households' Financial Assets (%)

Year	Currency	Deposit	Bonds	Stocks	Insurance Reserve	Total
1992	19.3	60.6	15.1	3.9	1.2	100
1993	22.4	66.6	5.9	3.9	1.2	100
1994	13.7	79.4	5.6	0.5	0.7	100
1995	5.0	87.1	6.6	0.3	1.0	100
1996	7.1	77.5	11.5	2.8	1.2	100
1997	10.9	67.1	11.9	7.7	2.5	100

Source: Data provided by PBOC, Survey and Statistical Bureau, quoted in Liu Hongru & Li Zhiling (1999).

In fact, shareholders in China know very well the risk of stock market price fluctuations due to the fact that they have experienced a number of stock market crashes in the past (as shown in Figure 2). There is no clear correlation between stock market price fluctuations and the overall economic growth in China. For example, during the economic boom of 1992-94, China experienced a stock market crash. Therefore, whilst fluctuations in the stock market may lead to temporary financial losses for shareholders, its impact on the overall wealth of households is not significant. From Table 2 it can also be seen that direct private finance (through the stock-market) constitutes only a small share of the total financial resources of Chinese enterprises (less than 5%). The financing of enterprises was not heavily dependent on the stock market, and as such does not have a significant influence on firms' financial position. Stock market fluctuations will therefore not lead to significant changes in the behavior of firms and households[4]. The proposition that the decline in stock market prices led to the contraction in total demand and is the primary reason underpinning the current period of deflation is unsupported.

Table 2. The Structure of Finance in Chinese Enterprises (%)

	1989	1990	1991	1992	1993	1994	1995	1996
Direct Finance	3.37	2.35	3.24	6.27	5.82	4.29	3.59	3.53
Indirect Finance	96.63	97.65	96.96	93.73	94.18	95.71	96.41	96.47

Source: Ming and Guoliang (1999).

In 1992, there was a nationwide 'development zone fever' and 'real estate fever' where real estate speculation was widespread, resulting in sharp increases in real estate prices. Real estate developers, as opposed to private households participating in increased land and home ownership, primarily drove the speculation. In 1993 and 1994 the central government's retrenchment program led to the collapse of the real estate bubble and a retraction in the real estate market. If the real estate bubble collapse had affected overall demand, the effect should have appeared in 1995 and 1996; however, aggregate deflation did not really appear until 1998.

The real estate market in China is quite different from that in other countries. Land is generally owned by the state instead of by households and as such the rise and fall of real estate prices has very little effect on the wealth of individuals. Real estate developers and the banks, which make many of the loans to developers, were the institutions that were mostly affected by realignments in the real estate market. With the exception of a few areas, the decline in real estate markets did not lead to a significant drop in real estate prices; instead, it only resulted in real

---

[4] This may explain why the boom in stock market from 1998 to 2001 coexisted with the deflation as shown in Figure 2.

estate market transactions coming to a halt and banks facing increased difficulties in ensuring loan repayments. Since most investments in real estate are as a result of bank loans and public funds, the pressure of repayment is limited. Loan providers do not especially want to see shrinking book values from the forced sale of real estate at discounted prices. It is safe to say that the retraction in the real estate market had a very limited effect on household consumption.

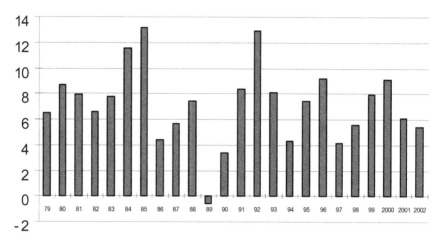

Figure 3. Annual Consumption Growth Rate
Source: SSB, *China Statistical Yearbook* (2002), p. 68.

It is important to note from Figure 3 that aggregate domestic consumption still grew above 5% in the years after 1997 during the deflationary period. Average growth rates were 6.8% in the period between 1998-2002, which was not very different from the average rate of 7.2% in the two decades between 1978 and 1997. From Figure 3, it can be inferred that the current deflation was not caused by any reduction in household consumption resulting from the decline in the stock and real estate markets[5].

---

[5] Lin (2000) examines the credit and monetary supply in China and concludes that the deflation was not caused by a credit squeeze.

As the deflation in 1998-2002 cannot be explained by changes in demand side factors, the only other possibility is that the deflation arose from a sudden shift or increase on the supply side. China's annual GDP growth rate averaged 9.8% between 1979 and 1998. Total GDP in 1998 was 6.4 times aggregate GDP in 1978 and the value added in the industrial sectors was 9.4 times that achieved in 1978 (SSB 1999a). The traditional pattern of economic shortages in a socialist economy had come to an end in China in the early 1990s following the abolition of all kinds of rationing activity. Immediately following the end of the rationing era, over-supply and competition prevailed in most markets and production capacity was widely underutilised.

Over-supply has become very common in the economy, as shown clearly in Table 3. By 1995, the production capacity utilisation rate was only around 50% in many important manufacturing industries; in some cases, the rate was even lower, standing at less than 40%. If high inventories are taken into account, the over-capacity problem is even more acute than the figures may initially suggest. It is estimated that in about half of the industries in China, production capacity utilisation rate is less than 60% with the lowest being 10% (Mao, 1999).

Table 3. Production Capacity Utilization Rates for Major Industries in 1995

Goods	Production Capacity Utilization rate	Goods	Production Capacity Utilization rate	Goods	Production Capacity Utilization rate
Black & white TV	47.8	Machine-Made Sugar	56.7	Partially Made Medicine	34.3
Colour TV	46.1	Chemical Fiber	76.4	Tyres/ Shoe	54.7
Household Refrigerator	50.4	Distilled Spirit	64.9	Chemical Fibre	76.4
Washing Machine	43.4	Car Manufacturing	44.3	Large and Medium Tractor Manufacturing	60.6
Popular Video Tape Recorder	40.3	Motor-Cycle Manufacturing	61.6	Small Tractor Manufacturing	65.9
Domestic Air Conditioning	33.5	Internal Combustion Machines	43.9	Oxidation Aluminium	66.3
Video Camera	12.3	Steel	62	Cement	72.9
Radio and Tape Recorder	57.2	Copper Processing	51.4	Chemical Pesticide	41.6
Printing and dyeing cloth	23.6	Metal Cutting Machinery Manufacturing	46.2	Heat-proof Materials	26.2

Source: SSB (1997), pp. 454-455.

3. Production Capacity

Increases in production capacity are mainly as a result of investment in fixed assets, such as machinery, assembly lines, factories, infrastructure and technological innovation, with the latter being usually embodied in new fixed assets. It is necessary to examine the state of fixed assets to understand the changes in production capacity. Figure 4 gives the lead coefficient of fixed asset investment over household consumption. The lead coefficient is defined as the difference between the index of fixed asset investment and the index of average household consumption level.

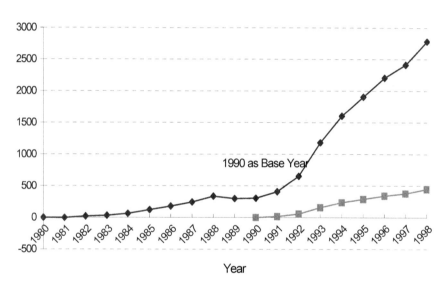

Figure 4. The Lead Coefficient of Fixed Asset Investment Growth over Consumption Growth

Notes:

1. Since 1997, with the exceptions of real estate, rural collective and individual investment, the statistical starting-point for basic construction, renovation and other forms of fixed asset investment rose from 50,000 to 500,000 RMB.

2. The lead coefficient is defined as the difference between the index of the fixed asset investment and the index of the average household consumption level. Taking 1980 as the base year means that the index of fixed asset investment and the index of household consumption level are both assumed to be 100 in 1980. Taking 1990 as the base year means that the index of fixed asset investment and the index of household consumption level are both set at 100 in 1990.

Source: SSB (1999c), pp. 27, 41.

Taking 1980 as the base year (=100), in 1990 the coefficient (of fixed asset investment over household consumption) had risen to 305.2. From 1991 it increased rapidly and the coefficient reached 2206.8 in 1996, and further increased to 2782.9 in 1998. If 1990 is taken as the base year, the coefficient was 342.1 in 1996, rising to 447.4 in 1998. The increase in the lead coefficient is mainly due to an increase in the growth rate of fixed asset investment, which was 19.5% and 16.5% per annum in the sixth Five-year Plan period (1981-1985) and the seventh Five-year Plan period (1986-90) respectively. However, the growth rate of fixed asset investment jumped to 36.9% in the eighth Five-year Plan period (1991-1995).

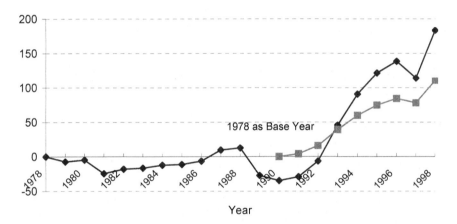

Figure 5. The Lead Coefficient of Growth of Net Value of Fixed Assets over Final Consumption

Note: The lead coefficient is defined as the difference between the index of net value of fixed asset and the index of final consumption. Taking 1978 as the base year means that the index of net fixed asset and the index of final consumption are both set at 100 in 1978. Taking 1990 as the base year means that the index of net value of fixed asset and the index of final consumption are both set at 100 in 1990.

Source: SSB (1999c), p. 76; SSB, State Economic Accounting Division (1997), pp. 42, 76.

As a result of the rapid growth of fixed asset investment, production capacity in the economy (represented by the net value of fixed assets) quickly exceeded the economy's final aggregate demand. Figure 5 depicts the lead coefficient of the net value of fixed assets (production capacity) over final consumption, which is defined as the difference between the index of the net value of fixed assets and the index of final consumption. Taking 1978 as the base year, the figures illustrate that since 1993, the growth in the net value of assets has begun to rapidly exceed the growth rate of final demand and that the difference is increasing.

In 1992 the difference in these two indices was still −6.5. In 1993 it turned positive to reach 45.9 with a further increase to 138.6 in 1996 and to 183.3 in 1998. If 1990 is used as the base year, the point can be seen more clearly. If the difference between the index of the net value of fixed assets and the index of final demand in 1990 is assumed to be zero, in 1996 the growth of the net value of fixed asset exceeded the growth in final demand by 84.4%; and in 1998 by 110.4 %. In other words, from 1990 to 1998, the formation of net fixed assets (production capacity) exceeded the growth in final consumption by over 100%.

Taking the state-owned economy as an example, the net value of fixed assets increased from 1,089 billion RMB in 1990 to 2,959 billion RMB in 1995, corresponding to a 273% increase. Since technological innovation is embodied in new fixed assets, the production capacity in 1995 is at least 2.7 times that of the capacity in 1990. The non-state-owned economy grew faster than the state-owned economy in the same period. However, the increase in consumption demand was constrained by the increase in income. During the eighth Five-year Plan period, income growth was only slightly higher than that of the 1980s[6], thus final consumption could not grow in line with the growth of production capacity. In the 1980s, the difference between production capacity growth and final demand growth was offset by economic shortages that existed long before the introduction of reforms. However, by the 1990s the long-existing shortages in the Chinese economy had come to an end and the difference between the growth of production capacity and demand led to the situation shown in Table 3.

---

[6] The GDP growth rates for sixth, seventh, and eighth Five-year Plans were 10.8%, 7.9%, and 11.6%, respectively.

In summary, it was primarily over-investment during the eighth Five-year Plan period and the resulting growth of production capacity that caused the situation of excessive production capacity and deflation.

4. Deflation and High Growth Rate in China

In most cases in other countries, deflation is accompanied by stagnating GDP. This is because deflation is in general caused by a significant reduction in household wealth (as a result of a significant decline in the prices of real estate and stock markets), and results in turn in a further decline in consumption. The appearance of excess capacity due to the decline in consumption demand subsequently results in the decline in the level of business investment. The simultaneous reduction of business investment and household consumption inevitably means a negative or close to zero growth of GDP.

In contrast to the deflationary experience in other countries, the Chinese economy still grew strongly with an average annual GDP growth rate of 7.8% between 1998 and 2002. This led some economists to question the reliability of Chinese GDP statistics especially when they found some apparent inconsistencies in the statistical data (Rawski 2002, Zhou 2002). For example, normally GDP growth will be associated with an increase in energy consumption. China's energy consumption dropped by 4.1% and 1.6% per annum in 1998 and 1999 respectively, whereas the GDP growth rates were 7.8% and 7.1% respectively in these two years.

The reason why it was possible for China to maintain high growth rates during the deflationary period was because the deflation was caused by a sudden increase in production capacity. There was no significant reduction in household wealth. Therefore, the annual growth rate of consumption remained relatively high at 6.8% between 1998 and 2002, as shown in Figure 3. While private business investment was repressed due to the lack of profitable investment opportunities, investment from public sector sources increased (as the discussion in the coming section will show) and the growth of overall investment was also maintained at 11.7% between 1998 and 2002. For these reasons, it was possible to achieve an average GDP growth rate of 7.8% over the period.

Meanwhile, the apparent contradiction in energy consumption and growth is possible because there was a change in technology structure in the Chinese economy before and after the deflationary experience. China was a typical shortage economy before the 1990s. Many township and village enterprises (TVEs) prospered in the 1980s under the shortage conditions with very low technology and energy efficiency levels. Significant levels of investment in the early 1990s came from firms in the state sector, foreign direct investment and joint ventures. Such firms possess better technology and are more energy efficient than the TVEs. As the level of excess capacity arose, a large number of TVEs were forced into bankruptcy. The more efficient and newly established firms replaced the less efficient TVEs and subsequently energy consumption declined while high GDP growth rates were maintained.

5. Can China Exit the Current Deflationary Environment?

As discussed in the previous section, the current growth rate of consumption in China is high. However, when over-capacity prevails in the economy, the business sector cannot easily find profitable investment opportunities. As a result, investment by private businesses will generally decline. At the same time, enterprises will continue to operate at less than full capacity, capital utilisation will be low and profits will fall. Businesses will face the possibility of bankruptcy and closure and the likelihood of unemployment will increase. A worker's *permanent* income expectation will drop and aggregate household consumption is likely to eventually decline[7].

---

[7] In the current situation in China, the decline of consumption is also exacerbated by the reforms in housing, medical care, education, pension, and social welfare system.

Investment demand by firms and household consumption are the main components of total final demand. Taking China as an example, these two components constituted 84.6% of GDP in 1998. If growth rates associated with these sources of demand drop and at the same time, production capacity continues growing at a faster rate than the growth in demand, then the effect of the economy's over-capacity will be even more acute. Investment and consumption demand will become even more depressed and deflation will persist. As in the deflation experienced by Japan, a vicious circle will emerge if the Chinese government does not take effective measures to eliminate the excess capacity.

The government has two main policy responses; monetary policy though the mechanism of changing interest rates; and fiscal policy through the direct creation or stimulation of demand.

Interest rates represent the cost of borrowing and hence the cost of investment. The interest rate also represents the relative price of current and future consumption. Theoretically, a reduction of interest rates should stimulate investment and current consumption (at the expense of future consumption). When investment and current consumption decline, the government often adopts expansionary monetary policy to reduce interest rates to stimulate investment and current consumption. In the case of China, interest rates were reduced three times in 1998 alone. When the government lowered interest rates again in June 1999, the one-year lending rate was 5.85%, only half that which prevailed in 1996. The interest rate for a one-year fixed-term deposit was 2.25%, only one quarter of the rate existing in 1996.

The frequency and the extent of interest rate reductions have been very strong but have not produced the expected results. The main reason for this ineffectiveness is, when significant over-capacity exists, firms cannot find profitable investment opportunities and are reluctant to borrow from banks to make investments, even when the interest rate is very low. In addition, when income growth expectations are low and the risk of unemployment increases, households become increasingly likely to save even when interest rates are relatively low (and falling).

Therefore, monetary policy aimed at stimulating investment and current consumption will be relatively ineffective[8]. At the same time, when the investment propensity of firms and the consumption propensity of households decrease, the money holding propensity of firms and households increases, and money velocity drops. The effect of increasing money supply will be negated by the decrease in the velocity of money. In these circumstances, the government cannot rely on simply increasing money supply to avert deflation.

When monetary policy, which indirectly affects firms' investment and households' consumption decisions, is ineffective, governments in many countries often switch to fiscal policy to stimulate the economy directly. Roosevelt's New Deal was the best-known example. In 1998, the Chinese government also began to implement expansionary fiscal policies and issued 100 billion RMB of special bonds to support infrastructure construction. By 2002, the government had issued a total of 660 billion RMB of long-term infrastructure construction bonds for this purpose. The government's expansionary fiscal policy made it possible to maintain at an average of 11.6% per annum growth in investment (in nominal terms) in the five years between 1998 and 2002.

However, the increase in consumption and investment is not enough to absorb the 30% over-capacity in the economy, especially when the growth rate of investment continues to exceed the growth rate of consumption. It is worthwhile mentioning that a common conclusion by scholars with respect to the Great Depression is that Roosevelt's New Deal had no substantial effect in helping the US economy exit from the Great Depression (Hall and Ferguson, 1998).

The monetary and fiscal policies detailed in economics textbooks are effective only when the total demand and supply in the economy is relatively balanced. However, with the current 30 percent or more excess

---

[8] Japan's case is a good example. The interest rates in Japan are close to zero now. However, due to the same reason of over-capacity, investment and consumption have not been stimulated by the low interest rates.

capacity in all major sectors of the Chinese economy, the implementation of any single policy or even the combination of monetary and fiscal policies will be ineffective in creating a large enough shift in demand to digest this over-capacity.

In fact, in Japan when the economic bubble burst in 1991 causing a reduction in household wealth and a decline in household consumption, production over-capacity and deflation, the Japanese government took various measures to stimulate the economy. In spite of this, the government has still not been able to get the economy back on track. The same happened in the US during the Great Depression of the 1920s and 1930s. The US economy grew out of the Depression only when the US mobilised its economy to engage in the Second World War in 1941. China must seek another way to solve the problems arising from the current deflation.

In a large economy, where exports constitute a small proportion of GDP, there are only two solutions to the problem of deflation, regardless of whether the deflation is caused by a sharp drop in consumption, as in the case of the Great Depression in the US, or by a sharp increase in supply, as in China's current situation.

The first policy (non) response is to let time dissipate the over-capacity. In this way, the national economy will experience a long-term depression. Inefficient firms will eventually go bankrupt and total supply will decrease. The economy will regain balance at a lower level of production capacity. The merit of this approach is the elimination of inefficient firms through competition and the improvement of resource allocation and utilisation levels, thereby making the economy more competitive when the economy eventually regains its dynamic equilibrium. However, the Chinese economy needs to create 8 million new jobs annually to meet urban employment demand. In addition, the Chinese economy also needs to create jobs to re-employ the 20 to 30 million workers that have been released from state-owned enterprises. Without decent growth rates, it would be difficult for the Chinese economy to maintain social stability.

The second solution is to unleash a large stock of unsatisfied demand[9] to fill existing over-capacity. In a developed market economy, if an agent has the ability to finance his/her demand, then this demand would normally be realised. Therefore, in a developed market economy, a large stock of unsatisfied demand with the ability to pay will generally not exist. This is one of the reasons why when deflation occurs, it normally lasts a significant length of time in a developed market economy unless some special event occurs to alleviate the deflation (such as the mobilisation for World War II in the United States in the 1940s). However, China is still in the transition from a planned economy to a market economy. In areas of the economy, the market is underdeveloped and there also exist many structural and institutional constraints on further investment and consumption. In at least four areas there are large stocks of unsatisfied demand in China.

The first area is foreign direct investment (FDI) demand. Prior to China's accession to the WTO, foreign direct investment was encouraged. However, foreign-owned companies were not allowed to sell their products directly to domestic markets without special approval from the Chinese government. These firms were supposed to export their products to international markets. China has the largest and fastest growing domestic market in the world and many foreign companies had the intention of investing in China with the specific expectation of selling into the domestic market. However, due to the Chinese government's restriction of access to domestic markets, they were discouraged from investing in China.

According to WTO accession agreements, China needs to provide foreign companies investing in the country with full access to the domestic market. Therefore, WTO accession will unleash foreign companies' unsatisfied demand for investment opportunities in China. In fact China has already become the largest recipient of FDI among all

---

[9] Unsatisfied demand is defined as the demand that cannot be realised due to the imbalance between demand and supply or the constraint of government's policies even though the agent has the ability to pay for the demand.

developing nations and China's WTO accession will further encourage the inflow of FDI into China.

The second area is private enterprises' investment demand. In the past, as a way of protecting state-owned enterprises (SOEs), the government restricted the entry of private enterprise to many sectors of the economy thus allowing SOEs monopoly positions in those sectors. After WTO accession, foreign-owned companies will be given the same market access as that of SOEs. Therefore, the privately owned domestic companies will also be given market access nationally. The government's removal of market access constraints is expected to encourage private sector investment.

The third area relates to urban consumption demand. A substantial number of urban residents are affluent enough to be able to afford home ownership and other significant purchases, such as cars. For such demand, the availability of consumer credit is important. However, at the time of the deflation, banks in China only gave loans to companies, especially SOEs, thus greatly depressing urban demand. Aware of this fact, banks in China have now begun giving consumer credit for the purchase of housing and consumer durables. As a result, urban consumption for housing and cars surged in 2002 and 2003.

The last and probably the most important area of latent demand relates to rural consumption. Currently 60.9% of the Chinese population lives in rural areas. There is a huge consumption demand from people who can afford consumer durables but whose demand is unsatisfied due to the constraints imposed by the existing market infrastructure. Using household electronic appliances as an example, urban markets are essentially saturated. However, in rural areas, the penetration rates per one hundred households in 2002 for colour televisions, refrigerators and washing machines were only 61, 15 and 32, respectively, which are only 48%, 17% and 34% of the levels reached in the urban areas in the same year (see Table 4).

Table 4. Durable Consumption Goods Penetration Rate Per One Hundred Households and Net Income Per Capita

	2002 Urban Households	2002 Rural Households	1991 Urban Households
Colour TV	126	61	68.4
Refrigerator	87	15	48.7
Washing Machine	93	32	80.6
Net Income Per Capita	7703	2476	2,025

Source: SSB (2003), pp. 352 and 375.

Colour televisions, refrigerators, and washing machines were the popular items in urban areas in the late 1980s and early 1990s, and contributed significantly to perceptions of economic prosperity. However, capacity utilisation rates in these sectors were only about 50% as shown in Table 3.

In absolute terms, the total number of rural households is 230 million, more than twice the 110 million households in urban areas. A 10% increase in the penetration rate of these three products in rural areas will be enough to consume the over-capacity of these products.

In the late 1980s, many people had already turned their attention to the rural markets. However, the effort expended has not achieved the results expected. The main constraint for rural households' consumption of modern appliances is not household income levels (even though rural income levels are lower than the urban levels). In 2002, per capita net income in rural areas was 2,476 RMB, which was only 22.3% higher than the 2,025 RMB urban per capita income level in 1991. In 1991 the penetration rates for colour televisions, refrigerators, and washing machines per one hundred urban households were 68.4, 48.7 and 80.6, which were substantially higher than the equivalent rates in rural areas in 2002. The lack of penetration in rural areas is despite the fact that prices for the three products were less than half the 1991 prices[10].

---

[10] For example, in 1991 the price for a 25-inch color TV was about 6000 RMB; it costs about 1200 now.

The lack of appropriate market infrastructure is the main reason for the low penetration rate of household electronic appliances in rural areas. The use of these appliances is dependent on the availability of electricity, a television signal and tap water.

In the countryside, the electricity network is old, the voltage unstable, and the cost expensive, usually three, five or even ten times the price level charged in urban areas. Television signals are also weak in rural areas, and almost 50% of rural households have no running water. All these factors greatly limit rural households' demand for these domestic appliances. If the quality of electricity network can be improved; the price of electricity lowered to that of the urban level; TV satellite signal receiving stations built in villages; and tap water towers constructed and running water provided, it might be expected that a consumption boom in household durable appliances will emerge and the over-capacity in household electronics industries will disappear.

It is the goal of economic development in China to narrow the disparities between rural and urban areas. The improvement of infrastructure in rural areas should have been part of the government's agenda a long time ago. For the purpose of exiting the current deflationary environment, the government could launch a nationwide new village movement to provide basic supporting infrastructure services such as electricity, running water and road networks. With running water supply, the demand for refrigerators and washing machines might increase significantly. This may even launch a revolution in kitchen, toilet and other modern living facilities in rural households. All these activities would create huge demand and the existing over-capacity in most industries could disappear.

Confronted with excess capacity, weak markets and deflation throughout the economy, it is necessary that the government adopt fiscal measures to stimulate the economy. To be effective, fiscal expenditure should be used on areas that might result in significant leverage effects inducing additional household consumption. The 'New Village Movement', which gives priorities to the construction of rural roads and the provision of electricity and running water, is one of the projects that will have the most significant leverage effects. These projects may remove the constraints that limit the realisation of the great potential for consumption demand in rural areas.

Compared to other large infrastructure projects, these investment initiatives have the following merits: they require less funds; create more employment opportunities due to the labour intensity of the projects; and stimulate more demand due to the use of more domestic inputs.

Rural infrastructural development needs to be implemented by local government and grass-root organisations due to their fundamentally small scale and its scattered nature. Central government and local government need to invest jointly, with the central government allocating special funds to the project and local government adding matching funds. The operational issues of how funding should be allocated can be explored in practice. It is unreasonable to depend on county, township and village level government to completely finance rural infrastructure projects. If they are undertaken in this way, the burden of financing those projects will unavoidably fall on rural households. In the past, the government had provided funds for the construction of urban infrastructure while rural peasants had to finance the development of rural infrastructure by themselves. This has been the main reason for the stagnation in the development of rural infrastructure. To expedite rural infrastructure development, government at all levels need to adapt their attitude and criteria for assessing performance in order to ensure that the government can really give higher priorities to rural infrastructure investments. The new government under the leadership of President Hu Jintao and Premier Wen Jiabao has given priority to rural development. With this effort, it might be expected that China will emerge from the current period of deflation soon.

6. Is China's Growth Sustainable?

Per capita income in China has just reached US$1,000 per annum. There is still a huge gap to close before China might be considered a developed country. Therefore, whether China can maintain dynamic growth in the coming decades is important for the Chinese people. China's trade dependency ratio, that is the sum of exports and imports as a percentage of GDP, reached 60% in 2003. If China is to maintain a dynamic growth path in the future, other countries in the world will also benefit greatly from trade with China due to the openness of the Chinese economy and its large economic size.

It is very likely that China will maintain a GDP growth rate of approximately 8 percent per annum for another 20 to 30 years. This is because technological innovation is the most important determinant of economic growth. As a developing country, China's technological level lags far behind that of developed countries. Therefore, China can adapt technological knowledge from advanced countries at a lower cost in order to achieve the necessary technological innovation for its economic development. As a result of their willingness to cheaply adapt and borrow technology from more advanced countries, Japan and the four small East Asian Tigers were able to achieve dynamic growth for almost 40 years after World War II.

Table 5. Comparison of Major Development Indicators between China and Japan

	China		Japan	
Life Expectancy (years)	Female 72 (1998)	Male 68	Female 72.9 (1965)	Male 67.7
Infant Mortality Rate (per thousand)	31 (1999)		30.7 (1960)	
Primary Sector as a Share of GDP (%)	15.9 (2000)		16.7 (1959)	
Engle's Coefficient in Urban Areas (%)	39.2 (2000)		38.8 (1960)	
Per Capita Electricity Consumption (kwh)	1071 (2000)		1236 (1960)	

Source: Kwan, C.H. "Overcoming Japan's China Syndrome," paper presented at "Asian Economic Integration: Current Status and Future Prospects" organized by Research Institute of Economy, Trade & Industry of Japan at Tokyo on April 22-3, 2002.

As shown in Table 5, all the major development indicators in China today are very similar to that of Japan in the early 1960s. China could have a similar technological potential as Japan in the early 1960s. For this reason, I am confident that China could achieve 8% annual GDP growth rate in the coming two or even three decades. If China can realise this potential it will be the largest economy in the world in the early 21st century.

However, this is only a potential scenario. In order to bring this scenario into full play, China needs to complete the transition from a planned economy to a market economy; strengthen its financial system; harden SOEs' budget constraints so as to improve their corporate governance; and mitigate regional income disparities, such as the disparities between urban and rural areas and those between the coastal and inland areas. It also needs to improve environmental sustainability, and maintain internal and external stability.

In addition, to realise its growth potential, China needs to follow an appropriate development strategy (Lin, 2003). Although technological potential had always existed, China had not benefited from this potential prior to 1978. The reason for this is that China had adopted the wrong development strategy. The right strategy should be one that promotes industrial development according to China's comparative advantage, namely China's cheap and abundant labour. In order to fully benefit from the technological gap between China and developed countries, China needs to focus on the labour intensive industries and the labour intensive segments of the capital/technological intensive industries.

At the same time, China also needs to integrate itself into the world economy so as to facilitate the adoption and adaptation of technology. China's entry into the WTO will greatly accelerate this integration process. The spirit of WTO is to lower tariff rates, eliminate non-tariff barriers for trade, and give foreign firms market access to domestic markets, commercial and professional services. In other words, China's domestic economy will be fully open to foreign competition except for the few remaining tariff areas. The accession to the WTO is certain to help China complete its transition to a market economy. At the same time, because the government will have fewer means to support or protect domestic firms, it will help accelerate China's reform of state-owned enterprises and ensure that China develops its economy in line with its comparative advantages (Lin, 2001). In this way, it will accelerate China's integration into the world economy and speed up China's economic development.

7. Conclusion

In the paper I argue that the deflation since the end of 1997 is the result of a surge in excess capacity due to the investment rush in the previous period brought on by Deng Xiaoping's famous tour to the South and his call for rapid growth in 1992. It was possible for China to maintain a high GDP growth rate alongside deflation because the deflation was caused by a sudden increase in production capacity instead of a sudden drop in consumption due to wealth reduction (following stock market of real estate retractions) as was the cases in many other countries. The best way for China to exit the current deflationary environment is to invest in its rural infrastructure so as to stimulate rural consumption.

I also argue that it is possible for China to maintain dynamic growth for another two or three decades due to the advantage of technological backwardness. However, China needs to complete the transition from the planned economy to a market economy, adopt a comparative-advantage following approach to its development strategy, and integrate fully with the global economy. If China can do so, the growth of the Chinese economy will make a great contribution to the improvement of welfare of the Chinese people and people in other parts of the world as well.

References

1. Bordo, M. and A. Redish, "Is Deflation Depressing? Evidence from the Classical Gold Standard," unpublished, Rutgers University (2001).
2. Hall, T. and J. Ferguson, *The Great Depression: An International Disaster of Perverse Economic Policies*, (University of Michigan Press, Ann Arbor, 1998).

3. Lin, J.Y., "The Current Deflation in China: Causes and Policy Options," *Asian Pacific Journal of Economics and Business*, Vol. 4, No. 2: 4-21 (2000).
4. Lin, J.Y., "WTO Accession and China's SOE Reform," in K.T. Lee, J.Y. Lin and Si Joong Kim, eds., *China's Integration with the World Economy: Repercussions of China's Accession to the WTO*, (Korean Institute for International Economic Policy, Seoul, 2001), pp. 55-79.
5. Lin, J.Y., "Development Strategy, Viability, and Economic Convergence," *Economic Development and Cultural Change*, Vol. 51, No. 2: 277-308 (2003).
6. Liu, H. and Z. Li, "The Reform of China's Financial System and the Role of the Stock Market," *Jingrong Yanjiu*, August (1999).
7. Mao, Z., "What were Covered by the Over-Capacity," *China's Nation Situation and Power*, No. 4 (1999).
8. Ming, L. and Y. Guoliang, "Debt Financing and Sustainable Development for Firms," *Jingrong Yanjiu*, 7 (1999).
9. Rawski, T., "Measuring China's Recent GDP Growth: Where Do We Stand," *Jingjixue Jikan China Economic Quarterly*, Vol. 2, No. 1: 53-62 (2002).
10. SSB (State Statistical Bureau) 1997, *Statistical Yearbook of China*, (State Statistical Press, Beijing, 1997).
11. SSB 1998, *Statistical Yearbook of China*, (State Statistical Press, Beijing, 1998).
12. SSB 1999a, *China Statistical Abstract*, (State Statistical Press, Beijing, 1999).
13. SSB 1999b, *China Statistics*, 2, 5, 8, 10 and various issues (1999).
14. SSB 1999c, *Statistical Yearbook of China*, (State Statistical Press, Beijing, 1999).
15. SSB 2002, *Statistical Yearbook of China*, (State Statistical Press, Beijing, 2002).
16. SSB 2003, *Statistical Yearbook of China*, (State Statistical Press, Beijing, 2003).
17. Yi, G., *A Study of Deflation in China, 1998-2000*, (Peking University Press, Beijing, 2000).
18. Zhou, N., W. Yunshi, and L. Thurow, "The PRC's Real Economic Growth Rate," mimio, (2002).

CHAPTER 3

MARKET INSTABILITY AND ECONOMIC COMPLEXITY: THEORETICAL LESSONS FROM TRANSITION EXPERIMENTS

Ping Chen[1]

China Center for Economic Research, Beijing University

Abstract: The 'Washington consensus' and 'shock therapy' approach to transition economies ignored the Keynesian lessons from the Great Depression, that market instability is a possibility and that there may be an active role of government in managing stability and growth. The severe output decline in Eastern Europe and the former Soviet Union (EEFSU) was triggered by a simplistic policy of liberalisation and privatisation, which ignored many economic complexities and the existence of multiple equilibria under alternative divisions of labour. Issues of fundamental importance, such as the chain reaction between macroeconomic instability and microeconomic behavior, the role of the government in creating learning space in development, interactions between economic openness, sustainable growth, and social stability, can all be revealed from comparative experiments between China and EEFSU. These include the role and impact of exchange rate regimes, price dynamics, trade policies, and reform strategies. The tremendous cost of the Transition Depression sheds new light on theoretical limitations of atomic demand and supply analysis, theory of hard-budget constraints, microfoundations in macroeconomics, and the property rights school in institutional economics. New development policy based on learning, innovation, and decentralised experiments will pave the way for new thinking in complex economics.

---

[1] Ping Chen is Professor of economics at China Center for Economic Research at Beijing University, Beijing, China; and Senior Research Fellow at Center for New Political Economy at Fudan University, Shanghai, China. Correspondence address: pchen@ccer.edu.cn

1. Introduction: The Forgotten Lessons from the Great Depression

There were two conflicting views on the nature of market economy and business cycles. The 'equilibrium school' in classical economics believes that the market economy is essentially stable because of a mean reverting mechanism of demand and supply forces, and as such, economic fluctuations are primarily driven by external shocks (Frisch, 1933). In contrast, the 'disequilibrium school' asserts that the market economy is like a biological organism (Schumpeter, 1939), which has both dynamic instability and a coherent structure. Innovation and technological progress are essentially unstable, and they are characterised by creative destruction, technology replacement, and biological rhythm. For policy analysis, the equilibrium school focuses on short-term deviations from equilibrium state, while the disequilibrium school mainly focuses on medium- and long-term dynamic patterns and structural changes.

Natural experiments play a key role in testing competing economic theories. The Great Depression shook a widespread belief in inherent market stability. The rise of Keynesian macroeconomics made a revolutionary contribution in relation to the definition of involuntary unemployment, destabilising financial markets, and role of government in managing economic business cycles (Keynes, 1936). However, the Keynesian revolution only partially succeeded in macroeconomic theory. The Keynesian school did not develop a general theory of dynamic disequilibrium that was capable of explaining financial crises and economic complexities. Methodologically speaking, equilibrium processes without history (nonlinearity) and diversity (multiple equilibria) are easier to model mathematically. Equilibrium theories are developed as a form of *armchair economics* and are without solid foundations in empirical observations. Microeconomic theory based on complete markets, perfect competition, and optimisation behavior leave no room for technology innovation and market instability.

There are a wide range of economic theories. The Arrow-Debreu general equilibrium model generates a utopian market with unique stable equilibrium that has no disruptive technology and learning space (Arrow and Debreu, 1954). The efficient market hypothesis in finance theory claims stock prices are always right, which implies that there is little chance of financial crisis occurring (Fama, 1970). The 'property rights school' further excludes path-dependence and multi-equilibrium from institutional evolution. According to the Coase theorem, optimal institutions can be established by the voluntary exchange of property rights, which is independent of initial conditions (Coase, 1990). The 'new classical school', led by Lucas, launched a counter-Keynesian-revolution in macroeconomics (Lucas, 1972). According to the theory of rational expectations and microfoundations, involuntary unemployment is no longer a significant problem in economic policy, since unemployment is re-defined as a rational choice between work and leisure at individual level. The main hypothesis within the so-called 'Washington consensus' might be considered part of this counter revolution, which not only rejects any contribution from socialist experiments in industrialisation and community-building, but also negates Keynesian policy in dealing with business cycles and financial crises.

If we accept that economics should be considered to be an empirical science, not simply a subset of philosophy, is it possible to test competing economic theories through policy experiments? Our answer is 'yes'. Recent events from the transition economies provide us with a good opportunity for testing economic theories.

The so-called 'Washington consensus' (or 'shock therapy approach') was derived from standard equilibrium theory. Based on their equilibrium-optimisation belief, the system of property-rights and hard-budget constraints could ensure firm level efficiency in a competitive marketplace; the flexible price system created by liberalisation policy should lead to both stability and efficiency in competitive market; economic growth would be driven by foreign direct investment and technology diffusion from developed economies after liberalising the exchange rate. Under these assumptions, economic transition and development is simply a convergent process without the need of policy experimentation and institutional innovation (Sachs and Woo, 2000). If we consider the rich physical and human resources in Eastern Europe and the former Soviet Union (EEFSU), it would be natural to predict that

EEFSU would grow at a much faster rate, while China would struggle with its poor natural resources, cultural burdens, and political institutions. The surprise of the large output decline in EEFSU and rapid development of China raises serious questions about the validity of textbook equilibrium economics, especially in relation to its theory on market mechanisms and economic development (World Bank, 2002).

Transition economies between the 1970's and 1990's have several features that are different from the industrial economies during the Great Depression. First, there were no major military conflicts or international crisis before or during the transition process. Secondly, severe output declines during the transition process were not driven by stock market crashes or banking crises. These two features made the background of transition experiment much simpler than that of the Great Depression in theoretical terms. Thirdly, the difference in economic performance during transition was mainly caused by policy differences between EEFSU and China; the former is characterised by "shock therapy" or liberalisation policies driven by the so-called Washington Consensus (Sachs, 2005; Williamson, 1990), while the latter is characterised by a gradual approach with decentralised experiments and a dual-track price system (Lin, 1992; Chen, 1993). In contrast, there was no theoretical dividing line emerging in policy debates during the Great Depression. Therefore, transition experiment can serve as a better touchstone in testing competing economic theories because of its relative simplicity in historical comparison.

The shock therapy approach originated in Latin America, and was then applied to EEFSU. The experimental approach was rooted in the East Asian mode of industrial policy, managed trade, and a dual-track price system for export-led growth. The different outcomes achieved in terms of economic growth can be seen in Table 1.

From Table 1, we can see two remarkable facts. Firstly, there was no evidence for the widespread belief that socialist economies collapsed in the 1970s and 1980s, even though there was a visible slow down in both developed countries and EEFSU. The wave of economic reform and

Table 1. Average GDP Growth Rate in Decades (%)

	1970s	1980s	1990s
East Asia	4.5	4.4	2.8
East Europe	4.8	2.4	-4.4 (46% in absolute decline)
West Europe	2.7	1.9	1.6
North America	3.3	3.0	2.8
South America	5.2	1.2	2.9
World	3.6	2.7	2.1
Japan	4.2	3.6	1.2
Germany	2.6	1.7	1.6
China	4.7	8.8	9.4
Vietnam	-0.1	5.0	6.9
Poland	6.1	0.9	3.2
Hungary	4.7	1.5	0.3
USSR	4.6	2.6	
Russia			-4.8
Ukraine			-8.9

Source: United Nations Statistics.

transition in socialist countries was driven mainly by political factors rather than economic crises in the 1980s. Secondly, there was a sharp contrast between the 'Transition Depression' in EEFSU and continued growth in China and Vietnam amongst the transition economies. We will consider the outcomes associated with transition economies as a natural experiment, in addition to the economic outcomes following the Great Depression, both of which are valuable in studying the unstable and complex nature of macroeconomic dynamics.

2. The Stylized Facts in the Great Depression and the Transition Depression

The main facts in the Great Depression and the Transition Depression are shown in Table 2 and Table 3. We can see that the degree of the Transition Depression is comparable or even more severe than the Great Depression. Polish economists even coined the term "The Greater Depression" for the recession that occurred in EEFSU (Kolodko, 2000).

Table 2. The Great Depression (1929-1942) Measured by Peak-to-Trough Decline in Industrial Production

Country	Decline (%)	Peak-Trough Date	Recovery Date	Length
US	46.8	1929.3-1933.2	1942	14 years
UK	16.2	1930.1-1932.4		
France	31.3	1930.2-1932.3		
Germany	41.8	1928.1-1932.3		
Canada	42.4	1929.2-1933.2		
Italy	33.0	1929.3-1933.1		
Poland	46.6	1929.1-1933.2		
Czechoslovakia	40.4	1929.4-1933.2		
Japan	8.5	1930.1-1932.3		

Source: "Great Depression," Christina D. Romer, Encyclopedia Britannica (2004).

Table 3. The Transition Depression in EEFSU Measured by Peak-to-Trough Decline in Real GDP

Country	Peak	Trough	Recovery	Length (yrs)	Decline (%)
Germany[2]	1992	1993	1994	1	-1.1
Czech Republic	1989	1993	1999	10	-13
Slovakia	1989	1992	1998	9	-22
Poland	1989	1991	1996	7	-18
Hungary	1989	1993	2000	11	-18
Romania	1987	1992	2005	18	-30
Bulgaria	1988	1997	>2006	>18	-34
Albania	1989	1992	2000	11	-40
Estonia	1990	1994	2002	12	-45
Latvia	1990	1995	2006	16	-50
Lithuania	1990	1994	2005	15	-44
Russia	1990	1998	>2006	>16	-43
Ukraine	1990	1999	>2006	>16	-61
Belarus	1990	1995	2003	13	-45
Georgia	1990	1994	>2006	>16	-73
Uzbekistan	1990	1995	2001	11	-20
Azerbaijan	1990	1995	2005	15	-58
Kazakhstan	1990	1998	2004	14	-38
Tajikistan	1990	1996	>2006	>16	-67
Turkmenistan	1990	1997	2006	16	-41
Mongolia	1989	1993	2002	13	-23

Sources: United Nations Statistics. For recent data, see CIA World Factbook (2006).

---

[2] East Germany declined 30% in 1991; its GDP in 1992 was only 7% of unified Germany.

We were surprised by the depth of the Transition Depression. US industrial output was down 47%, its real GDP declined by about 25% and the recovery to pre-Depression level took approximately 14 years while China's economic depression (caused by famine in late 1950s) lasted 5 years with 32% decline in GDP. However, the Transition Depression in Romania, Bulgaria, and three other countries in the former Soviet Union lasted more than 16 years and GDP levels are still below those levels achieved before the transition. The decline in real GDP ranged from 43% in Russia, 60% in Ukraine, and even 73% in Georgia. The magnitudes of the Transition Depression were more severe than those in the Great Depression in the US and most other European countries at that time.

There are several theories proposed to explain the Great Depression: The financial instability caused by World War I in Europe; the stock market crash in the US; the deflation caused by the British return to the Gold Standard; and the human error in the determination of monetary policy (Romer, 2004). Many economists share the consensus that the endogenous instability in the financial market played a major role in the Great Depression. In contrast, there was only a minor slowdown and no financial crisis in socialist economies in EEFSU, before the transition in early 1990s. The rapid transition in Eastern Europe was marked by the fall of the Berlin Wall in 1989 and the break-up of the Soviet Union in 1991. There was wholesale liberalisation in exchange rates, trade, prices, and rapid privatisation carried out with ideological fever in EEFSU. On the other hand, China and Vietnam were cautious in preserving social stability and export-led growth.

The central question should examine the main cause of the Transition Recession in EEFSU. Let us start with the simplest case in transition process — East Germany after German unification.

3. Monetary Power and Trade Imbalance in Non-Equilibrium World

Some economists blamed the Transition Recession on "bad politics" rather than "bad economics" (Roland, 2000). For example, Sachs pointed out that insufficient level of Western aid was the main cause of Russia's failure to stabilise its currency (Sachs, 2005). Disruption of production chains and credit tightness were significant factors in output decline (Blanchard and Kremer, 1997; Calvo and Coricelli, 1992). However, the case of German unification offers a clear clue to the primary reason for output decline in EEFSU. This reason is exchange rate liberalisation.

The best example of transition shock therapy (without Sachs' concern over the problem of insufficient aid) occurred not in Poland, but in East Germany (Kolodko. 2000; Burda. 2006). After German re-unification in 1989, East Germany completely imported from their West German neighbours its system of property rights and its legal infrastructure. West Germany provided the most generous financial transfer in history, approximating 80-90 billion Euros per annum or 20% of East German GDP. This is much larger than the amount allocated as part of the Marshall Plan following the Second World War or indeed any amount of foreign aid to a single developing country. As a consequence, there was essentially zero inflation and macro instability in East Germany. Using Barror's convergence measurement, the wage rate, consumption, productivity, and other economic indicators in East Germany, converged to those of West Germany more rapidly than that predicted by neoclassical growth theory (Burda, 2006; Barro, 1991). However, there is slow economic growth and the unemployment rate in East Germany is still rising 15 years after unification. Why has convergence theory and the property rights hypotheses failed to produce an East German miracle under the most favorable transition conditions in industrial history?

In 2004, we undertook a field observation at the famous Zeiss Optical Company in Jena, Eastern Germany. We were surprised by the large negative shock of switching exchange rate regime. Although Zeiss products were the most advanced and competitively produced in the global market, the company suddenly lost more than 90% of the market share in Eastern Europe after German reunification, mainly due to the fact that existing customers could not afford to pay in former Soviet block currencies. Accumulation of hard currencies used in the West is a relatively slow process in developing countries and in transition economies. It is an outcome of learning process, including increasing competitiveness, building market-networks, and the accumulation of foreign reserve, rather than reaching the equilibrium state overnight in an exchange rate market. We may speculate that the breakdown of the CMEA (Council for Mutual Economic Assistance) and industry overkill in EEFSU was mainly caused by radical liberalisation in foreign trade and the exchange rate.

The slow convergent process in international trade can be revealed from China's dual-track foreign exchange system, which lasted about 15 years from April 1980 to January 1995. China's international trade had a deficit of $1.8 billion US dollars in 1980. However, this grew to a trade surplus of $5.4 billion in 1994, and $24.1 billion in 2000. Accordingly, its accumulation of foreign reserves increased from $0.8 billion US dollars in 1979, to $51.6 billion in 1994, to $165.6 billion US dollars in 2000. China's dual-track foreign exchange system successfully merged in 1994, at a time when its foreign trade had moved from deficit into surplus after 15 years of reform and export-led growth (Figure 1).

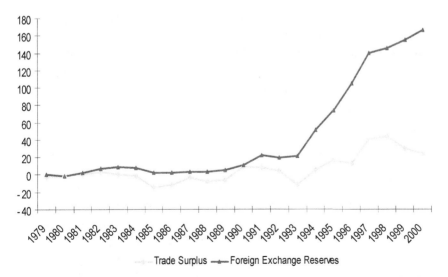

Figure 1. China's Trade Surplus and Foreign Reserves (billion US$)
Source: China Statistics 2001.

China's annual export growth rate was 26% in the 15 years from 1979 to1994, which was more than twice the growth rate of annual GDP growth rate in the same period (9.5%). In contrast, the trade liberalisation in EEFSU induced a flood of imports rather than an increase in export growth. As observed by a Polish economist, "the more rapid the liberalisation of trade, the bigger the initial shock and the deeper the ensuing recession" (Kolodko, 2000).

After the Asian financial crisis in 1997, there were an increasing number of economists who realised the danger of excess international capital mobility since it encourages international speculation in financial markets. Mainstream economists argue for a flexible exchange rate in order to create an anchor for macroeconomic stability. However, these economists ignore the reality of unequal competition and the monetary power associated with international trade and finance. In neoclassical monetary theory, money and exchange rates are simply treated as the media of exchange in a utopian general equilibrium world. In the far-from-equilibrium real world, hard currency also engenders market power associated with political economy (Goodhart, 1998).

There is no role for the 'selective filter effect' created by currency control in equilibrium theory of monetary economics. Evolutionary economics has more to learn from evolutionary biology, where the emergence of biological structures, such as cell membranes, plays an important role in the origins of life. Selective open membranes in organisms are equivalent to a *Maxwell demon* in a living system, which allows positive matter, energy flow, and information flows, but rejects harmful flows for maintaining dissipative structures in open system (Prigogine, 1984). Without the protection of biological borders, no living being can maintain a living organism under far from equilibrium conditions. This is an essential difference between mechanical creations and biological organisms. In political economy terms, custom, credit, visa, and other security systems closely guard developed economies, which are *not "free"*, but *selectively open* to the world market. Those individuals promoting free trade and free capital markets simply ignore the needs of developing countries for creating learning space and a defense wall against potential negative shocks from the international marketplace. The argument for liberalisation policy is that it attracts foreign direct investment (FDI). However, trade liberalisation plus macro instability led to additional capital flight and asset stripping in EEFSU. China's success in attracting FDI mainly resulted from a growing market and a sound macroeconomic policy, not from property rights or liberalisation policy.

4. Complex Dynamics, Path Dependence and Learning Space

According to neoclassical microeconomics, a complete market economy (without innovation space and product cycles) has a unique equilibrium in general equilibrium microeconomics. This equilibrium is inherently stable because of the atomic mechanism (i.e. no supply chains or networks in the division of labour) of supply and demand (Arrow and Debreu, 1954). An optimal system of property rights can be achieved by exchange without historical constraints (Coase, 1990). Therefore, the 'convergence school' hypothesis predicted a relatively quick stabilisation process after price liberalisation and the establishment of property rights. Surprisingly, the immediate results of liberalisation policies in EEFSU led to inflation spirals, the excessive devaluation of currencies, and widespread output decline (see Table 4 and Table 5).

Table 4. Peak Inflation Rate during the Transition Measured by the Implicit Price Deflator in National Currency

Country	Peak Inflation (%)	Year	Length of High Inflation (>40%)
Germany	9	1990	0
China	13, 20	1988, 1994	0
Poland	400-581	1989-1990	5 yrs (1988-1992)
Bulgaria	334-1068	1991-1997	7 yrs (1991-1997)
Romania	295-300	1991-1992	9 yrs (1991-2000)
Ukraine	3432	1993	6 yrs (1991-1996)
Russia	1590-4079	1992-1993	8 yrs (1991-1998)

Source: United Nations Statistics Database.

Table 5. Devaluation of Currency (Exchange Rate set at 1 in 1980 or 1991)

	1980	1985	1990	1991	1993	1995	2000
Germany	1	1.62	0.89	0.91	0.91	0.79	1.17
China	1	1.96	3.19	3.55	3.85	5.57	5.52
Czech			0.77	1	1.04	0.95	1.38
Slovakia			0.61	1	1.04	1.01	1.56
Hungary	0.44	0.67	0.85	1	1.23	1.68	3.78
Poland		0.01	0.90	1	1.71	2.29	4.11
Bulgaria				1	1.55	3.78	0.12
Romania	0.22	0.24	0.29	1	9.55	26.62	284
Belarus			0.51	1	191	47937	108
Russia				1	195	897	5534
Ukraine			0.50	1	634	20602	76087

Note: The exchange rates are measured against the dollar. All exchange rates are re-scaled by the base year, which are 1980 for Germany and China and 1991 for the rest. Source: Penn World Table 2002.

Equilibrium theory such as the purchasing power parity has little power to understand the large currency depreciation during transition. For example, from 1990 to 1998, Russia's real GDP measured by 1990 US Dollar declined 43%, but its currency depreciated 13,860 times. This is a clear case of non-equilibrium process.

One visible feature in China is its remarkable stability in the inflation rate and exchange rates, which can be seen in Table 4 and Table 5. However, situations vary greatly in EEFSU. Can we understand these differences by new thinking in evolutionary economics and complex dynamics? We propose two possible explanations: path-dependence and learning space.

4.1. Inflation constraints and path-dependence

One interesting finding is that those countries with low inflation rates, including China, Germany, the Czech Republic, Slovakia, and Hungary, suffered painful periods of hyperinflation in the first half of 20th century. The collective memory of previous hyperinflations during the civil war in China and between the two world wars in central Europe created a behavioral constraint in monetary policy in these countries. In contrast, new hyperinflation occurring in the former Soviet Union, which had a long history of fixed prices under a command economy, was without recent historical precedent. History or path-dependence *matters in economic behavior* (David, 1985; Arthur, 1994)! It is often assumed in macroeconomic dynamics that price movements follow Markovian processes, which has no historical memory. Now we understand it is rarely true under nonlinear dynamics (Chen, 2005). History tells us a different story.

4.2. Complex patterns under a dual-track price system: Production cycle and round-about production

The most visible innovation in China's reform was the introduction of the dual-track price system in the mid-1980s and continued after the failed attempt of shock therapy in terms of the price reforms in 1988. There were two-fold objectives in introducing the dual-track price system. The first was to maintain social stability with fixed prices and food rationing under the central planning system. The second was to provide production incentives by ensuring payment at market prices when firm production exceeded the levels of government quotas. The resulting price dynamics varied greatly in product markets, which provided rich evidence of industrial structure and complex dynamics.

The most rapid price convergence and output growth was achieved in the market for farm products, such as meat and vegetables. Foodstuff prices did increase initially, but several months later the prices quickly stabilised or even fell after a rapid growth in farm supply. For basic goods such as grain and cotton, price controls were in place (on and off) for more than 10 years, and never fully liberalised. The price of industrial products were rapidly liberalised and deflation for consumer goods and luxury products occurred in places, but market liberalisation for basic consumption goods occurred much more slowly. The prices for energy, utility, education, and health are still under tight control despite a persistent trend of price inflation, because their supply persistently falls behind social demand when income grows rapidly (see Figure 2). Price dynamics are complex with complicated interactions within changing microeconomic behavior, varying product cycles, interdependent industrial structures, and a cyclic macroeconomic environment.

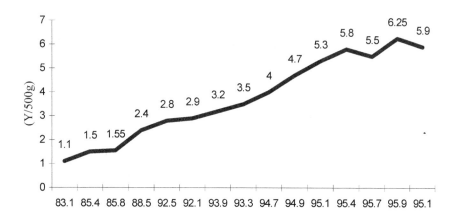

Figure 2a. Price History in China's Shanghai Local Market: (a) Fresh pork meat price in retailed market (1983-1995)

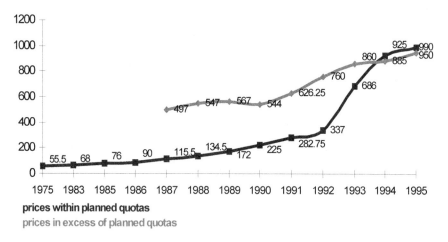

Figure 2b. Price History in China's Shanghai Local Market: (b) Heavy oil dual-track price in Shanghai industrial market (1975-1995)

One possible explanation for the varied pattern in price dynamics is the varied length of production cycles. The production cycle for vegetables and meat is several months; however, the investment cycle for power stations is several years. Additional complexity can be added as a result of roundabout production in division of labour (Hayek, 1935). This is greatly different from the simple supply and demand mechanism among farmers without network constraints. Grain and cotton have a similar production cycles (in terms of length) as those of vegetable and meat. However, cotton and grain can also be used as input for later industrial production, and as such price fluctuations in grain and cotton markets are much greater and more persistent than those in vegetable and meat markets. China's price reform in grain and cotton markets was much slower than other agriculture markets. The existence of inventory cycles and future markets introduce additional complexity in the grain and cotton markets. The Chinese government made great efforts in managing price stability and stimulating growth to ensure social support during reform process.

The difference in industrial structure between China and EEFSU may have partially contributed to the difference in agriculture reform. The family contract system worked well for China's small-scale farm production, but failed to work for large-scale mechanised farms in the former Soviet Union.

In summary, the simplistic picture of a Robinson Crusoe economy in neoclassical economics cannot explain business cycles and divergent evolution in division of labour (Chen, 2002). Modern farm industries are also highly correlated because of industrial supply of seeds, fertilizers and other farm production inputs. The observed price cycles in grain, cotton and many industrial prices have significant degrees of volatility. A market system will be remarkably stable under external shocks, if supply and demand curves have a unique equilibrium and negligible time-lag. However, market dynamics will be unstable or even chaotic when there exists multiple equilibria or substantial time-lags (Chen 1987; 2005). Dynamic complexity and transition uncertainty created the room for decentralised experiments and dual-track reform, which would create a learning space for adapting policy. The blind confidence in general equilibrium theory led to the naïve strategy of shock therapy in EEFSU.

5. Conflicting Analysis in Equilibrium Thinking and Economic Policy

The Washington consensus seems to provide an integrated approach for transition and development economies. However, the Washington consensus proposes too many conflicting goals without an operational strategy or reform sequence. For example, while large scale privatisation and rapid institutional change created fiscal crises and weak government; it has shaken social confidence in market economy. The Lucas idea of microfoundations of macroeconomics ignores the complex nature of economic market organism and the whole entity being greater than the sum of the parts. We will discuss lessons from transition economies, in order to seek a better alternative than the equilibrium perspective and methodological individualism.

5.1. Hard-budget constraints and credit crunch

Kornai singled out the soft-budget constraint (in the form of government subsidy to loss-making firms) as the main cause of inefficiency of firms under socialist economies (Kornai, 1986). This logic is true only for a closed economy without technology progress or credit markets. This is the fundamental weakness of the complete market hypothesis. In industrial societies, soft-budget constraints widely exist in various forms, including bank credit, venture capital, and bankruptcy law. American bankruptcy law offers a re-organisation opportunity for firms in financial difficulties and a chance of eventual survival. Chrysler and the Long-Term Capital are well-known example of "too big to fail" or soft-budget constraints in capitalism. In practice, the credit crunch through the imposition of "hard budget-constraints" is an additional cause of the output decline in EEFSU (Calvo and Coricelli, 1992).

When open-door policies introduce international competition to domestic firms, the critical choice is how to upgrade technology for a domestic firm's survival. A favorable macroeconomic environment, including access to bank credit and capital markets, is very important in a firm's effort to survive in a globally competitive marketplace. Sachs and Woo (2000) argue that China's market-oriented reform should be much easier than Russia's since China's rural population has no social security. If this is true, developing countries such as Bangladesh may grow faster than China! The real reason behind China's rapid technological progress is its state insurance during the learning process. Farmers' down-side risk is protected by collective ownership of land, thus preserving positions for those in business adventures. China achieved rapid economic growth and technological advancement under the policy of so-called soft-budget constraints. Many state owned enterprises (SOEs) and township and village enterprises (TVEs) made rapid progress in terms of international competitiveness, which can be seen from double-digit growth of manufacturing exports in China. From the view of the property rights school of thought, both SOEs and TVEs have no clearly defined property rights. In financial practice, shares of local government could enhance firm's credit for bank loan. Certainly, growth under soft-budget constraints does have a cost in the form of non-performing loans (NPL) accumulated in state banks. China's growth under soft-budget constraints creates a *trial and win* scenario through informal privatisation. If SOEs or TVEs succeed in new product markets, they are privatised; when failure occurs, the state owned banks absorb the financial loss. In this way, China's state sector absorbed the main costs in technology acquisition and business venture activities in the non-state sector. The NPL contains both components of efficiency loss and social burden. Comparing to credit tightness under the policy of hard-budget constraints, the cost of transition depression in EEFSU is much larger than the NPL in China. Whether China's growth under soft budget-constraints can be continued does not depend on the cost of soft budget constraints, but the productivity gain over and above the social cost. The same is true of the US's growing trade and budget deficit. China's growth-oriented development strategy is a new type of Keynesian policy, while Konai's policy of hard-budget constraints is simply a new form of the new classical counter-Keynesian-revolution. The history in transition economies provides strong evidence that the macro environment for micro (firm) behavior is more significant than the so-called microfoundations of macro stability.

Theoretically speaking, the theory of soft-budget constraints is a somewhat naïve exercise in microeconomics, but a dubious theory in macroeconomics. If the survival of majority rather than minority of socialist firms only depends on state subsidies, socialist countries would have much higher inflation than market economies. This is not true historically. Persistent budget deficits and hyperinflation rarely occurred in planned economies but frequently occurred in market economies such as in Latin America. Kornai has postulated the wrong diagnosis of the trade-off between planned economies and market economies. As Schumpeter pointed out, capitalism is driven by innovation, which is intrinsically unstable. Business cycles and financial crises are the price paid for creative destruction in open economies. In contrast, socialism is more stable in closed society. The main weakness of planned economies is not the lack of incentives, but the stagnation of technology. Therefore, the right direction for reforming socialist economies is not creating a pure private economy with hard-budget constraints, but a mixed economy open to world market and new technology.

5.2. The MM theorem and the property right school

The property rights school of thought claims that private ownership is a necessary condition for market efficiency, which is the main belief behind privatisation policy. However, the MM theorem in financial economics implies that the debt structure, or alternatively, the ownership structure, does not matter in determining a firm's value in competitive market (Modigliani and Miller, 1958). From a governance point of view, there is no essential difference between state firms without clear ownership and private firms with diversified ownership. Technology, management, corporate strategy, and economies of scale all matter in market competition. There is no question that excessive state ownership crowds out private innovation; that is why privatisation of small and medium firms is successful in many countries. However, there is no solid evidence that privatising large firms would improve competitiveness and efficiency (Von Weizsacker *et al.*, 2005). China's secret of low labour costs in export industries is rooted in its mixed social security system. In particular, the social security of large rural population is based on the collective ownership of land. If China privatised collectively owned land, its infrastructure development and export growth would slow down dramatically.

5.3. Privatisation vs. competition policy

Under socialist systems, large state firms often have monopolistic positions in industry. Large oil and utility firms generate important revenues for government. Competition policy is a means of breaking down state monopolies, just like breaking-up AT&T in US was an effective way of improving efficiency in the telecommunications market. This type of success story is also seen from the break-up of China Airways into several competing companies. However, privatising large firms without mitigating monopoly power has made the situation worse in Russia. The government has not only lost significant revenues, but also public support for privatization. Local government was forced to change from a "helping hand" approach into a "grabbing hand" (Frye and Shleifer, 1997). The collapse of public finances led the rise of mafia economy. The simultaneous liberalisation, stabilisation (financial squeezing under the name of hard-budget constraints), and privatisation policies created vicious cycles and chain reactions of output decline, hyperinflation, currency devaluation, fiscal crisis, capital flight, and asset stripping. The Transition Depression was a man-made disaster, while the Great Depression was an outcome of market bubbles and financial crises.

6. Conclusions

Both the Great Depression and the Transition Recessions are two natural experiments, which have stimulated new economic thinking for generations of economists. Keynes learned an important lesson on macro instability and emphasised the role of active government in maintaining social stability. Certainly, the experiences of the welfare state in industrial countries also revealed the limits of large government in job creation and technology advancement. The transition experiments in EEFSU and China provide new lessons on co-evolution of changing economies and innovative government, which is relevant not only for developing economies, but also for developed economies. We need a more general framework, which could integrate historical lessons from market instability and economic complexity in the evolution of the division of labour. We will briefly discuss the theoretical lessons from transition economies.

Stiglitz rightly concluded that "the (oversimplified) Washington consensus did not provide the answer for development strategy. There was a failure in understanding economic structures within developing countries" (Stiglitz, 2004). Roland pointed out the importance of "the evolutionary-institutionalist perspective" in understanding transition economies (Roland, 2000). Sachs also realised that "economies (like the human body) are complex systems; ... economists, like medical clinicians, need to learn the art of differential diagnosis" (Sachs, 2005). These observations are worthy of further theoretical analysis.

First, general equilibrium theory in neoclassical microeconomics is a static model. Many economists admire its mathematical simplicity and theoretical elegance, but few realise the limitations in terms of its policy implications. In the utopian model of complete markets under perfect competition, consumers have no subsistence threshold or interdependencies; all products have infinite life without technology replacement and product cycles; price is the only variable available for adjusting resource allocation (without the need of business strategies and product innovation); and the speed of adjustment is infinite without any delay or possibility of overshooting. Any violation of one of these "perfect" conditions results in the price equilibrium being neither unique nor stable. That is why shock therapy in price liberalisation led to inflation spirals in EEFSU but the gradual approach with dual-track prices made smooth transition in China's price reform. Future microeconomics should construct more realistic market models with nonlinear dynamics and complex networks.

Second, methodological individualism or the Robinson Crusoe economy in neoclassical macroeconomics abstracts out the critical link of financial intermediates between micro firms and the macro economy. There is little understanding of financial crisis through the efficient market hypothesis in finance theory. There is weak evidence of "micro-foundations" of macro economies, but strong evidence of the "macro environment" for micro behavior because of the Principle of Large Numbers (Chen, 2002). Macro economy can be better described by three layer model: macro — meso (financial intermediate and industrial structure) — micro. It is the original idea of financial Keynesian economics that financial instability is an important source of macroeconomic boom and bust (Minsky, 1985).

Third, social evolution and institutional development in an open economy is a divergent process like biological evolution, while the prediction of transaction costs or property rights school is a convergent story in closed systems. Historical constraints and institutional innovation play no role in the Washington consensus. Under uneven distribution and non-equilibrium development, a 'disciplined hand' in positive development requires more constraints than protecting property rights (i.e. the 'invisible hand') during the reform process. Protecting competition and innovation is indispensable in market economies. Monopoly, corruption, organised crime, and income polarisation may destroy the social foundation of a market economy. The modern history of science and capitalism reveals the importance of checks and balance in mixed economies with private, public, and non-profit non-government sectors. Institutional economics should better understand the historical lessons of mixed economies and study new international order in 21st century.

Fourth, the equilibrium perspective in global development is simply a linear trajectory towards the 'end of history' (Fukuyama, 1993). The question is how to understand the rise and fall of nations in transition economies. From the view of complex science, there is a trade-off between complexity and stability in evolutionary dynamics (Chen, 1987; 2005). Under a stable environment with moderate fluctuations, development of division of labour will increase economic diversity while severe fluctuations will reverse the trend back into barter or self-sufficient economies. The ecological dynamics of learning competition may help understand the nature of evolutionary dynamics (Chen, 2005).

In sum, the equilibrium approach ignores two main sources of market instability and economic complexity: nonlinear interactions with multiple equilibria and collective behaviour. Market forces without government management and social coordination cannot achieve healthy development under rapid technology advancement and unequal global competition. Complex economics with evolutionary perspective offers a better alternative in understanding economic development and institutional changes.

Acknowledgements

I would like to thank the participants for their stimulating discussions, including German-Sino Workshop on Evolutionary Economics at Max-Planck-Institute in Jena, Germany; the CCER-LSE (London Economic School) forum at Peking University in Beijing, China; International Symposium on Transition and Development at Fudan University in Shanghai; and International Symposium on China and Development at University of Stockholm in Sweden; all meetings hold in 2005. I also thank the valuable comments on the Washington consensus by Joseph Stiglitz, James Galbraith, Hans-Walter Lorenz, Wing Thye Woo, Guido Buenstorf, Charles Goodhart, Ziyuan Cui, Chang Liu, Zhengfu Shi, Jun Zhang, Weisen Li, Ziwu Chen, Danny Quah, and Linda Yueh. Financial support from National Science Foundation of China under the Grant of #70471078, the 211 Project from China Center for Economic Research at Peking University, and Center for New Political Economy at Fudan University in Shanghai is also acknowledged.

References

1. Arrow, K. J. and G. Debreu, "Existence of an Equilibrium for a Competitive Economy," *Econometrica*, 22(3), 265-290 (1954).

2. Arthur, W. B., *Increasing Returns and Path Dependence in the Economy*, (University of Michigan Press, Ann Arbor, 1994).
3. Barro, R., "Eastern Germany's Long Haul," *Wall Street Journal*, May 3 (1991).
4. Blanchard, O. and M. Kremer, "Disorganization," *Quarterly Journal of Economics*, 112(4), 1091-1126 (1997).
5. Burda, M. C., "What Kind of Shock Was It? Regional Integration of Eastern Germany after Unification," *AEA 2006 Annual Meeting* (2006).
6. Calvo, G. and F. Coricelli, "Stabilizing a Previously Centrally Planned Economy: Poland 1990," *Economic Policy*, 14, 175-208 (1992).
7. Chen, P., "Origin of Division of Labor and Stochastic Mechanism of Differentiation," *European Journal of Operational Research*, 30(3), 246-250 (1987).
8. _____, "China's Challenge to Economic Orthodoxy: Asian Reform as an Evolutionary, Self-Organizing Process," *China Economic Review*, 4, 137-142 (1993).
9. _____, "Microfoundations of Macroeconomic Fluctuations and the Laws of Probability Theory: the Principle of Large Numbers vs. Rational Expectations Arbitrage," *Journal of Economic Behavior & Organization*, 49, 327-344 (2002).
10. _____, "Evolutionary Economic Dynamics: Persistent Business Cycles, Disruptive Technology, and the Trade-Off between Stability and Complexity," in Kurt Dopfer ed., *The Evolutionary Foundations of Economics*, Chapter 15, pp. 472-505, (Cambridge University Press, Cambridge, 2005).
11. Coase, R. H., *The Firm, the Market, and the Law*, (University of Chicago Press, Chicago, 1990).
12. David, P. A., "Clio and the Economics of QWERTY," *American Economic Review* (Papers and Proceedings), 75, 332-337 (1985).
13. Fama, E. F., "Efficient Capital Markets: A Review of Theory and Empirical Work," *Journal of Finance*, 25, 384-433 (1970).
14. Frisch, R., "Propagation Problems and Impulse Problems in Dynamic Economics," in *Economic Essays in Honour of Gustav Cassel*, (George Allen and Unwin, London, 1933).
15. Frye, T. and A. Shleifer, "The Invisible Hand and the Grabbing Hand," *American Economic Review* (Papers and Proceedings), 87, 354-358 (1997).
16. Fukuyama, F., *The End of History and The Last Man*, (Harper, New York, 1993).
17. Goodhart, C.A.E., "Two Concepts of Money: Implications for the Analysis of Optimal Currency Areas," *European Journal of Political Economy*, 14, 407-432 (1998).
18. Hayek, F. A., *Prices and Production*, (Routledge, London, 1935).

19. Keynes, J. M., *The General Theory of Employment, Investment, and Money*, (Macmillan, London, 1936).
20. Kolodko, G. W., *From Shock to Therapy: The Political Economy of Postsocialist Transformation*, (Oxford University Press, Oxford, 2000).
21. Kornai, J., "The Soft Budget Constraints," *Kyklos*, 39(1), 3-30 (1986).
22. Lin, J. Y., "Rural Reforms and Agricultural Growth in China," *American Economic Review*, 82(1), 34-51 (1992).
23. Lucas, R.E. Jr., "Expectations and the Neutrality of Money," *Journal of Economic Theory*, 4, 103-124 (1972).
24. Minsky, H. P., "The Financial Instability Hypothesis: A Restatement," in P. Arestis and T. Skouras eds., *Post Keynesian Economic Theory*, (Sharpe, 1985).
25. Modigliani, F. and M. H. Miller, "The Cost of Capital, Corporation Finance, and the Theory of Investment," *American Economic Review*, 48(3), 261-297 (1958).
26. Prigogine, I., *Order Out of Chaos, Man's New Dialogue with Nature*, (Bantam Books, New York, 1984).
27. Roland, G., *Transition and Economics: Politics, Markets, and Firms*, (MIT Press, Cambridge MA, 2000).
28. Romer, C. D., "The Great Depression," *Britannica Encyclopedia* (2004).
29. Sachs, J. D., *The End of Poverty*, (Penguin Books, New York, 2005).
30. Sachs, J. D. and W. T. Woo, "Understanding China's Economic Performance," *Journal of Policy Reform*, 4(1), 1-50 (2000).
31. Schumpeter, J. A., *Business Cycles, A Theoretical, Historical, and Statistical Analysis of the Capitalist Process*, (McGraw-Hill, New York, 1939).
32. Stiglitz, J., *Post Washington Consensus Consensus*, Initiative for Policy Dialogue (2004).
33. Von Weizsacker, E. U., O. R. Young and M. Finger, *Limits to Privatization: How to Avoid too Much of a Good Thing*, (Earthscan Publications, London, 2005).
34. Williamson, J., "What Washington Means by Policy Reform?" In John Williamson ed., *Latin America Adjustment: How Much Has Happened?* (Institute for International Economics, Washington DC, 1990).
35. World Bank, *Transition, the First Ten Years, Analysis and Lessons of Eastern Europe and Former Soviet Union*, (World Bank, Washington DC, 2002).

CHAPTER 4

THE IMPACT OF PRIVATISATION ON FIRM PERFORMANCE IN CHINA

Ligang Song* & Yang Yao** [*]

*Australia-Japan Center, Australian National University

**China Center for Economic Research, Beijing University

Abstract: This paper analyses the impact of privatisation on firm performance in China. Privatisation has had a significantly positive impact on firm profitability, but has had a weak or insignificant impact on unit costs and labour productivity. Increasing private share ownership has had a positive effect on profitability but only under the condition that the proportion of private share ownership passes a certain threshold. The presence of external share ownership has both statistically and economically significant effects on profitability, labour productivity and to a lesser extent, on unit costs. When there is no external share ownership, it takes time for an internally privatised/ gaizhi-ed firm to overcome the inertia inherited from being a former state enterprise. For gaizhi (enterprise restructuring) to be effective in improving firm performance, it has to be connected with a certain degree of privatisation.

[*] Ligang Song is a fellow at the Australia-Japan Center, Australian National University; Yang Yao is a professor at the China Center for Economic Research, Beijing University and visiting professor, Stanford Center for International Development, Stanford University. The authors thank the International Finance Corporation for permission to use the survey data. Yang Yao thanks Stanford Center for International Development for hosting him while part of the paper was written. Email addresses: yyao@ccer.pku.edu.cn and ligang.song@anu.edu.au

1. Introduction

While early reforms have improved the efficiency of the Chinese state-owned enterprises (SOEs) in various aspects (Gordon and Li, 1995; Groves *et al*, 1994; Groves *et al.*, 1995; and Li, 1997), market liberalisation in the 1990s has increased the competition from the private sector and encouraged local governments to privatise their SOEs (Li *et al.*, 1999; Tian, 2001; Guo and Yao, 2003; Su and Jefferson, 2003). The privatisation drive started in the early 1990s and has accelerated considerably since the mid-1990s when the Chinese central government formally sanctioned *gaizhi* ("changing the system" in Chinese) as a way to reform the Chinese SOEs. *Gaizhi* covers a wide variety of forms of enterprise restructuring ranging from incorporation of the SOE to an outright sale of the firm to an external private buyer. Through *gaizhi*, local governments have relinquished their control over a large number of SOEs. Figure 1 shows the trend of privatisation in China as a whole and for the 11 cities contained in the data set used in this study for the period between 1996 and 2001. The figure indexes the number of state-controlled firms in 1996 at 100 and shows the percentage of the remaining state-controlled firms in each subsequent year. For this analysis, state-control has been defined as those firms with more than

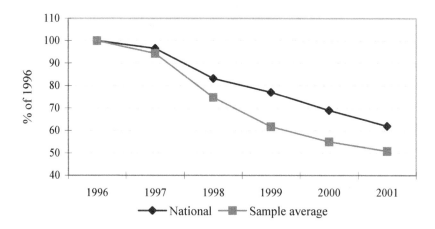

Figure 1. Dynamics of Firms Controlled by State Shares
Sources: *China Financial Statistical Yearbook: 1997-2002* and the survey data.

50 per cent (inclusive) of their share issue controlled by the government. Treating those firms no longer under majority state control as being privatised[1], it is possible to see that about 40 per cent of the SOEs were privatised in China during the period of 1996-2001. The pace of privatisation was even faster according to our sample. Only about half of the state-controlled firms of 1996 remained by 2001. Garnaut *et al.* (2003) found that about 80 per cent of the SOEs nationwide had finished *gaizhi* by the end of 2002, and about 70 per cent of the *gaizhi* cases involved at least partial transfer of the ownership from the state to private owners. A quiet revolution of state ownership of firms has occurred in China.

Despite the significance of this revolution, there are surprisingly few empirical studies assessing the privatisation process and its impacts (Megginson and Netter, 2001; Djankov and Murrell, 2002). This deficiency is largely related to the lack of data. Thanks to a recent large scale survey of 683 firms in 11 cities in the period between 1995 and 2001, Garnaut *et al.* (2003) are able to provide a comprehensive study of China's *gaizhi* process. This paper extends that study by providing an in-depth assessment of the impact of privatisation and *gaizhi* on firm performance in China. In a way it is a continuation of the earlier studies on the incentive schemes adopted during the earlier reforms, but the sheer magnitude of the events in this study singles it out from earlier studies. In addition, with the help of the panel structure of our data, we are able to effectively deal with the estimation difficulties, in particular the selection bias associated with privatisation, which is frequently encountered in the transition economics literature (Megginson and Netter, 2001 and Djankov and Murrell, 2002). To our knowledge, this is the first study that provides systematic evidence on the impact of SOE privatisation in China.

---

[1] Such treatment is subject to two qualifications, though. First, some firms may have vanished not because of privatisation but because of simple closing-up, which implies that our measure of privatisation is upward-biased. Second, new SOEs may be established over the period, which implies that the measure is downward-biased.

We are interested in the impact of three aspects of privatisation/*gaizhi*: private share ownership versus state share ownership, external versus internal private share ownership, and different forms of *gaizhi*. The central theme of privatisation is the introduction of private ownership into SOEs. We study the productive implications of the amount of private share ownership in a firm and compare the efficiency of fully state-owned firms (with 100 per cent state share ownership), state controlled firms (the extent of state share ownership is no less than 50 per cent but less than 100 per cent), and privately controlled firms (the amount of private share ownership is no less than 50 per cent of total shares issued). The introduction of external share ownership has been proven to be the most effective means of raising productivity in Eastern European countries (Djankov and Murrell, 2002). Internal privatisation is more common in China than in the other transition countries (Garnaut *et al.*, 2003). Does this mean that internal privatisation has a stronger rationale in China than in the other transition countries? Answering this question will contribute to our understanding of the comparison between China and other transition economies. Although *gaizhi* does not necessarily lead to privatisation, there may still exist some efficiency gains when a firm undertakes restructuring measures. As the market has become more and more competitive, even SOEs have been forced to respond to the market more closely, which often requires organizational restructuring inside the firm, a task frequently accomplished by *gaizhi*. It has been argued by some authors that a SOE can perform no worse than a private firm if the market is sufficiently competitive (Lin *et al.*, 1996). A comparison of *gaizhi* with genuine or full privatisation will shed light on the validity of this claim.

The indicators that we adopt to measure efficiency are pre-tax profit rates over total assets, cost per unit revenue, and labour productivity. These three indicators have been frequently used in the literature (Megginson and Netter, 2001; Djankov and Murrell, 2002). We find that increasing the proportion of private share ownership has a positive effect on profitability but only under the condition that the proportion of private share ownership exceeds a certain threshold. A firm controlled through state share ownership outperforms a fully state-owned firm by 2.7

percentage points in terms of profit margin, and a firm controlled through private share ownership outperforms a fully state-owned firm by 1.24 percentage points. Compared with the yearly average profitability of −0.93 per cent to −1.17 per cent in the sample, these differences have a high economic significance. However, unit costs and labour productivity do not respond in the same manner depending on the extent of private share ownership. The most robust and also economically significant results relate to the presence of external share ownership: when external share ownership increases by one percentage point, profitability increases by 0.020 percentage points; unit costs decrease by 0.024 percentage points; and labour productivity increases by 0.121 percentage points. It is important to note that external share ownership can relate to ownership by another SOE. In fact, a further analysis finds that institutions comprising external state share ownership have done no worse, or sometimes even better, than institutions characterised by private share ownership. Finally, *gaizhi* has been found to have no statistically significant positive impact on any of the three measures of efficiency and in some cases has even had a negative impact on the three measures of efficiency.

We attribute the inability of privatisation to improve cost effectiveness and labour productivity to Chinese SOEs' inferior production technology and management skills and the strict government employment policy. The finding that external share ownership' contributes to efficiency is consistent with the findings relating to Eastern European countries. Our findings, which indicate that organisations characterised by state share ownership have performed as well as organisations characterised by external private share ownership, suggest that the mechanism for external share ownership's positive impacts in China may be different than elsewhere. Besides attracting capital, the introduction of external share ownership may serve to break up the personal working relationships inherited from the old state enterprises that may undermine existing management authority within the firm. The contrast between *gaizhi* and privatisation measures shows that *gaizhi* needs to be connected with a certain degree of privatisation for it to be effective in improving firms' performance. The result also refutes the claim that market competition is enough for an SOE to perform equally as well as a private firm does.

The remainder of the paper is arranged as follows. Section 2 describes the data and re-samples the data to correct selection biases arising during the implementation stage of the survey. This section also describes the variables under consideration. Section 3 discusses the econometric issues, emphasising those that concern the potential selection biases associated with privatisation. Section 4 presents the main results regarding the impact of privatisation on firm performance. It then extends this analysis to deal with the time trends in privatisation, and assesses the effects of some other factors, including firm size, worker redundancy and soft budget constraints on firm profitability and productivity. The latter analysis provides some interesting results. Specifically, incorporating the "prettier daughters effect", i.e., better performing SOEs are privatised initially, does have an impact on our estimates; heavier burdens associated with making workers redundant have a strong negative effect on firm efficiency; and soft-budget constraints do not have a significant impact on firm efficiency. Finally, Section 5 concludes the paper.

2. Data and Measurement

2.1. Data issues

The data used in this study come from a 2002 International Finance Corporation survey conducted on 683 firms in 11 Chinese cities: Harbin, Fushun, Tangshan, Xining, Lanzhou, Chengdu, Guiyang, Weifang, Zhenjiang, Huangshi, and Hengyang. Some of these cities are large provincial capitals, while others are medium sized cities. Detailed information about these cities and approach adopted for implementing the survey can be found in Garnaut *et al.* (2003). The initial design of the survey was to contact all SOEs managed by each city as of the end of 1995. 1995 was chosen because large-scale privatisation commenced in 1996. Several problems arising during the implementation stage of the survey need to be addressed before we move on to discuss the variables.

The first problem relates to firm attrition due to bankruptcy. Current Chinese bankruptcy law only applies to SOEs, and bankruptcy does not necessarily lead to the liquidation of the bankrupt firm. It is often the case that the firm is re-organised and operates under a new name[2]. Therefore, the sample includes firms that have experienced bankruptcy. In addition, there must be firms that had actually been liquated by the sate of the survey and thus were not captured by the survey. Due to the fact that those firms tended to be those with poor performance, our sample was potentially biased upwards in terms of performance. This bias may not have a significant impact on our estimates of the effect of privatisation due to the fact that of those dissolved firms remaining in operation, they could have either remained as an SOE or been privatised (as with any other former SOE).

The second problem concerns merger activity and firms either splitting or de-merging. It is usually the case that poor performing firms participating in merger activity lose their name and the better performing firm retains their name following the merger. As such there is a potential upward bias in the aggregate performance in the sample. However, because the poor performing firms could have either remained as a SOE or been privatised, this bias does not necessarily lead to a biased estimate of the effect of privatisation.

To avoid data discontinuities, data were recorded from the year of the merger. That is, only the new firm was surveyed. In the case of de-mergers, the largest of the newly active firms was surveyed and data were recorded from the year of the split. It was often the case that the

---

[2] Bankruptcy is often used as a means to evade state bank debts. Because the banks are owned by the central government, local governments have an incentive to collude with local firms to use bankruptcy to evade bank debts (see Garnalt *et al.*, 2003 for more discussion and Gao and Yao (1999) for a theoretical treatment of the issue).

de-merger took the form of spin-off, that is, the old firm spun off a new firm and moved all of its production to this new firm, leaving the old firm only with a name, bank debts, and the pension burden of retired former employees (Garnaut *et al.*, 2003). As a result, the only truly active firm is the new firm. Since spin offs were recorded as one method of *gaizhi* in the survey, there is the potential for an upward bias in the estimate of the effect of *gaizhi*. However, the estimate of the effect of privatisation is not likely to be affected because spin-offs do not necessarily lead to additional privatisation.

The third problem is the potential selection bias associated with the timing of when the questionnaires were administered. Self-selection on the part of the firms in returning the questionnaire was one factor, and selection on the part of the particular city's Economic and Trade Commission (the local agency that administered the survey) was another. The first is unavoidable in any voluntary survey, but hopefully the selection was not systematically related to the decision to privatise. However, the second factor may cause real concern as local officials might encourage the firms that had closer ties with the government, usually the larger firms and non-privatised SOEs, to complete the questionnaire. While sample selection is hard to avoid in such a survey, the selection may cause over-sampling of non-privatised SOEs. Therefore, the sample could produce biased estimates if one is considering the effects of privatisation. However, we have information on the number of firms that were fully owned or controlled by the government in each city in each year, so weighted regressions can be adopted to correct for this source of bias. To accommodate different methods of regression analysis, however, we have adopted a different strategy to re-sample the SOEs in each city by adopting the following method.

Let s_{it} stand for the share of fully state-owned and state-controlled SOEs in city i in year t out of the total the number of such SOEs in the city at the end of 1995. That is, s_{it} measures the extent of privatisation in the city. Let $\hat{s}_{it}$ be the share of those firms in the sample. Then the weight for the SOEs in city i in year t is defined as $w_{it} = s_{it} / \hat{s}_{it}$, which will be used when weighted regressions are performed. It would also be ideal to use these weights to re-sample the SOEs in each city in each year. To maintain the panel structure of the data, we first create a weighted weight for each city $\hat{w}_i = \sum_t w_{it}(N_{it} / N_i)$, where N_{it} is the number of SOEs for city i in year t in the sample, and N_i is the sum of those numbers in the period of 1995-2001. Then this weight is used to sample the SOEs of 2001 in each city, and data of the earlier years are matched to this new sample accordingly.

The validity of the above re-sampling strategy relies on the assumption that randomness is preserved among the SOEs and among the privatised firms in each city, respectively. There is no doubt that this assumption does not strictly hold for data collected as part of this survey, but we contend that this is the best approach that can be adopted. The new sample has 608 firms. By the end of 2001, 39.8 per cent of these firms had experienced some form of *gaizhi*, 24.5 per cent had some private share ownership, and 19.1 per cent had external share ownership.

2.2. Performance indicators

Three indicators - profitability, unit cost, and labour productivity - are used in this study to determine the impact of privatisation on firm performance. Profitability is defined as the rate of return to assets, that is, the percentage of pre-tax profit over the total value of assets. The total value, instead of the net value is used because many firms had a negative net value of assets. Profitability is the most comprehensive measure of firm efficiency.

Unit cost is the percentage of the material and operational costs over revenue. In this case, costs do not include wages and as such the definition adopted here is different from that adopted by Frydman *et al.* (1999) who include both material and labour costs in the total cost. The unit cost would become the mirror index of profitability if we adopted this alternative definition and it is for this reason that we have avoided it. Labour costs are partly reflected by labour productivity. Similar to the definition of Frydman *et al.* (1999), our definition of unit cost also allows us to account for a firm's passive restructuring measures focused on cost reduction.

Labour productivity is defined as the revenue contributed by an on-duty worker. A salient feature of the Chinese SOEs relates to worker inactivity. A considerable proportion of the workforce is not economically active although it is attached to a particular firm[3]. For this reason, we use the number of on-duty workers in the model estimation. Revenue has been adjusted using China's overall GDP price deflator. Labour productivity captures the features of both passive adjustments by the firm, (i.e. laying off workers) and positive expansion (i.e., expanding production).

2.3. Explanatory variables

To study the impacts of *gaizhi* and privatisation on the three performance indicators, we construct three sets of explanatory variables. The first set is constructed along the lines of private share ownership. Private shares can be 'internal' or in other words owned by either firm insiders such as managers and employees or 'external' and owned by outsiders (mainly external private firms). In addition to the percentage of private share ownership, we also construct two dummy variables to control for share ownership. To be consistent with official Chinese statistics, the threshold for controlling share ownership is set to be 50 per cent (inclusive). With

---

[3] There are two categories of redundant workers. One is internal retirement, and the other is the so-called *xiagang*, i.e., a situation in which a worker is legally attached to a firm but nevertheless does not work. The first type of workers is fully supported by individual firms, and the second type is supported by both the firm and the local government (See Garnaut *et al.*, 2003). Official retirees also place a burden on an SOE.

the reference group being defined as the firms fully owned by the government, the first dummy is defined for firms that are not fully owned, but nevertheless controlled by government (state-controlled firms), and the second dummy is for firms that are controlled or fully owned privately (privately controlled firms). We classify shares privately owned by other SOEs also as being government owned. The percentage of private share ownership and the controlling dummies are widely used in the literature to capture the extent of privatisation (Djankov and Murrell, 2002).

The second set of explanatory variables is constructed along the lines of internal versus external ownership. The presence of external share ownership is found to have the most significant effect on post-privatisation performance in the literature (Djankov and Murrell, 2002). We are concerned about the different impacts of internal state share ownership, internal private share ownership, and external share ownership on firm performance. Internal state share ownership corresponds to those shares that are directly held by the government.

Internal private share ownership can be decomposed into shares held by the management of the company and shares owned by the employees of the company. The decomposition is a meaningful one as management and employee incentives are often studied separately in the transition literature. Early studies have found that managerial and employee incentives, mainly in the form of bonuses, improve the efficiency of the Chinese SOEs (Groves *et al.*, 1994, 1995). Our study will determine whether share ownership accomplishes the same thing.

External share ownership can be further decomposed into external private share ownership and external state share ownership. External private share ownership is mainly associated with external private firms, and external state share ownership associated with external SOEs. Studies have found that external block share ownership is more effective than external individual share ownership in improving firm performance (Djankov and Murrell, 2002). Our data do not make a fine distinction between external block share ownership and external individual share ownership, so such a comparison cannot be performed. Nevertheless, external SOE shares can serve as a proxy for block share ownership.

The third set of variables is constructed along the line of *gaizhi*. A dummy variable is first constructed to indicate whether a firm has conducted *gaizhi*. Even without changing ownership, *gaizhi* may help an SOE to improve efficiency through various forms of restructuring. For the current purpose, however, the form of *gaizhi* is of more interest. The survey identifies a series of forms of *gaizhi*, which can be summarised into five types: internal restructuring, bankruptcy, employee shareholding, open sales and leases, and 'others'. Internal restructuring includes incorporation, spin offs, introducing new investors[4], and debt-equity swaps[5], which through re-organisation of departments, setting up new branches, and downsizing, may have some efficiency implications.

Bankruptcy is often used by SOEs to shake off bank debts. It is also used to reorganise the firm, noticeably, to remove the burdens associated with inactive or redundant workforce (Garnaut *et al.*, 2003). Therefore, a firm reorganised through bankruptcy may perform better than before.

Employee shareholding is the most common form of *gaizhi*. It is equivalent to the insider privatisation in Russia, which has been found to be an inferior means of privatisation compared with external takeovers (Boycko *et al.*, 1996). It is thus interesting to find out whether this is the case in China. Open sales and leases are theoretically open to everyone, insider or outsider, but in reality the firm is often sold or leased to insiders. There has been an increasing trend in outside private participation (Garnaut *et al.*, 2003). A lease contract is adopted often for the reason that the buyers of the lease do not have enough cash to pay for the assets at a single point in time. Eventually, buyers will buy the firm

---

[4] Private investors may be introduced in this process. Here the emphasis is that the stock of assets does not change ownership.

[5] Starting in 1999, the Chinese government set up four asset management companies to handle the non-performing loans in the four major state banks. One measure adopted has been debt-equity swap that converts a firm's debt into shares held by an asset management company and then sold to potential investors.

after they have accumulated enough funds. So sales and leases constitute the most radical form of *gaizhi* and are more likely to introduce outside private participation. However, this form of *gaizhi* may not be equivalent to 100 per cent privatisation because the government may keep shares in the firm.

The category of "others" mainly includes publicly listed and joint venture activities with foreign firms. A small number of *unclassified* firms are also included in this category. Until very recently, China's two stock exchanges were only the marketplace for trading shares in SOEs. A publicly listed SOE was still controlled by the government as by law 50 per cent of the shares could be traded. The number of publicly listed SOEs and the number of joint ventures in the sample are both small, so it is not feasible to define them as separate categories in the later regression models. To the extent that joint ventures help SOEs to acquire external finance, combining them into one category is not a totally unreasonable approach. A dummy variable is constructed for each of the above five forms of *gaizhi* and will be compared with the SOEs that had not undergone any form of *gaizhi*.

Figures 2 to 4 show the time trend of the three performance indicators according to the three sets of explanatory variables. In Figures 2 and 3, comparisons are made between categories of controlling shares rather than by share ownership itself. The three figures show that *gaizhi* and privatisation have significant positive effects on all three measures of performance (though weaker in the case of labour productivity). However, these effects are only indicative because other factors are not controlled for in this comparison. In particular, there may be a selection bias in privatisation and *gaizhi* in the sense that better performing firms may be selected to undertake *gaizhi* or be privatised first (this issue will be discussed in Section 3).

2.4. Control variables

Two sets of control variables were used in our regressions. The first set contains several firm-level variables. Employment in SOEs is largely controlled by the government, so it can be regarded as being an external factor that influences a SOE's performance. Two variables are adopted to measure employment. One is the logarithm of the number of on-duty workers, which controls for firm size. The second is the redundancy rate, which controls for firms' social burdens[6]. The redundancy rate is the number of "redundant" workers as a percentage of the number of on-duty workers. "Redundant" workers include official retirees, internal retirees, and *xiagang* workers (see footnote for a discussion of these categories of workers). Official retirees are counted as a social burden because in many cases firms are still directly responsible for paying retirement wages despite the fact that China has established a new pension system that in most cases maintains a centralised system of provision up to provincial level[7]. While the firm size may have either a positive or negative impact on firm performance, a higher redundancy rate is likely to result in poor performance.

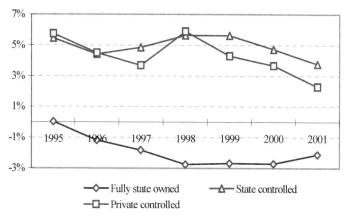

Figure 2a. Comparison of Performance by Private and State Controlling Shares: Profitability
Source: Calculated and plotted using the survey data.

---

[6] See Lin and Tan (1999) for a discussion on implications of social burdens of SOEs.
[7] However, there are serious problems in the transition from the old firm-based system to the new system. The central issue is how to finance workers that will not have paid for enough years upon their retirement. One of the difficulties faced by SOEs in privatisation is related to this issue (Garnaut *et al.*, 2003).

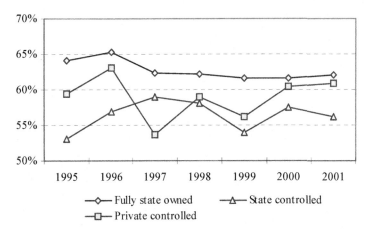

Figure 2b. Comparison of Performance by Private and State Controlling Shares: Unit Costs

Source: Calculated and plotted using the survey data.

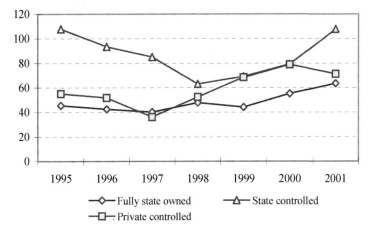

Figure 2c. Comparison of Performance by Private and State Controlling Shares: Labour Productivity (1,000 yuan)

Source: Calculated and plotted using the survey data.

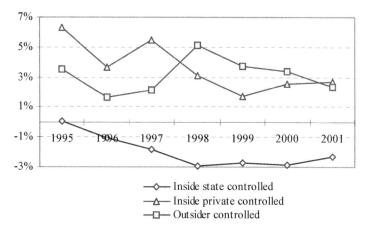

Figure 3a. Comparison of Performance by External and Internal Controlling Shares:
Profitability
Source: Calculated and plotted using the survey data.

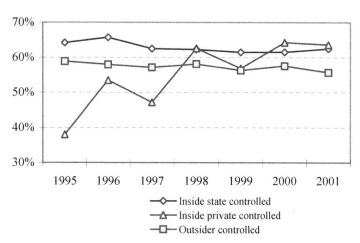

Figure 3b. Comparison of Performance by External and Internal Controlling Shares: Unit
Cost
Source: Calculated and plotted using the survey data.

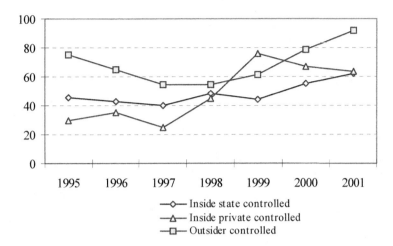

Figure 3c. Comparison of Performance by External and Internal Controlling Shares: Labour Productivity (1,000 yuan)
Source: Calculated and plotted using the survey data.

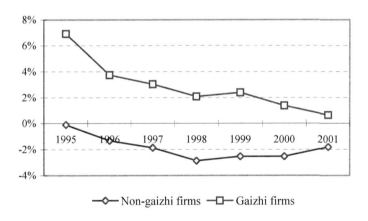

Figure 4a. Comparison of Performance by *Gaizhi:* Profitability
Source: Calculated and plotted using the survey data.

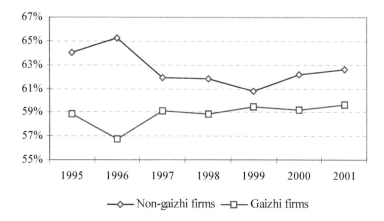

Figure 4b. Comparison of Performance by *Gaizhi:* Unit Costs
Source: Calculated and plotted using the survey data.

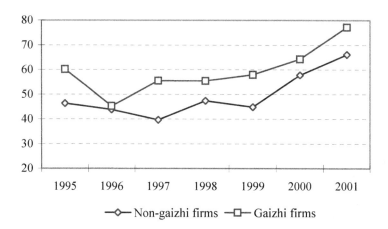

Figure 4c. Comparison of Performance by *Gaizhi:* Labour Productivity (1,000 yuan)
Source: Calculated and plotted using the survey data.

We use debt/equity ratio to control for a firm's financial standing. It would be expected that a higher debt/equity ratio would be associated with worse firm performance because it indicates that the firm has accumulated a large quantity of unpaid debts. In addition, we include three variables to measure a firm's budget constraints imposed by the banking sector and the government. They are the percentage of accumulated overdue bank loans and interest as a proportion of the year-end stock of outstanding loans (bank arrears); the quantity of accumulated overdue taxes as a proportion of tax payments in a particular year (tax arrears), and the quantity of accumulated overdue social security as a proportion of social security payments (social security arrears) in a particular year. While the first variable measures the *soft budget* constraint problem in a firm's dealings with the banking sector, the last two variables measure the same problem when a firm deals with the government, although perhaps with different implications because firms are likely to face a harder budget constraint in the case of taxes than in the case of paying for social security (Garnaut *et al.*, 2003). Garnaut *et al.* (2003) find that firms are more likely to evade liabilities owned by the government than those liabilities owned by the bank. It is interesting to find whether the soft-budget constraint with the government is more damaging to efficiency than the equivalent constraint with the banking sector.

There is an endogeneity problem associated with the three soft-budget constraint variables. Indeed, the same problem may happen with respect to the other control variables. To deal with this problem and smooth out time variations, we use the lagged three-year moving averages of the above control variables in the regressions. To save data, however, we use the data of 1995 and the averages of 1995 and 1996, respectively, for the years of 1996 and 1997 that do not have three preceding years in our data set. In adopting this approach, we drop the information from 1995 from our data and the analyses cover only the period between 1996 and 2001. Table 1 reports the basic statistics of the transformed control variables as well as of the performance indicators and explanatory variables.

Table 1. Descriptive Statistics of the Variables in the Re-drawn Sample (608 firms, 1996-2001)

	Number of valid cases	Min	Max	Mean	Std. Dev.
ROA (per cent)	3642	-101.54	89.48	-.91	10.83
Unit cost (per cent)	3618	1.79	99.77	62.43	18.37
Labor productivity (1,000 RMB)	3648	.00	88.8318	5.41	8.04
Private shares (per cent)	3290	.00	102.35	10.09	28.18
State controlled firms dummy	3290	.00	1.00	0.04	.20
Private controlled firms dummy	3290	.00	1.00	0.10	.30
Inside state shares (per cent)	3290	.00	100.00	85.33	34.42
Insider shares (per cent)	3290	.00	100.00	4.91	20.35
Management shares (per cent)	3290	.00	100.00	2.22	11.86
Employee shares (per cent)	3290	.00	100.00	2.69	12.55
Outside shares (per cent)	3290	.00	100.00	9.76	28.14
Outside state shares (per cent)	3290	.00	100.00	4.57	18.85
Outside private shares (per cent)	3290	.00	100.00	5.19	19.81
Gaizhi *dummy*	3648	.00	1.00	.24	.43
Internal restructuring	3648	.00	1.00	0.06	.24
Bankruptcy	3648	.00	1.00	0.03	.16
Employee shareholding	3648	.00	1.00	0.06	.23
Sales & leases	3648	.00	1.00	0.05	.22
Others	3648	.00	1.00	0.05	.21
Number of on-duty workers	3646	.00	15245	632.81	1168.40
Worker redundancy (per cent)	3646	.00	100.00	32.74	24.66
Debt/assets (per cent)	3526	.00	992.92	61.47	68.71
Bank arrears (per cent)	3646	.00	6332.76	83.62	213.89
Tax arrears (per cent)	3526	.00	1940.23	3.32	49.91
Social security arrears (per cent)	3526	.00	27.73	.30	1.26
List-wise valid cases	3168				

The second set of control variables is comprised of sector, city, and year dummies. Industrial concentration in the sample is considerable, so the two-digit classification system is inadequate. We aggregate the two-digit industries into ten sectors as follows:

- Primary (agriculture, mining, and logging) ;
- Food, beverage, and tobacco production;
- Textile and garment production;
- Furniture and toy production, and printing;
- Chemical production;
- Metal refinement and products;
- Ordinary manufacturing;
- Electronics;
- Public utilities; and
- Services.

This aggregation has an arbitrary element to it, but classifying industrial activity into ten sectors should be adequate for our attempt to control for sectoral variations in performance. China's *gaizhi* program varies from city to city (Garnaut *et al.*, 2003). Adding city dummies in the regressions will control for differences in *gaizhi* and privatisation, as well as for the regional disparities in economic and social conditions. Year dummies are added to control for time-wise *gaizhi* variations and changes in macroeconomic conditions in general.

3. Econometric Issues

The panel structure of our data allows us to deal with the selection problem frequently encountered in the literature. Using the same data set, Guo and Yao (2003) show that better performing firms in our sample are indeed privatised in the first instance. Therefore, we have to deal with the selection problem in our regression analysis.

One way to correct for selection bias is to adopt the instrumental variables (IV) method. However, this method is confined by the availability of instruments. Often the researcher has to face the "spurious exclusion" problem, namely, it is hard to justify the exclusion of the instruments from the performance equations. Therefore, except for a few studies (e.g., Anderson *et al.*, 2000), most of the studies in the literature do not adopt this approach.

Two other correction methods used in the literature rely on the assumption that the selection bias is time-invariant. The first rests on the premise that selection is based on a firm's pre-privatisation performance, so controlling for pre-privatisation performance can effectively correct the bias (Megginson and Netter, 2001). However, this method does not fully control the bias if the selection is not solely based on pre-privatisation performance, but also relies on a firm's long-term profitability. In addition, it is not feasible to identify a pre-privatisation date if privatisation is a gradual process and illustrated by private share ownership increasing incrementally over the years. This is exactly the case for two of the three sets of explanatory variables in this study - private share ownership versus state share ownership and external share ownership versus internal share ownership.

The second method is to adopt the standard fixed-effect (FE) panel method (e.g., Frydman *et al.*, 1999). This method is based on the premise that the selection is based on a firm's intrinsic and long-term time invariant properties. In effect, it also takes care of the possibility dealt with by adopting the first correction method, that is, firms are only selected based on their pre-privatisation performance.

However, the FE method may impose too much control if the selection is only based on pre-privatisation performance. In addition, this method may not be as effective in our analysis because for a considerable number of firms the explanatory variables do not have much variation in the period covered by the data. For example, among the 144 firms that had some degree of private share ownership, 19 of them, or 13.2 per cent did not undergo any change in the extent of the holdings held privately in the period 1996-2001. If the FE method were used, these firms would be treated the same as those that had no private share ownership at all. The problem is more severe in the case of external share ownership and *gaizhi*. Among the 112 firms that had external share ownership, 22.3 per cent did not experience any change, and among the 242 firms that experienced *gaizhi*, 27.7 per cent finished during or before 1996.

The above discussion leads us to adopt a compromise approach to our baseline regressions that controls the lagged three-year moving averages of the three performance indicators. This approach takes a position between controlling for pre-privatisation/*gaizhi* conditions and controlling for intrinsic firm characteristics. It takes care of the problem of gradual privatisation that cannot be handled by merely controlling the initial conditions and avoids the possible over-control of the FE model. To the extent that reverse causality exists running from performance to privatisation/*gaizhi* measures, this approach also bears some of the functions of the instrumental variable method.

The method of generating the data on the lagged performance variables is the same as that which we have adopted for the control variables. However, putting these lags directly into the regressions would appropriate the statistical significance of most other variables if strong time persistency exists in the performance indicators, which was indeed the case shown during preliminary tests. To deal with this problem, we extract two principal components from the three lagged average performance indicators by adopting the standard *principal component* method. The two components together explain 75.4 per cent of the total variance of the three variables. The correlation coefficients between the first component and profitability, unit cost, and labour productivity are 0.32, 0.58, and 0.84, respectively; and between the second component and the three performance indicators are 0.82, -0.65, and 0.13, respectively. We call the first component the "expansion factor" because it has relatively high correlation with labour productivity and unit cost and a low correlation with profitability; conversely, we call the second component the "saving factor" because it has a high correlation with profitability and strong negative correlation with unit costs, but exhibits a low correlation with labour productivity. These two factors will be used in our regressions to control for the selection bias. Our baseline regression specification is as follows:

$$Y_{it} = \alpha_0 + P_{it}\beta + \overline{X}_{it-1}\gamma + \overline{Y}_{it-1}\phi + \alpha_s + \alpha_c + \alpha_t + e_{it},$$ (1)

where Y_{it} is a performance measure, P_{it} is an explanatory variable, $\overline{X}_{it-1}$ is the set of the lagged three-year averages of the control variables, $\overline{Y}_{it-1}$ contains the expansion factor and the saving factor, α_0 is the constant terms, α_s, α_c and α_t are the sector, city, and year dummies with proper omission of the reference groups, and e_{it} is the stochastic error term with the usual probabilistic properties.

Admittedly, the expansion and saving factors do not control for all the selection bias in an exact way. However, the direction of the discrepancy is hard to predict. If the selection bias were only related to pre-privatisation (or *gaizhi*) performance, using the two factors might undermine the effect of privatisation because too much of the performance would be attributed to their influence at the time after privatisation was first introduced for three or more years. Conversely, the control would not be sufficient if the selection bias were based on intrinsic firm characteristics. To test the sensitivity of our estimates, we also estimate the following firm fixed-effect (FE) model:

$$Y_{it} = \alpha_0 + P_{it}\beta + \overline{X}_{it-1}\gamma + \overline{Y}_{it-1}\phi + \alpha_i + \alpha_t + e_{it},$$ (2)

where α_i is the i th firm's fixed effect. The sectoral and city dummies have to be dropped because of possible double counting relating to the firm fixed effects. The FE model is likely to provide the lower bounds of estimates of the impacts of privatisation/*gaizhi*, for two reasons, which have been discussed before. First, it would put too much of a constraint on the data if the selection bias were only related to pre-privatisation (or *gaizhi*) performance; and secondly, it only allows for within-firm comparison. However, the FE model may provide even stronger results if the firms that did not change the extent of privatisation/*gaizhi* just happened to be those that performed poorly. Therefore, the FE model of equation (2) is best viewed as an alternative specification to the baseline specification (1). More confidence should be put on the estimates that are significant in both specifications.

In addition to the average effects of privatisation/*gaizhi*, we are also interested in performance over time. Specifically, we are concerned with two kinds of time trends. One is related to post-privatisation/*gaizhi* performance, and the other is related to the year of the introduction of the first privatisation/*gaizhi* measures.

For the first kind of time trend, Frydman *et al.* (1999) point out two kinds of selection bias that may distort the estimation of the effects of privatisation. First, the manager may under-report the firm's performance (or deliberately perform poorly) before privatisation in order to achieve a better deal during and after privatisation, so the better post-privatisation performance may be artificial. Secondly, a firm may have taken efficiency-enhancing measures (such as installing new equipment) just before privatisation so their effects are only felt after privatisation. Those two kinds of selection biases suggest that privatisation would have stronger effects in the early years of privatisation.

In addition to these two sources of selection biases, post-privatisation/ *gaizhi* performance may also exhibit a temporal pattern for other reasons. The positive effects of privatisation/*gaizhi* may diminish or become stronger over the years, depending on the forms of privatisation/*gaizhi* and other firm-specific characteristics. For example, privatisation in the form of employee shareholding may have a significant effect on firm performance in the earlier years of privatisation because of enhanced incentives, but this effect may quickly diminish in the later years as the shortcomings of employee share ownership overtakes the positive effects of enhanced incentives[8]. On the other hand, the effects of privatisation/ *gaizhi* may also be enhanced over the years because these measures generally take time to have an effect.

We test the post-privatisation/*gaizhi* time trend by estimating the following equation

---

[8] Employee shareholding gives most employees shares so it is not so different from SOEs in terms of the free-riding problem.

$$Y_{it} = \alpha_0 + \beta_0 P_{it} + \beta_1 P_{it} \times Year\_after_{it} + \overline{X}_{it-1}\gamma + \overline{Y}_{it-1}\phi + \alpha_s + \alpha_c + \alpha_t + e_{it}$$

(3)

where *Year_after$_{it}$* is the year difference between the *t*th year and the year when the first private share ownership or outside share ownership appeared in a firm, or when the firm first undertook *gaizhi*. That is, it takes a value of $(t-f)$ for $t \geq f$, and a value of zero for $t < f$, where *f* is the year of the appearance of the first privatisation/*gaizhi* measure[9]. We would expect β_1 to take the opposite sign to that of β_0 (provided β_0 takes the expected sign) if the two selection biases proposed by Frydman *et al.* (1999) were the major factors driving the trend[10].

For the second kind of time trend, we notice that later privatised/*gaizhi*-ed firms may not perform as well as early privatised/*gaizhi*-ed firms because privatisation may be determined by unobserved firm characteristics that have productive implications only after privatisation and are unobservable before privatisation. These characteristics may include the competence of the management team working independently of the government; its ability to set up the right corporate governance structure; possible industrial relations difficulties between the management and the workers after privatisation, and so forth. As long as local governments are aware of these factors, they might postpone the privatisation for some and choose better performing firms to be privatised in the first instance (Guo and Yao, 2003). So the saying goes: "the prettier daughters are married out first." There is of course a possibility that the "prettier daughters" marry out later. In both cases, the privatisation/*gaizhi* effect would be over-estimated. To accommodate this possibility, we are again concerned about the year in which a firm

---

[9] This means that firms that had not taken any privatisation/*gaizhi* measure by 2001 take a value of zero for any year. There are a few firms that first took privatisation/*gaizhi* measures before 1995. For those firms, we assume that their first privatisation/*gaizhi* measures were as if introduced in 1995.

[10] In equation (3), we use a continuous variable of the years, rather than a set of dummies to denote each year after the first measures of privatisation/*gaizhi* was taken because under the dummy approach the degree of freedom in some years is too small to get reliable estimates. The same consideration applies to equation (4).

first introduced its privatisation/*gaizhi* measures. Unlike the previous case, though, here we are interested in the difference in years between that year and 1995. We let this difference be denoted by *Years_before$_{it}$*. For a firm that first introduced any privatisation/*gaizhi* measure in year *f*, this variable takes a value of $(f - 1995)$ for $t \geq f$, and a value of zero for $t < f$.[11] Then we estimate the following equation

$$Y_{it} = \alpha_0 + \beta_0 P_{it} + \beta_1 P_{it} \times Years\_before_{it} + \overline{X}_{it-1}\gamma + \overline{Y}_{it-1}\phi + \alpha_s + \alpha_c + \alpha_t + e_{it}.$$

(4)

If the selection problem existed, β_1 would be significant. The coefficient would be negative if the "prettier daughters" were married out first, but positive if they were married out late.

4. Impacts of Privatisation/*Gaizhi*

The baseline specification (1) is estimated separately for profitability, unit cost, and labour productivity, with different sets of explanatory variables. As we pointed out in the last section, the FE model is best seen as an alternative specification to the baseline model. Here we discuss its results together with the results form the baseline model. We are especially interested in the estimates that are significant under both specifications.

4.1. Private versus state share ownership

The results in Table 2 show the comparison between private and state share ownership under the baseline specification. For each performance indicator, two regressions are run. One uses the continuous variable of the percentage of private share ownership, and the other uses the two dummy variables indicating state controlled and privately controlled firms, respectively. The results concerning the effects of privatisation are

---

[11] Again, firms that had not taken any privatisation/*gaizhi* measure by 2001 get zero for this variable for any year.

Table 2. Private versus State Shares: Baseline Results

Variable	Profitability I	Profitability II	Unit cost I	Unit cost II	Productivity I	Productivity II
Private shares	0.016***		0.007		-0.051	
	(0.005)		(0.009)		(0.042)	
State controlled firms		0.988		-2.369**		4.689
		(0.723)		(1.151)		(5.178)
Private controlled firms		1.731***		0.804		-4.212
		(0.502)		(0.798)		(3.589)
Ln(on-duty workers)	-0.268**	-0.276**	0.280	0.325	-3.042***	-3.142***
	(0.128)	(0.129)	(0.204)	(0.205)	(0.922)	(0.923)
Redundancy	-0.023***	-0.023***	-0.009	-0.009	-0.093*	-0.092*
	(0.007)	(0.007)	(0.011)	(0.011)	(0.051)	(0.052)
Debt/equity ratio	-0.003	-0.003	0.004	0.004	0.001	0.001
	(0.002)	(0.002)	(0.003)	(0.003)	(0.010)	(0.011)
Bank arrears	0.000	0.000	-0.0017*	-0.0018*	0.001	0.001
	(0.001)	(0.001)	(0.001)	(0.001)	(0.010)	(0.010)
Tax arrears	-0.001	-0.001	0.003	0.003	0.001	-0.010
	(0.003)	(0.003)	(0.004)	(0.004)	(0.021)	(0.021)
Social security arrears	-0.072	-0.076	0.015	0.034	0.191	0.154
	(0.112)	(0.112)	(0.178)	(0.178)	(0.801)	(0.802)
Expansion factor	2.520***	2.513***	9.365***	9.382***	55.044***	54.989***
	(0.146)	(0.146)	(0.232)	(0.232)	(1.044)	(1.044)
Saving factor	6.108***	6.090***	-10.197***	-10.154***	10.752***	10.645***
	(0.149)	(0.149)	(0.237)	(0.238)	(1.072)	(1.073)
R^2	0.443	0.444	0.563	0.563	0.546	0.547
No. of cases	3166	3166	3166	3166	3166	3166

* Significant at the 10 per cent significance level; ** significant at the 5 per cent significance level; *** significant at the 1 per cent significance level.
Figures in parentheses are standard errors.

mixed. While privatisation is highly significant in increasing firm profitability, the percentage of private share ownership has no significant impact on unit cost and labour productivity. State controlled firms are only more efficient than fully government owned firms in terms unit cost, and privately controlled firms are only more efficient in terms of profitability. The economic significance of private share ownership is considerable.

According to our point estimate, a fully privately owned firm (that has 100 percent of private share ownership) has a profit rate that is 1.6 percentage points higher than that of a fully owned state firm. The average profit rate of the sample in each year in the period of 1996-2001 was between −0.93 per cent to −1.17 per cent, so a gap of 1.6 percentage points is substantial. This gap is also verified by the estimate of the private control dummy, which shows that the profit rate of a privately controlled firm is 1.73 percentage points higher than that of a fully state owned firm. The economic significance of state controlled firms' cost advantage over fully state owned firms is not high if one compares it with the average unit cost in the sample, which is between 55 per cent and 60 per cent of the sales volume. However, a reduction in unit cost implies an increase in profitability (in terms of sales), so the 2.4 percentage point advantage is substantial.

The two control factors are highly significant in all the regressions and have the expected signs. The expansion factor is positively correlated with all the three performance measures, and the saving factor is positively correlated with profitability and labour productivity, but negatively correlated with unit cost. These results remain unchanged in the other two sets of regressions. Comparing the trends shown in Figures 2-4 and the regression results, one realises that the two control factors siphon off most of the advantages of the privatised/*gaizhi*-ed firms. This implies that selection biases indeed existed and the two control factors are effective in controlling for them.

The results of the FE model are presented in Table 3. It has a much higher R^2, indicating that firm fixed effects are strong. The F-test shows that the firm dummies are jointly significant in all regressions. The number of significant variables, however, has decreased considerably. Private share ownership now turns out to have no significant impact on any of the three performance indicators. If the comparison is made between fully government owned, state controlled, and privately controlled firms, however, the latter two types of firms are both shown to have significantly higher profitability, but there is no difference in respect of unit cost and labour productivity.

Table 3. Private versus State Shares: FE Results

Variable	Profitability I	Profitability II	Unit cost I	Unit cost II	Productivity I	Productivity II
Private shares	0.010		-0.009		-0.035	
	(0.007)		(0.009)		(0.042)	
State controlled firms		2.704**		-1.919		5.203
		(1.258)		(1.709)		(7.994)
Private controlled firms		1.242**		-1.176		-3.349
		(0.634)		(0.870)		(4.037)
Ln(on-duty workers)	-2.594***	-2.596***	0.072	0.075	0.193	0.204
	(0.542)	(0.541)	(0.737)	(0.737)	(3.438)	(3.439)
Redundancy	-0.064***	-0.062***	-0.040*	-0.042*	-0.070	-0.067
	(0.016)	(0.016)	(0.022)	(0.022)	(0.102)	(0.102)
Debt/equity ratio	0.004	0.004	0.012***	0.013***	0.013	0.013
	(0.004)	(0.004)	(0.005)	(0.005)	(0.022)	(0.022)
Bank arrears	-0.000	-0.000	-0.001	-0.001	-0.001	-0.001)
	(0.001)	(0.001)	(0.001)	(0.001)	(0.010)	(0.010)
Tax arrears	0.000	0.000	-0.001	-0.001	-0.001	-0.001
	(0.005)	(0.005)	(0.007)	(0.007)	(0.035)	(0.034)
Social security arrears	-0.095	-0.092	-0.037	-0.039	0.337	0.338
	(0.174)	(0.174)	(0.236)	(0.236)	(1.104)	(1.105)
R^2	0.701	0.701	0.831	0.830	0.807	0.808
Number of cases	3187	3187	3167	3167	3192	3192

* Significant at the 10 per cent significance level; ** significant at the 5 per cent significance level; *** significant at the 1 per cent significance level.

Figures in parentheses are standard errors.

Putting together the baseline results and the FE results, we have the following two conclusions regarding the effect of privatisation. First, privatisation only has a significant positive impact on profitability, but has a weak or insignificant impact on unit cost and labour productivity. This finding is consistent with the finding of Frydman *et al.* (1999) in three Eastern European countries. Secondly, while increasing private share ownership has a positive effect on profitability, only the private control dummy is significant under both the baseline and the FE specifications. This result seems to suggest that the degree of private share ownership has to pass a certain threshold in order for it to have a significant effect on firm performance.

The reason that privatisation does not have any significant impact on unit costs is related to the technological and managerial conditions of many SOEs pre-privatisation. Garnaut *et al.* (2003) find that many SOEs had not spent on R&D or even purchased new equipment for more than 10 years. SOEs were used to an expansionary business model to increase profits. This historical approach has had a great impact on privatised SOEs. In our sample, the profit rate is positively correlated with unit cost, and the expansion factor is positively correlated with all the three performance indicators.

The failure of privatisation to improve labour productivity has a great deal to do with government policy to maintain full employment in the country. It is well known that the Chinese SOEs have a serious problem of disguised unemployment and a high level of worker redundancy or inactivity. The survey found that all the sample cities set a limit, usually 10 per cent of a firm's workforce, for layoffs in the privatisation/*gaizhi* package. In practice, a privatised/*gaizhi*-ed firm was often required to retain all its employees, with concessions/subsidies from governments in terms of cheaper privatisation prices and/or the retaining of land use rights (Garnaut *et al.*, 2003). Although firms could use internal or early retirement to deal with worker redundancy and inactivity, there was a limit to this in practice. It was commonly found that firms had to set up auxiliary branches (mostly engaged in services and producing low-skill products) just to digest the redundant workers. The function of these branches was more to provide welfare to redundant workers (who were usually less skillful) than to produce marketable products, so their productivity was lower. As a result, the firm's overall efficiency was compromised.

The result that privatisation has only significant impacts on return to assets suggests that a privatised firm is keener to adopt capital-saving technology than an old-style SOE. Chinese SOEs are characterised by a much higher degree of capital intensity than private firms, indicating certain levels of inefficiency (Lin and Tan, 1999). When an SOE is transferred into private hands through privatisation, it is natural for the new owner(s) to reduce capital intensity by more efficient use of the current stock of assets.

4.2. External versus internal share ownership

There are more significant results for the comparison between external and internal share ownership (Tables 4 and 5). The baseline results in Table 4 show that, consistent with the previous results, internal private share ownership has a significant impact on profitability, but not on unit costs and labour productivity. External share ownership has a significant effect on profitability and labour productivity. Calculated by our point estimates, the profit rate of a fully externally owned firm would be 1.6 percentage points higher than that of a fully state owned firm, and its workers would on average contribute 6,200 yuan more of revenue than their counterparts in the latter type of firm. Both effects are economically significant (the average labor productivity in the sample was in the range of 46,000 to 62,000 yuan for different years).

When internal share ownership is broken up into management and employee share ownership, we find that the positive effect of internal share ownership on profitability comes solely from employee share ownership. The profit rate of a fully employee owned firm is 2.8 percentage points higher than that of a fully state owned firm. However, increasing employee share ownership has a negative effect on unit costs

Table 4. Outsider versus Insider Shares: Baseline Results

Variable	Profitability I	Profitability II	Unit cost I	Unit cost II	Productivity I	Productivity II
Insider private shares	0.015**		0.017		-0.078	
	(0.007)		(0.012)		(0.052)	
Outsider shares	0.016***		0.002		0.0620*	
	(0.005)		(0.008)		(0.040)	
Management shares		0.001		-0.012		-0.174**
		(0.013)		(0.021)		(0.089)
Employee shares		0.028**		0.043**		0.001
		(0.012)		(0.019)		(0.092)
Outside state shares		0.014**		0.007		0.138***
		(0.007)		(0.012)		(0.053)
Outside private shares		0.018***		-0.003		-0.012
		(0.007)		(0.012)		(0.051)
Ln(on-duty workers)	-0.270**	-0.273**	0.295	0.297	-3.189***	-3.131***
	(0.129)	(0.129)	(0.205)	(0.205)	(0.919)	(0.918)
Redundancy	-0.022***	-0.022***	-0.008	-0.008	-0.089*	-0.087*
	(0.007)	(0.007)	(0.011)	(0.011)	(0.053)	(0.052)
Debt/equity ratio	-0.003	-0.003	0.004	0.004	0.001	0.001
	(0.002)	(0.002)	(0.003)	(0.003)	(0.012)	(0.011)
Bank arrears	0.000	0.000	-0.001	-0.001	0.001	0.001
	(0.001)	(0.001)	(0.001)	(0.001)	(0.014)	(0.009)
Tax arrears	0.000	-0.001	0.003	0.003	-0.009	0.001
	(0.003)	(0.003)	(0.004)	(0.004)	(0.019)	(0.018)
Social security arrears	-0.075	-0.067	0.011	0.023	0.234	0.233
	(0.112)	(0.112)	(0.178)	(0.178)	(0.878)	(0.789)
Expansion factor	2.509***	2.517***	9.366***	9.385***	54.892***	54.956***
	(0.146)	(0.146)	(0.232)	(0.233)	(1.043)	(1.041)
Saving factor	6.098***	6.099***	-10.198***	-10.190***	10.589***	10.654***
	(0.149)	(0.149)	(0.237)	(0.237)	(1.071)	(1.066)
R^2	0.444	0.444	0.563	0.563	0.547	0.548
Number of cases	3166	3166	3166	3166	3166	3166

* Significant at the 10 per cent significance level; ** significant at the 5 per cent significance level; *** significant at the 1 per cent significance level.
Figures in parentheses are standard errors.

and no effect on productivity. Management share ownership does not have a positive effect on profitability, nor does it have an effect on unit costs. In the case of labour productivity, increasing management share ownership has a significantly negative impact. A one percentage point increase of the degree of management share ownership reduces a worker's contribution by 170 yuan.

Both external private and external state share ownership contribute to the positive effect of external share ownership on profitability, but the former is more significant than the latter. In contrast, the positive contribution of external share ownership to labour productivity only comes from external state share ownership.

In the FE model (Table 5), internal private share ownership turns out to be insignificant for all the three performance indicators, but under external share ownership all become statistically significant. The result that external share ownership reduces unit cost is particularly interesting because the baseline regression did not illustrate this point. The reduction has some economic significance: an increase of one percentage point in external share ownership would reduce unit costs by 0.024 percentage points. In addition, the positive effect of external share ownership on labour productivity is greatly enhanced: a one percentage point increase in external share ownership would lead to an increase of 121 yuan (as compared with 62 yuan before) in labour productivity.

When internal share ownership is broken into management and employee share ownership, only management share ownership has a significant impact. This effect occurs in respect to labour productivity for which the estimate repeats the baseline result that more management share ownership leads to lower labour productivity. Within external share ownership, external state share ownership have significantly positive effects on profitability and labour productivity, but no effect on unit costs; external private share ownership has exactly the opposite effects.

Reviewing the results from both the baseline and the FE regressions, we find that the most robust results are those relating to external share

Table 5. Outsider versus Insider Shares: FE Results

Variable	Profitability I	Profitability II	Unit cost I	Unit cost II	Productivity I	Productivity II
Insider private shares	0.008		0.002		-0.060	
	(0.008)		(0.011)		(0.050)	
Outsider shares	0.020**		-0.024**		0.121**	
	(0.009)		(0.012)		(0.057)	
Management shares		-0.001		0.002		-0.230***
		(0.001)		(0.019)		(0.089)
Employee shares		0.002		0.002		0.135
		(0.002)		(0.022)		(0.103)
Outside state shares		0.032**		-0.009		0.274***
		(0.015)		(0.020)		(0.092)
Outside private shares		0.013		-0.033**		0.024
		(0.011)		(0.015)		(0.070)
Ln(on-duty workers)	-2.646***	-2.619***	0.125	0.139	-0.395	0.018
	(0.542)	(0.543)	(0.738)	(0.739)	(3.439)	(3.437)
Redundancy	-0.062***	-0.061***	-0.041*	-0.041*	-0.059	-0.046
	(0.016)	(0.016)	(0.021)	(0.022)	(0.102)	(0.102)
Debt/equity ratio	0.004	0.004	0.012***	0.012***	0.011	0.012
	(0.004)	(0.004)	(0.005)	(0.005)	(0.022)	(0.022)
Bank arrears	-0.000	-0.000	-0.001	-0.001	-0.001	-0.001
	(0.001)	(0.001)	(0.001)	(0.001)	(0.035)	(0.001)
Tax arrears	0.000	0.000	-0.001	-0.001	-0.002	-0.002
	(0.005)	(0.005)	(0.007)	(0.007)	(0.035)	(0.035)
Social security arrears	-0.088	-0.081	-0.045	-0.043	0.403	0.503
	(0.174)	(0.174)	(0.236)	(0.236)	(1.104)	(1.103)
R^2	0.701	0.701	0.830	0.830	0.808	0.809
Number of cases	3187	3187	3167	3167	3192	3192

* Significant at the 10 per cent significance level; ** significant at the 5 per cent significance level; *** significant at the 1 per cent significance level.
Figures in parentheses are standard errors.

ownership. The presence of external share ownership, irrespective of whether the shares are owned privately or by another SOE, has both statistically and economically significant effects on profitability and labour productivity, and to a lesser extent, on unit costs. The difference between external state share ownership and external private share ownership is interesting. While greater external state share ownership help a firm improve its profitability and labour productivity, greater external private share ownership helps reduce costs. This seems to suggest that a firm is more likely to adopt expansionary measures to improve its efficiency if it has greater external state share ownership, but is keen to adopt passive measures to reduce costs if it has a greater degree of external private share ownership. This distinction makes sense in terms of the risk embedded in the two different approaches. In the Chinese setting, an SOE may be less risk averse than a private firm because it has easier access to bank loans and other sources of finance and faces weaker financial constraints.

The finding that external state share ownership helps a firm is interesting and somewhat puzzling. Our earlier results have shown that internal state share ownership hurts firm efficiency, so why can external state share ownership have a positive effect? Research on other transitional countries has found that outside block shares are more helpful than scattered private share ownership because block shares make it easier to establish better corporate governance (Djankov and Murrell, 2002). To the extent that external state share ownership are all owned by external SOEs and thus qualify as block shares, our finding seems to be consistent with the findings in the literature. However, external private shares are usually also owned by private firms rather than scattered individuals, but their presence seems not to be as effective as external state share ownership. External SOEs have to have certain advantages in order to outperform external private firms. The SOEs' advantageous position in attracting external finance is still key. The state sector enjoys an obvious advantage over the private sector in accessing bank credit. The state sector contributes to barely over 20 per cent of the nation's industrial output, but it takes up 80 per cent of bank credit. In addition, the Chinese stock market is disproportionately dominated by state controlled firms.

Often, the private sector relies on the funds leaked from the state sector to gain finance (Lu and Yao, 2003). Consequently, an external SOE is in a better position to bring more finance to the recipient SOE than an external private firm.

However, a question still remains: why is external SOE ownership different from internal employee ownership? This has something to do with the mindset under these two ownership structures. In the latter case, each employee tends to regard himself as one of the "masters" of the firm because he is assigned to the firm by the government as one of the guardians of the state assets. This kind of mindset considerably weakens managerial authority and makes worker discipline very difficult. Firing workers is not in the manager's capacity. However, when the state shares are owned by an external SOE, employees' attitudes change. There is no ground for them to think that they have privileges toward the assets brought in by an external SOE, which enables the outside SOE to impose discipline on the employees. The external SOE may not be able to properly handle its own employees, but its status of an outsider gives it more leverage to deal with the employees in the new firm creating room for improving its efficiency. The survey found evidence to support the role of external SOE in improving firm efficiency[12].

While internal employee shares do not help improve firm efficiency (a result that is also found in other transitional countries), the finding that management share ownership does not help, and may hurt, firm efficiency is contradictory to some early findings by Groves *et al.* (1994; 1995), Gordon and Li (1995) and Li (1997). These studies have shown that contractual incentives (such as performance-based bonus schemes) in the early reform period did help the Chinese SOEs to improve efficiency. It seems reasonable to believe that ownership incentives

---

[12] For example, the tractor giant Luoyang Tractor Factory has serious problem in its headquarters in Luoyang, Henan province, but it runs a successful joint venture (through a subsidiary registered in Great Britain) with another SOE in Zhenjiang, Jiangsu province. Indeed, one of the purposes of many failing SOEs' seeking joint venture with another SOE is to find an opportunity to get rid of the excessive workforce (Garnaut *et al.*, 2003).

should play at least the same role as contractual incentives because the manager gains more autonomy when he owns part of the firm.

So our findings are puzzling. One possibility is that our use of share ownership as the measure for incentives may be too stringent. To double-check the validity of our results, we re-run the baseline regressions with the four types of shares each substituted by a dummy variable that represents the group of firms that have the corresponding type of shares[13]. The results largely repeat those in Table 4, so our finding is not specific to our econometric method. Another explanation of our finding is that we did not control for the autonomy of the manager. In the literature (e.g., the above quoted studies relating to China; more comprehensive discussion can be found in Djankov and Murrell, 2002), management autonomy is found to be as important as managerial incentives in achieving firm efficiency. However, privatisation may not automatically give the manager autonomy (Garnaut *et al.*, 2003). Therefore, a control for management autonomy is needed in our regressions to obtain an accurate assessment of management incentives. However, we do not have a comprehensive series of data on management autonomy so we cannot perform this test in the panel framework[14].

4.3. Gaizhi versus non-gaizhi firms

In the baseline regression, *gaizhi* is shown to have a significant effect on profitability (Table 6). On average, a *gaizhi* firm has a profit rate 0.78 percentage points higher than achieved by a non-*gaizhi* firm. In terms of different forms of *gaizhi*; bankruptcy, employee shareholding, and sales and leases have strong positive effects, but internal restructuring has a strong negative effect, and "others" has no effect. Contrasting with its

---

[13] Among 587 firms with valid data, the percentages of the four groups of firms are 12.6 per cent for management shares, 14.7 per cent for employee shares, 9.3 per cent for outside state shares, and 14 per cent for outside private shares.

[14] We have data on the distribution of decision rights in the firm for 2002, the year when the survey was conducted, that allow us to perform some form of the test based on cross-sectional comparison in future research.

Table 6. Different Forms of *Gaizhi*: Baseline Results

Variable	Profitability I	Profitability II	Unit cost I	Unit cost II	Productivity I	Productivity II
Gaizhi	0.784**		0.624		0.345	
	(0.350)		(0.534)		(2.456)	
Internal restructuring		-1.519***		-0.487		0.018
		(0.602)		(0.921)		(4.244)
Bankruptcy		2.104***		3.225***		6.654
		(0.866)		(1.325)		(6.101)
Employee shareholding		1.544***		0.144		-4.450
		(0.620)		(0.948)		(4.356)
Sales and leases		1.750***		1.370		-0.362
		(0.653)		(0.999)		(4.598)
Others		1.016		0.267		3.742
		(0.678)		(1.037)		(4.778)
Ln(on-duty workers)	-0.398***	-0.328***	0.122	0.158	-2.514***	-2.542***
	(0.128)	(0.129)	(0.195)	(0.197)	(0.901)	(0.914)
Redundancy	-0.026***	-0.025***	-0.015	-0.015	-0.114**	-0.114**
	(0.007)	(0.007)	(0.010)	(0.010)	(0.051)	(0.051)
Debt/equity ratio	-0.002	-0.001	0.005	0.005	-0.011	-0.010
	(0.002)	(0.002)	(0.003)	(0.003)	(0.013)	(0.012)
Bank arrears	0.000	0.000	-0.001	-0.001	0.001	0.001
	(0.001)	(0.001)	(0.001)	(0.001)	(0.008)	(0.011)
Tax arrears	0.000	0.000	0.003	0.003	0.001	-0.001
	(0.003)	(0.003)	(0.004)	(0.004)	(0.019)	(0.020)
Social security arrears	-0.119	-0.136	0.000	-0.036	-0.045	-0.101
	(0.113)	(0.114)	(0.173)	(0.174)	(0.798)	(0.801)
Expansion factor	2.782***	2.788***	9.572***	9.567***	53.414***	53.378***
	(0.145)	(0.145)	(0.221)	(0.221)	(1.018)	(1.022)
Saving factor	6.543***	6.531***	-9.918***	-9.919***	9.196***	9.158***
	(0.144)	(0.144)	(0.220)	(0.221)	(1.013)	(1.018)
R^2	0.463	0.546	0.524	0.461	0.565	0.524
No. of cases	3494	3494	3494	3494	3494	3494

* Significant at the 10 per cent level; ** significant at the 5 per cent level; *** significant at the 1 per cent level.
Figures in parentheses are standard errors.

strong effect on profitability, however, *gaizhi* has no positive effect on unit costs and labour productivity, and bankruptcy actually has a negative impact on unit cost.

The FE model largely agrees with the baseline regression on unit cost and labour productivity, but erases most of the statistically significant results concerning profitability (Table 7). The overall significant effect of *gaizhi* on profitability disappears, as do those of the specific forms of *gaizhi*. Nevertheless, the positive signs of the estimates are unchanged. The strong negative effect of internal restructuring remains, however, and increases in terms of magnitude. In addition, internal restructuring is shown by the FE model to have a strong negative effect on labour productivity: compared with a counterpart in an old-style SOE, a worker in a restructured SOE produces 15,119 yuan less in revenue. A final difference between the FE model and the baseline regression is that the FE model shows that a firm sold or leased has a significantly lower unit cost than an old-style SOE.

The fact that most of the significant estimates of the baseline model vanish in the FE model may imply that the selection biases of *gaizhi* were more based on longer-term firm specific characteristics rather than short-term performance records. However, some caution needs to be taken in interpreting this result. As we pointed out before, 27.7 per cent of the *gaizhi* firms finished *gaizhi* before 1996. These firms are treated by the FE model as the same as those that had not undertaken *gaizhi* at all, so the FE model tends to put too much of a limitation on the data and its results are best taken as providing the lower bounds on the estimates for the *gaizhi* effects. Combining the baseline and the FE results, therefore, it may be appropriate to conclude that *gaizhi* has had moderate effects on profitability.

Bankruptcy is often used by SOEs to shake off bank debts and reorganise the firm in terms of management and employment, so an SOE that has 'emerged' from bankruptcy can easily improve its profitability. Indeed, the baseline regression shows that bankruptcy has the largest effect on

Table 7. Different Forms of *Gaizhi*: FE Results

Variable	Profitability I	Profitability II	Unit cost I	Unit cost II	Productivity I	Productivity II
Gaizhi	0.119		-0.256		-4.172	
	(0.511)		(0.689)		(3.264)	
Internal restructuring		-2.033**		-0.852		-15.119***
		(0.859)		(1.156)		(5.499)
Bankruptcy		0.216		2.602		-2.869
		(1.253)		(1.687)		(8.021)
Employee shareholding		1.146		1.057		-7.589
		(0.793)		(1.074)		(5.081)
Sales and leases		0.877		-2.643**		6.800
		(0.881)		(1.187)		(5.583)
Others		0.803		-0.729		9.700
		(1.202)		(1.619)		(7.699)
Ln(on-duty workers)	-2.462***	-2.368***	0.227	0.184	1.617	1.873
	(0.519)	(0.520)	(0.700)	(0.702)	(3.325)	(3.331)
Redundancy	-0.068***	-0.067***	-0.048**	-0.046**	-0.122	-0.120
	(0.015)	(0.015)	(0.021)	(0.020)	(0.097)	(0.097)
Debt/equity ratio	0.004	0.004	0.011**	0.011**	0.014	0.013
	(0.004)	(0.004)	(0.005)	(0.005)	(0.023)	(0.023)
Bank arrears	0.000	0.000	-0.000	-0.001	-0.002	-0.002
	(0.001)	(0.001)	(0.001)	(0.001)	(0.005)	(0.005)
Tax arrears	0.001	0.001	-0.001	-0.001	0.001	0.001
	(0.005)	(0.006)	(0.007)	(0.007)	(0.036)	(0.036)
Social security arrears	-0.299*	-0.310	-0.106	-0.096	0.170	0.013
	(0.172)	(0.173)	(0.232)	(0.233)	(1.104)	(1.106)
R^2	0.714	0.715	0.820	0.820	0.788	0.789
Number of cases	3519	3519	3495	3495	3525	3525

* Significant at the 10 per cent level; ** significant at the 5 per cent level; *** significant at the 1 per cent level.
Figures in parentheses are standard errors.

profitability (2.1 percentage points versus an average of 0.78 percentage points for all kinds of *gaizhi*). Employee shareholding and sales and leases are means of privatisation, so they improve firm profitability as expected. The reason why public listing and joint venture with foreign firms (grouped under the title of "others") does not have any significant effect may have something to do with the fact that the state ownership is largely intact in those two types of restructuring. The strong negative effect of internal restructuring on profitability (and on labour productivity in the FE model) is puzzling. Research on other transitional countries even finds that incorporation helps an SOE to improve efficiency in some cases (Djankov and Murrell, 2002).

While an exact explanation requires detailed research, we suggest that this may have much to do with the corporate governance of the incorporated SOEs. In an old-style SOE, the government has strong managerial control. While the responsibilities on the manager are enhanced without corresponding rewards being offered, his relative incentive to provide effort is lost. Incorporation gives more independence to the managerial cadre, but a sound corporate governance structure is not easily established when a tangible owner is missing. As a result, the manager obtains much control and power within the firm, however, this power is not matched by the manager's proper adoption of the objective of increasing the long-term growth of the firm. This discrepancy may well lead the manager either to shirk or to steal from the firm, so firm performance may be sacrificed.

The baseline model and the FE model do agree on most of *gaizhi*'s effects when considering unit cost and labour productivity. Both models show that *gaizhi* has few significant effects on those two performance indicators, a result that is largely consistent with those of the previous two sets of regressions.

To summarise the findings presented in this section, we have the following major conclusions regarding the effects of privatisation/*gaizhi*. First, privatisation/*gaizhi* varies in terms of its effects on different aspects of performance. It is more effective in raising the return to assets (profitability) than raising labour productivity and cutting costs. We attributed this finding to a privatised/*gaizhi*-ed firm's additional incentive to use capital-saving technology, its constraints in terms of employment policy, and its expansionary business model inherited from its SOE predecessor.

Second, different measures of privatisation/*gaizhi* have different degrees of impact on performance. The most robust result is for the introduction of external share ownership: regardless of whom they belong to, external share ownership has significantly positive effects on all three performance indicators. The introduction of private share ownership has a positive effect on the return to assets when their amount exceeds a certain threshold. In comparison, *gaizhi* has the weakest effects on performance.

In cases where it does have a positive effect, *gaizhi* has to be in conjunction with a degree of privatisation. We attributed the superb performance of external share ownership to the commonly found advantage associated with block share ownership in other transitional countries, but also pointed out the financial advantage associated with external state share ownership and their key difference with internal state share ownership.

Finally, management incentives in the form of firm shares do not have any significantly positive impact on any of the three performance indicators. This finding contradicts both the findings on other transitional countries and the findings on early Chinese reforms that give managerial staff contractual incentives. We pointed out that further research might improve on our findings by controlling for the extent of management autonomy.

4.4. Time trends

In this section, we test the post-privatisation/*gaizhi* time trend and the "prettier daughters" hypothesis. The test is only performed for three variables, private share ownership, external share ownership, and *gaizhi*.

The tests for the break-up variables are omitted because the results in Section 4 have shown that most of the effects of privatisation and *gaizhi* can be found on those three variables. Equations (3) and (4) are each run in turn for profitability, unit cost and labour productivity, respectively. Tables 8 and 9 present the main results of those regressions.

4.4.1. Post-privatisation/gaizhi time trend

As shown in Table 8, time trend estimate is weak. There are only two cases in which β_1 has the expected sign and is significant. In both cases, this happens when unit cost is regressed on private share ownership and external share ownership, respectively. However, there is no significantly reverse time trend either, that is, there is no evidence to show that firms' performance is significantly improved over the years after privatisation/ *gaizhi* measures are first introduced. This contrast reflects the uniqueness of the unit cost. It is important to note that the "pure" effect of private share ownership on unit costs is not significant, but the "pure" effect of external share ownership is. If the selection biases proposed by Frydman *et al.* (1999) exist, this latter result seems to suggest that the manager tends to inflate costs (instead of hiding profit) ahead of the introduction of external share ownership, or the unrealised efficiency gains are more related to cost-saving technology than to expansionary technology. However, the finding can also be taken as the evidence for the external investor(s)' keener intention to save costs in its earlier years post purchase. This saving is accompanied by stronger growth of profitability and labour productivity.

Our baseline results show that all the three measures of privatisation/ *gaizhi* have positive effects on profitability. Private share ownership and *gaizhi* are shown to have no significant "pure" effect (that is, the estimate of β_0 is not significant) but have weakly positive time trends. The significant positive effects in the baseline regressions thus can be thought as the average effects associated with these weak time trends. It is noteworthy that the "pure" effect of external share ownership still has the expected signs and significance for all the three performance indicators.

Table 8. Test Results of the Post-Privatisation/*Gaizhi* Time Trend

Model and Variable	Profitability	Unit cost	Productivity
Private vs. state shares			
Private shares	0.008	-0.013	0.002
	(0.009)	(0.015)	(0.007)
Private shares	0.003	0.0085*	-0.003
× Years_after	(0.003)	(0.005)	(0.002)
Outsider vs. insider shares			
Outsider shares	0.019*	-0.053***	0.013*
	(0.010)	(0.016)	(0.007)
Outsider shares	-0.001	0.019***	-0.002
× Years_after	(0.003)	(0.005)	(0.002)
Gaizhi vs. non-gaizhi firms			
Gaizhi	0.535	-0.073	-0.205
	(0.599)	(0.913)	(0.420)
Gazhi	0.093	0.260	0.089
× Years_after	(0.181)	(0.276)	(0.127)

* Significant at the 10 per cent significance level; ** significant at the 5 per cent significance level; *** significant at the 1 per cent significance level.
Figures in parentheses are standard errors.

This contrast suggests that the positive effects of private share ownership and *gaizhi* are evenly distributed over the years after they are first introduced, but the positive effects of external share ownership are most likely to show up immediately after their initial introduction.

When there is no external participation, it takes time for an internally privatised/*gaizhi*-ed firm to overcome the inertia inherited from the old

SOE. The manager neither has significant power nor will to discipline the workers in an SOE. For one thing, he does not have much personal gain from undertaking worker discipline; in addition, he is held accountable to workers by the sections of Enterprise Law that govern the operation of SOEs, so accommodating workers is to his own advantage. Privatisation/*gaizhi* is supposed to empower the manager, but nevertheless this does not automatically prepare him to administer these new responsibilities, nor does privatisation/*gaizhi* automatically prepare the workers to accept this change authority. In contrast, an external investor does not have the historical burden and can more easily introduce restructuring measures into the firm.

4.5. The "prettier daughters" effect

The test of this effect provides mixed results (see Table 9). For profitability, the year of the introduction of the first external share ownership does not have a significant impact, but the year of the introduction of the first private share ownership or *gaizhi* has a strong effect. The positive effects of private share ownership and *gaizhi* decline quickly for the later privatised/*gaizhi*-ed firms. Indeed, they have vanished for firms that introduced private share ownership or *gaizhi* in 2001. However, the trend is reversed when we turn to the example of unit cost. The "pure" effects of private share ownership, external share ownership, and *gaizhi* are all to increase unit costs, but the time trend for the later privatised/*gaizhi*-ed firms is to produce a reducing unit cost. This reversed trend is also weakly presented in the case of labour productivity.

The contrasting results described above generate two conclusions. To the extent that profitability is the most comprehensive measure of efficiency, we first conclude that the "prettier daughters" effect does exist with the introduction of private share ownership and *gaizhi*. However, viewing the reverse trend in the cases of unit costs and labour productivity, we conclude that the "prettier daughters" must have relied to a greater extent on expansionary measures to increase their profitability, but have faced greater constraints in their ability to adjust their employment structure compared to the "uglier daughters".

Comparisons between those privatised/*gaizhi*-ed firms in 1996–1998 and those in 1999-2001 show that, in their post-privatisation/*gaizhi* years, the first group of firms reached an average investment rate of 13.3 per cent, but only reduced their on-duty workforce by an average pace of 2.7 per cent per annum; in contrast, the latter group only achieved an investment rate of 8.6 per cent, but reduced their on-duty workforce by an annual rate of 8.0 per cent.

Table 9. Test Results of the "Prettier Daughters" Effect

Model and Variable	Profitability	Unit cost	Productivity
Private vs. state shares			
Private shares	0.034***	0.043***	-0.015**
	(0.010)	(0.016)	(0.007)
Private shares	-0.0056**	-0.012***	0.0033*
✕ *Years_before*	(0.003)	(0.004)	(0.002)
Outsider vs. insider shares			
Outsider shares	0.017**	0.045***	-0.007
	(0.008)	(0.013)	(0.006)
Outsider shares	-0.001	-0.021***	0.007***
✕ *Years_before*	(0.003)	(0.005)	(0.002)
Gaizhi vs. non-gaizhi firms			
Gaizhi	1.564***	1.803**	0.215
	(0.552)	(0.843)	(0.388)
Gazhi	-0.340*	-0.514*	-0.079
✕ *Years_before*	(0.186)	(0.284)	(0.131)

* Significant at the 10 per cent significance level; ** significant at the 5 per cent significance level; *** significant at the 1 per cent significance level.
Figures in parentheses are standard errors.

4.6. Other factors

The baseline and the FE models have revealed interesting results concerning the factors other than privatisation/*gaizhi*. Indeed, some of these results are very robust to different specifications. In this section we discuss two sets of these results, namely, those concerning firm size and worker redundancy/inactivity and those concerning soft budget constraints.

4.6.1. Firm size and worker redundancy

The three baseline regressions show that firm size as defined by the number of on-duty workers has significant negative effects on profitability and labour productivity and insignificant effects on unit cost (Tables 2, 4, and 6). The estimates in the three sets of regressions are fairly stable. A one percentage point increase of the firm size would reduce profitability by about 0.27 percentage points (larger in the *gaizhi* regression) and reduce labour productivity by about 3,100 yuan. The effects of worker redundancy exhibit the same pattern. An increase of one percentage point in worker redundancy would reduce profitability by 0.022 to 0.026 percentage points and reduce labor productivity by 90 to 110 yuan.

The FE regressions provide the same results for profitability, however, the negative effects associated with labour productivity vanish (Tables 3, 5, and 7). The negative effects of firm size and worker redundancy on profitability have been augmented. A one percentage point increase in firm size would reduce profitability by 2.6 to 2.7 percentage points, and a one percentage point increase in worker redundancy would reduce profitability by about 0.06 percentage points. However, worker redundancy is shown to have a positive effect on unit costs. One percentage point increase in worker redundancy would reduce unit costs by about 0.04 percentage points.

The negative impact of worker redundancy on profitability are results that would be expected as more redundant workers increase the firm's payroll, social security, and healthcare burdens. What are not so transparent are the reasons behind worker redundancies' positive effects on unit costs and negative effects on labour productivity. One explanation for the positive effect on unit cost is that firms with more acute worker burdens are keener to save material costs. Firms do not have much flexibility in adjusting their workforce, nor do they have much flexibility in wage and benefit payments, so they are forced to save the costs of materials. The negative effects on labour productivity have to be understood by considering the firm's opportunity costs in dealing with redundant workers. Financial resources and management time spent on redundant workers have a crowding out effect on a firm's efforts to increase its revenues elsewhere.

The negative coefficients associated with firm size show that larger firms are less efficient than smaller firms. Larger firms are usually found to have higher levels of technical efficiency but lower levels of allocative efficiency than smaller firms in China (Wang and Yao, 2002). Our results seem to support this finding. However, these results may also be caused by the rigidity in employment that forces the firms to keep a greater than efficient workforce. In other words, the firm size may be another indicator for worker redundancy.

4.6.2. *The soft budget constraint*

Research on other transitional countries find mixed results on the efficiency implications of the soft budget constraint. While Djankov and Murrell (2002) document several studies showing that soft budget constraints hurt firm efficiency, Frydman *et al.* (2000) find that the hardening of the budget constraint alone does not improve efficiency. In our study, we have three variables to represent the soft budget constraints faced by a firm. We use the rate of overdue bank loans and interest to represent the magnitude of the problem when a firm deals with the bank, and use the rate of overdue taxes and social security payments to represent the magnitude of the problem when a firm deals with the government. However, none of the regressions under either the baseline specification or the FE model show significant negative impacts on any of the three variables (bank dues are even shown to have weakly significant positive impacts on unit costs when the variable is regressed with the private shares under the baseline specification, as presented in Table 2). Therefore, it seems that the soft-budget constraint does not have an efficiency implication in our sample.

However, the results may be produced by the lack of sufficient variation in the three variables as 20.1 per cent of the sample firms have never had overdue bank loans or interest repayments, 51.5 per cent have never had overdue taxes, and 66.9 per cent have never had overdue social security payments. To take into account this possibility, we replace the three overdue rates by three dummy variables indicating, respectively, whether a firm had overdue bank loans/interests, overdue taxes, or overdue social security payments, and re-run the regressions in Table 2 and Table 3 (that is, the two regressions that study the effects of private/state share ownership). In the baseline regressions, the soft-budget constraint is shown to have a negative impact on efficiency on two occasions: overdue taxes and overdue social security payments are shown to have a significantly negative impact on profitability. Firms with overdue taxes have a profit rate 1.3 percentage points lower than that of the firms without overdue taxes, and firms with overdue social security payments have a profit rate 0.62 percentage points lower than that of those without overdue social security payments. However, even these two significant results vanish in the FE regressions. Therefore, we conclude that the soft budget constraint related to the banking sector does not have any efficiency implications and the soft budget constraint related to the government has weak efficiency implications that only show up at the group-mean level when cross-firm comparison is allowed.

Judging by the strong negative impacts found by some studies on other transitional countries (e.g., Coricelli and Djankov, 2001), the weak or even non-existence of these variables in our case needs closer scrutiny. In standard OLS regressions, without controlling the two performance factors, all three variables of the soft-budget constraint are shown to have highly significant negative impacts on profitability. Comparing this with our baseline and FE results, this suggests that the soft budget constraint is endogenously determined by a firm's long-term performance potential. Other things being equal, a firm with a low potential is more likely to face a soft budget constraint. When a firm's long-term performance potential is controlled for, the baseline and the FE results show that facing a soft budget constraint does not lead a firm to perform less efficiently than it would otherwise do under a hard budget constraint.

However, the finding that the soft budget constraint does not lead to worsening firm performance cannot be taken as evidence to completely absolve the soft budget constraint for lower efficiency. Our results have shown that government and bank resources do flow to poorly-performing firms, so there is a cost to the society. In addition, we did not study the "demonstration effect" that is at the heart of the soft-budget constraint problem: in a setting where firms expect to have no obligation to honour their budget constraints, everyone's profit incentive is lowered. Central to the demonstration effect is the contagious effect of some firms being subject to the soft budget constraint within properly defined subgroups of firms (e.g., firms in the same city). Future research can be conducted along these lines.

5. Conclusions

Chinese privatisation was not initiated by a conscious pursuit of efficiency. Nonetheless, our results show that it has brought considerable efficiency gains. We found that privatisation has a significantly positive impact on firm profitability, but has a weak or insignificant impact on unit costs and labour productivity. Increasing private share ownership has a positive effect on profitability but only under the condition that the degree of private share ownership passes a certain threshold. The presence of external share ownership has both statistically and economically significant effects on profitability and labour productivity and to a lesser extent, on unit cost. For *gaizhi* to be effective in improving firms' performance, it has to be connected with a certain degree of privatisation.

We found some time trends in the performance of privatised/*gaizhi*-ed firms. The positive effects of private share ownership (*gaizhi*) on firm performance are evenly distributed over the years after they are first introduced, but the positive effects of external share ownership are more likely to show up immediately after their introduction. There is a strong trend for better performing SOEs to be privatised/*gaizhi*-ed in the first instance. We also found strong evidence that Chinese firms are characterised by excessive employment and worker inactivity. However, we did not find significant and robust linkages between the soft-budget constraint problem and firm performance.

Our findings contribute to the transition economics literature in two ways. The first is that we have provided the first set of system evidence for the positive impact of privatisation in China, an important but under-studied transition country, and the second is that we are able to provide robust results controlling for the endogeneity of privatisation and variables that are often missing in other studies.

Our findings have a further implication for the question of why Chinese SOEs have failed. The conventional wisdom believes that failure is because public ownership provides an inadequate incentive structure in the firm. While we do not refute this claim, our results nonetheless suggest that the causes may be more subtle than SOEs simply lacking incentives. The ineffectiveness of *gaizhi* and the effectiveness of the participation of outside SOEs are two seemingly contradicting findings. To reconcile those two findings, we hypothesise that the deficiency in Chinese SOEs relates to the lack of managerial authority caused by the public ownership that give employees *de facto* equal ownership of the firm. Interpreting the findings in this way, we contend that the introduction of private share ownership and external share ownership serve the same purpose, that is, to break up insiders' sense of ownership and restore managerial authority in the firm.

References

1. Anderson, J., Y. Lee and P. Murrell, "Competition and Privatisation amidst Weak Institutions: Evidence from Mongolia." *Economic Inquiry*, Vol. 38(4): 527-546 (2000).
2. Boycko, M., A. Shleifer and R. Vishny, *Privatizing Russia*, (MIT Press, Cambridge, 1996).
3. Coricelli, F. and S. Djankov, "Hardened Budgets and Enterprise Restructuring: Theory and an Application to Romania." *Journal of Comparative Economics*, Vol. 29(4): 749-763 (2001).
4. Djankov, S. and P. Murrell, "Enterprise Restructuring in Transition: A Quantitative Survey." *Journal of Economic Literature*, Vol. XL (3): 739-792 (2002).
5. Frydman, R., C. Gray, M. Hessel and A. Rapaczynski, "When Does Privatisation Work? The Impact of Private Ownership on Corporate Performance in the Transition Economies." *Quarterly Journal of Economics*, Vol. 114(4): 1153-1191 (1999).
6. Frydman, R., C. Gray, M. Hessel and A. Rapaczynski, "The Limits of Discipline: Ownership and Hard Budget Constraints in the Transition Economies." *Economics of Transition*, Vol. 8(3): 577-601 (2000).
7. Gao, S. and Y. Yao, "Implementation of Socially Optimal Outcomes in the Process of Dissolving Public Enterprises in China." *China Economic Review*, Vol. 10(2): 41-58 (1999).
8. Garnaut, R., L. Song, S. Tenev and Y. Yao, *A Study of Firm Restructuring in China*, (World Bank, Washington, D.C., 2003).
9. Gordon, R. and W. Li, "The Change in Productivity of Chinese State Enterprises, 1983-1987." *Journal of Productivity Analysis*, Vol. 6(1): 5-26 (1995).
10. Groves, T., Y. Hong, J. McMillan and B. Naughton, "Autonomy and Incentives in Chinese State Enterprises." *Quarterly Journal of Economics*, Vol. 109 (1): 183-209 (1994).
11. Groves, T., Y. Hong, J. McMillan and B. Naughton, "China's Evolving Managerial Labor Market." *Journal of Political Economy*, Vol. 103(4): 873-892 (1995).
12. Guo, K. and Y. Yao, "Testing among Several Theories of Privatisation in China," Working paper, (Center for International Development, Stanford University, 2003).
13. Li, S., S. Li and W. Zhang, "The Road to Capitalism: Competition and Institutional Change in China." *Journal of Comparative Economics*, Vol. 28 (2): 269-292 (2000).

14. Li, W., "The Impact of Economic Reform on the Performance of Chinese State Enterprises, 1980-1989." *Journal of Political Economy*, Vol. 105(5): 1080-1106 (1997).
15. Lin, J., F. Cai and Z. Li, *Sufficient Information and SOE Reform in China*, (Shanghai Sanlian Press, Shanghai, 1996).
16. Lin, J. and G. Tan, "Policy Burdens, Accountability and the Soft Budget Constraint." *American Economic Review*, Vol. 89(2): 426-431 (1999).
17. Lu, S. and Y. Yao, "The Effectiveness of the Law, Financial Development, and Economic Growth in an Economy of Financial Repression: Evidence from China," Working paper, (Center for International Development, Stanford University, 2003).
18. Megginson, W. and J. Netter, "From State to Markets: A Survey of Empirical Studies on Privatisation." *Journal of Economic Literature*, Vol. XXXIX (June): 321-389 (2001).
19. Qian, Y., "A Theory of Shortage in Socialist Economies Based on the Soft Budget Constraint." *American Economic Review*, Vol. 84 (1): 145-156 (1994).
20. Su, J. and G. Jefferson, "A Theory of Decentralized Privatisation: Evidence from China." Working paper, (Department of Economics, Brandeis University, 2003).
21. Tian, G., "A Theory of Ownership Arrangements and Smooth Transition to a Free Market Economy." *Journal of Institutional and Theoretical Economics*, Vol. 157(3): 380-412 (2001).
22. Wang, Y. and Y. Yao, "Market Reforms, Technological Capabilities and the Performance of Small Enterprises in China." *Small Business Economics*, 18(1-3): 197-211 (2002).

PART II

EXTERNAL REFORMS AND IMPACT

CHAPTER 5

PUTTING THE CART BEFORE THE HORSE? CAPITAL ACCOUNT LIBERALISATION AND EXCHANGE RATE FLEXIBILITY IN CHINA

Eswar Prasad*, Thomas Rumbaugh* & Qing Wang**[1]

International Monetary Fund

**Bank of America*

Abstract: This paper reviews the issues involved in moving towards greater exchange rate flexibility and capital account liberalisation in China. A more flexible exchange rate regime would allow China to operate a more independent monetary policy, providing a useful buffer against domestic and external shocks. At the same time, weaknesses in China's financial system suggest that capital account liberalisation poses significant risks and should be a lower priority in the short term. This paper concludes that greater exchange rate flexibility is in China's own interest and that, along with a more stable and robust financial system, it should be regarded as a prerequisite for undertaking a substantial liberalisation of the capital account.

1. Introduction and Overview

Like their counterparts in many other emerging market economies, Chinese policymakers are facing a complex set of questions related to the desirability and appropriate mode of implementing exchange rate flexibility and capital account liberalisation. The Chinese authorities have stated publicly that both exchange rate flexibility and capital

---

[1] Eswar Prasad (eprasad@imf.org), former Chief of the International Monetary Fund's (IMF) China division, is now the Chief of the Financial Studies division in the Research Department. Thomas Rumbaugh (trumbaugh@imf.org) is an Advisor in the IMF's Asia and Pacific Department, and was Deputy Chief of its China Division when this paper was written. Qing Wang (qwang@imf.org) was an economist in the China Division when this paper was written. He is now with Bank of America.

account convertibility are their medium-term objectives, but they have resisted recent calls from the international community for an early move toward more flexibility.

The issue has come to the fore in the context of discussions about the appropriateness of maintaining the current exchange rate regime — wherein the renminbi is effectively linked to the US dollar — given the rapid pace of China's reserve accumulation. Many observers have interpreted this surge in reserve accumulation over the last two years, which has reflected a rapid expansion of China's exports as well as large inflows of foreign direct investment (FDI), as clear evidence of undervaluation of the renminbi. However, it also reflects large speculative capital inflows, suggesting that the evidence on whether the renminbi is substantially undervalued in terms of fundamentals is far from conclusive[2].

A more important reason for recommending exchange rate flexibility is that it is in China's own interest. As its economy matures and becomes closely integrated with the global economy, China will inevitably become more exposed to different types of macroeconomic shocks, both internal and external. It would therefore benefit from having some flexibility in its exchange rate and, by extension, a more independent monetary policy to help the economy better adjust to such shocks. Thus, a strong argument can be made for an early move toward greater exchange rate flexibility in China, irrespective of whether or not the renminbi is substantially undervalued. A corollary to this argument is that it is a move toward flexibility rather than a revaluation of the rate

---

[2] On the one hand, IMF (2004) and Funke and Rahn (2005) conclude that there is no strong evidence that the renminbi is substantially undervalued. Goldstein (2004) and Frankel (2004), on the other hand, argue that the renminbi is undervalued by at least 30–35 percent. Market analysts have a similarly diverse range of views. The role of speculative capital inflows in accounting for pressures on China's exchange rate appears to have increased substantially since 2001. For instance, about half of the increase in international reserves in 2003 can be accounted for by non-FDI capital inflows (for more details, see IMF, 2004, and Prasad and Wei, 2006).

that is desirable[3]. As experiences of other countries have shown, rapid economic growth and a strong external position constitute relatively favorable circumstances for making such a move.

An interesting point in this public discussion is that the Chinese authorities as well as a number of observers on both sides of the exchange rate flexibility debate have conflated the issue of exchange rate flexibility with that of capital account liberalisation[4]. One of the main points of this paper is that these are related, but distinct issues. They do not necessarily have to be implemented simultaneously, and neither one necessarily implies the other.

The juxtaposition of these issues appears to have come about in the context of the notion that exchange rate flexibility could pose major problems for the financial sector. Indeed, a number of observers (and the Chinese authorities themselves) have argued that the weaknesses in China's banking system are a reason to defer making a move toward greater exchange rate flexibility. The logic appears to be that such flexibility could expose the financial system's vulnerabilities by facilitating outflows from the banking system as domestic economic agents take advantage of investment opportunities abroad.

---

[3] See Prasad (2004) for a further discussion of this point. Goldstein and Lardy (2003) argue for a two-step approach to exchange rate reform in China—a revaluation followed by a widening of the trading band. At the other end of the spectrum, the most prominent proponents of the view that China should not alter its current exchange rate regime include McKinnon and Schnabl (2003) and Mundell (2003).

[4] To cite a prominent example, Alan Greenspan has been quoted as saying that "Many in China fear that removal of capital controls that restrict the ability of domestic investors to invest abroad and to sell or to purchase foreign currency–which is a necessary step to allow a currency to float freely–could cause an outflow of deposits from Chinese banks, destabilizing the system" (*Wall Street Journal*, March 2, 2004). News reports interpreted his statement as indicating "...that before floating its exchange rate China should fix its banking system" (Ip, 2004). Standard & Poor's has also said, in their evaluations of China, that "risk control systems are ill-prepared to deal with rapid liberalisation of the exchange rate and capital controls," suggesting that the two issues are linked (Standard & Poor's, 2003).

We argue that with existing capital controls in place, even if these are somewhat porous, the banking system is unlikely to be subject to substantial stress simply as a result of greater exchange rate flexibility. Domestic banks do not have a large net exposure to currency risk, and exchange rate flexibility by itself is unlikely to create strong incentives (or channels) to take deposits out of the Chinese banking system. Furthermore, the introduction of greater flexibility would create stronger incentives for developing the foreign exchange market and for currency risk management, including developing the hedging instruments and forward markets that are currently absent. In this way, the introduction of exchange rate flexibility could, in fact, facilitate capital account liberalisation by better preparing the economy to deal with the impact of increased capital flows.

Capital controls do, however, tend to become less effective over time. Expanding trade and the increasing sophistication of domestic and international investors invariably generate new ways to get around capital controls. In addition, the experiences of numerous emerging market countries have shown the risks associated with maintaining a fixed exchange rate in tandem with a capital account that is open in either *de jure* or *de facto* terms, especially if there are weaknesses in the domestic financial system. Thus, the authorities' recent efforts to gradually liberalise capital outflows in the context of the current exchange rate regime could well prove counterproductive. Moreover, these factors suggest that delaying a move toward greater exchange flexibility could precipitate the need for an adjustment in the future under far less desirable circumstances.

At the same time, given the weaknesses in China's banking system, a cautious and gradual approach to capital account liberalisation would, indeed, be appropriate. There are substantial risks associated with exposure to capital flows in the absence of sufficient institutional development, especially in the financial sector. The liberalisation of capital flows should be sequenced in a manner that reinforces domestic financial liberalisation and allows for institutional capacity building to manage the additional risks. A more stable financial system and experience over time with greater flexibility in the exchange rate should, in fact, be regarded as prerequisites to fully opening the capital account[5].

What does it mean to have exchange rate flexibility if the country's currency is not convertible on the capital account? The exchange rate can still be allowed to fluctuate in response to the evolution of supply and demand for foreign exchange, even though there may be constraints on capital flows. A move toward more flexibility also does not necessarily mean immediate adoption of a free float[6]. In fact, a period of "learning to float" can be advisable to overcome "fear of floating," a term used to characterise policymakers' initial aversion, upon exiting a fixed exchange rate regime, to allow the nominal exchange rate to move significantly. At the same time, the maintenance of capital controls can, to some degree, support this process by providing protection from potential instability arising from capital flows while institutional arrangements needed to support capital account convertibility are allowed to develop.

The remainder of this paper develops the case for two key points: that a move toward greater exchange rate flexibility is in China's own interest and that it should precede capital account liberalisation (Eichengreen, 2004 reaches similar conclusions). It does not deal with a whole host of related (and equally important) issues including how the move toward greater exchange rate flexibility should be managed, what the best alternative exchange rate regime would be, what form an alternative monetary anchor could take, or how much financial sector and institutional development is adequate to minimise the risks of capital account liberalisation.

---

[5] Yu (2004) has argued that it would be optimal for gradual capital account liberalisation and moves towards greater exchange rate flexibility to proceed simultaneously.

[6] IMF (2004) notes that an initial move toward flexibility could take the form of a widening of the renminbi trading band, a peg to a currency basket, or some combination of these.

2. The Case for Exchange Rate Flexibility

With China's increasing integration into the global economy, its exposure to external shocks has increased. This has heightened the need for an autonomous monetary policy and greater use of market-oriented instruments such as interest rate changes to control economic activity. Indeed, the constraints on the use of such instruments have been highlighted by the capital inflows since 2001 that have increased liquidity in the banking system and complicated domestic monetary management. During this period, rapid growth of bank credit has contributed to a surge in investment growth, leading to the possible build-up of excess capacity and associated nonperforming loans in several sectors of the economy, as well as potential problems of more generalised overheating. Increases in interest rates to control these problems have perforce been limited by the increased incentives for capital inflows that would result.

In this context, it is worth reiterating that the Chinese authorities themselves have clearly articulated the desirability of having a more flexible exchange rate and independent monetary policy; the main focus of the recent debate has been about the appropriate timing for such a move. It is useful to set the stage for the case for an early move to flexibility by reviewing the economic concerns that could be inhibiting it.

2.1. Concerns about greater exchange rate flexibility

China's export growth is widely regarded as playing an important role in catalysing overall economic and employment growth. Thus, a key concern about allowing more flexibility is that an appreciation of the renminbi could hurt China's external competitiveness, thereby reducing export growth and weakening prospects for continued FDI inflows (see Mundell, 2003). However, the direct impact on exports of a moderate appreciation of the exchange rate is likely to be considerably muted by the high import content of China's exports, as well as China's strong productivity growth and low labour costs. Indeed, during the period 1999-2002, China's total exports (in value terms) rose by 37 percent despite a 7 percent real effective appreciation. Trade data show that over 50 percent of Chinese export operations involves the final assembly of products using intermediate inputs produced by other countries. Despite the high gross value of Chinese exports, the domestic value-added content of these exports to the rest of the world in general, and to the United States in particular, is only about 30 percent and 20 percent respectively (Lau, 2003). An appreciation of the renminbi, while raising the cost of processing and assembly in China, would also lower the cost of imported intermediate inputs. Hence, an appreciation of the renminbi may not put much of a dent in China's external competitiveness[7].

Another concern is that an exchange rate appreciation could adversely affect the agricultural sector. There is believed to be a large amount of surplus labour in the rural areas approximating 150 million workers by the Chinese authorities' own estimates. This, in conjunction with the notion that the Chinese agricultural sector is not internationally competitive, has raised considerable concerns among policymakers that a fall in domestic prices of food imports that would result from an appreciation of the renminbi could have significant adverse consequences. While this is a plausible and relevant concern, there is as yet little empirical evidence to support it. In addition, recent research suggests that the competitiveness of China's agricultural sector has improved significantly in recent years, making it less sensitive to external shocks (see Rosen *et al.*, 2004)[8].

As noted earlier, a greater concern is that exchange rate flexibility could imperil the health of the banking system. Indeed, this is a typical problem in countries where a devaluation imposes a large burden on firms and banks that have large amounts of debt denominated in foreign currencies. The situation in China is of course quite the opposite as current pressures

---

[7] Anderson (2004) makes a similar point. Lau (2003) estimates that a 10 percent real appreciation of the renminbi would increase the cost of Chinese exports to the United States by only about 2 percent.

[8] This study notes that, contrary to expectations, the agricultural sector was able to cope quite well with the opening up of China's agricultural markets that resulted from WTO accession commitments.

are for an appreciation, but the fact that domestic banks have a positive net foreign asset position implies that there could still be costs to the banking sector.

The current overall exposure of the corporate sector and banks in China to foreign exchange risks appears to be low; however, there are some indications that the degree of exposure has been on the rise in recent years. As shown in Table 1, in 2003, banks' net foreign assets accounted for 3 percent of broad money and 6 percent of GDP, and foreign currency lending constituted about 5 percent of domestic credit and 9 percent of GDP. These indicators seem relatively innocuous when compared with those of other countries. Their recent evolution, however, points to a trend that bears watching closely: during 2001-03, banks' foreign currency loans to domestic residents have increased by over 60 percent, net foreign currency liabilities are up by nearly 50 percent, and total short-term external debt (which is denominated in foreign currencies) has risen by over 50 percent. These are trends that are likely to continue with China's increasing global integration and the opening of the financial system as part of the terms of World Trade Organization (WTO) accession[9].

There are some caveats to be borne in mind in interpreting the aggregate figures in Table 1. Detailed information on exposures of large financial institutions, including the currency composition and maturity of foreign currency assets and liabilities, would have to be analysed in detail to determine the exposure of specific institutions and any possible systemic spillovers that could result from the effects of an exchange rate appreciation on any of these institutions. Moreover, there is currently little information available on hedging practices in the corporate sector. Anecdotal evidence suggests that the use of hedging instruments is limited; however, other forms of hedging, particularly "natural" hedges (e.g., denomination of processing imports and related exports in the same currency) may be more prevalent.

---

[9] More recent data show that total short-term external debt as of end-September 2004 was 29 percent higher than its end-2003 level.

Table 1. China: Foreign Currency Exposures of Financial and Corporate Sectors
(In billions of US dollars)

	2001	2002	2003
Net foreign assets of People's Bank of China	234	276	370
Net foreign exchange-denominated assets of the banking system[1]	31	60	67
Of which, net foreign assets	85	108	85
(in percent of broad money)	4.6	4.8	3.2
(in percent of GDP)	7.3	8.5	6.1
Net domestic foreign currency assets	-54	-48	-19
Banks' foreign currency loans to domestic residents	81	103	130
(in percent of total credit)	5.0	4.9	5.2
(in percent of GDP)	6.9	8.1	9.2
Net foreign currency exposure of corporate sector	-103	-121	-150
Corporates' foreign currency assets[2]	45	52	52
Corporates' foreign currency liabilities[3]	149	172	202
Total external debt	170	171	194
Of which: short-term	44	48	73
Of which: corporate	68	70	82

Sources: CEIC; and IMF staff estimates.
[1]Sum of net foreign assets (net claims against foreign residents) and net foreign currency-denominated assets against domestic residents.
[2]The estimates are based on corporate foreign currency deposits in domestic banks.
[3]Sum of corporate external debt and domestic foreign currency loans.

A more general concern is that nominal exchange rate volatility under a more flexible exchange rate regime could affect trade flows and FDI inflows, both of which have been important to China's growth. On the former, recent studies find little evidence that exchange rate volatility has a significant adverse effect on trade flows (see Clark *et al.*, 2004). It is also worth noting that, by maintaining an effective peg to the dollar, China's currency is stable relative to its major trading partner—the United States—but it still fluctuates relative to most of China's other trading partners. This does not appear to have hurt China's trade expansion in other industrial country markets.

There is also little evidence in the literature that exchange rate volatility has a significant role in determining the level of FDI a country receives. The most important factors affecting FDI include market size, GDP growth, productivity growth, political and macroeconomic stability, the regulatory environment, and the ability to repatriate profits (United Nations, 1999; Lim, 2002). Nevertheless, some recent papers have suggested that China's maintenance of an undervalued exchange rate is crucial for its ability to attract strong FDI inflows[10]. Our view is that, given China's strong productivity growth, increasing access to world markets, and rapidly expanding domestic demand, there is little reason to believe that an exchange rate appreciation would have a substantial negative effect on FDI inflows. Indeed, the prospects of greater macroeconomic stability that could result from exchange rate flexibility could well offset any negative effects from an appreciation.

In summary, our assessment is that the net adverse effects on the Chinese economy of any appreciation in the renminbi resulting from a move towards greater flexibility would be quite modest. There could, however, be significant distributional effects, with some sectors such as agriculture potentially facing larger adjustment costs.

All of these potential costs would, in any case, depend on the persistence of any appreciation of the currency. Under current circumstances, a near-term appreciation of the renminbi is widely regarded as a sure thing. Over the medium term, however, the trend in the real exchange rate is much harder to predict as it will depend on a number of additional factors with potentially offsetting effects. Forces for appreciation include the continuing strong productivity growth in China's traded goods sector, aided by structural reforms and further improvement in access to world markets. Forces for depreciation

---

[10] For instance, this is implicitly suggested by the work of Dooley *et al.* (2004), although it is not their central thesis.

include the further liberalisation of China's domestic market that will take place as part of WTO accession commitments, and the expected gradual liberalisation of the capital account which could lead to more outflows if domestic agents sought to undertake some international diversification of their portfolios. Moreover, as noted earlier, recent upward pressure on the exchange rate reflects strong capital inflows that in large part appear to be driven by speculative inflows in anticipation of a currency appreciation. Such inflows are likely to be transitory and could easily reverse. Thus, it is far from obvious that greater flexibility will result in a persistent appreciation of the renminbi.

2.2. The potential costs of not having exchange rate flexibility

We now turn to a discussion of the costs of delaying a move towards exchange rate flexibility. In this context, it is first worth reviewing why countries adopt fixed exchange rate systems in the first place. A crucial consideration for developing economies is that such regimes provide a well-defined nominal anchor and, in principle, impose discipline on macroeconomic policies. This discipline can be useful for countries with institutional and policy weaknesses that tend to manifest themselves in higher inflation, problems of debt sustainability, fragile banking systems, and other sources of macroeconomic volatility. Empirical studies have shown that fixed or relatively rigid exchange rate regimes have indeed provided some benefits in terms of macroeconomic stability, especially to low-income countries where financial market development is limited and the capital market closed (e.g., Rogoff *et al*, 2004). However, these benefits tend to erode over time while exchange rate flexibility becomes more valuable as economies mature and become integrated with global markets.

In fact, maintenance of a fixed exchange rate regime can often mask underlying policy and institutional weaknesses and result in the build-up of various sorts of imbalances. These problems can be exacerbated by an open capital account. For instance, governments may accumulate external debt in order to get around constraints to domestic financing of budget deficits. Domestic firms and financial institutions may also react to the perception of limited foreign exchange risk by taking on foreign currency debt. Given the relative riskiness of lending to emerging markets as perceived by international investors, much of this debt tends to be short term. The presence of large amounts of short-term external debt denominated in foreign currencies is now widely recognised as being a key risk factor in precipitating balance of payments crises.

In addition to these general considerations, the particular circumstances that China faces also generate some specific costs of maintaining a fixed exchange rate. The sterilisation of capital inflows has been facilitated by the fact that domestic interest rates related to the main sterilisation instrument (central bank bills) have been lower than interest rates on medium and long-term industrial country treasury bonds, which is where much of China's reserves are presumed to be held. Thus, the traditional net costs of sterilisation are absent in this case. However, maintaining such low domestic interest rates, which have recently been negative in real terms, requires domestic financial repression, which in turn creates large distortions and efficiency losses (see Prasad and Rajan, 2005).

Moreover, the depreciation of the US dollar since 2003 suggests that the terms of trade for China have worsened. This effectively acts as an implicit tax on consumption and, while such costs are difficult to detect directly, they are likely to be significant in terms of potential welfare losses, especially in view of China's high level of trade openness.

Furthermore, if fundamental factors such as relative productivity growth create persistent pressures for real exchange appreciation, these pressures eventually tend to force adjustment through one channel or another. Even in an economy with capital controls and a repressed domestic financial sector, these pressures can be bottled up for only so long (Rajan and Subramanian, 2004). It is typically better to allow the required adjustment to take place through changes in the nominal exchange rate rather than through inflation. Particularly in a developing economy, such inflationary dynamics can pose serious risks as expectations of rising inflation can feed on themselves and become entrenched.

For an independent monetary policy (with exchange rate flexibility) to be most effective, further institutional and operational improvements would be needed to establish a credible monetary policy framework and improve the monetary policy transmission mechanism. However, the movement toward an independent monetary policy regime should not be delayed. While it may indeed be possible to maintain China's present exchange rate regime for a long period, the explicit and implicit costs of maintaining this regime are potentially large and likely to grow over time, especially in view of China's increasing integration with global markets and the authorities' stated objective to gradually liberalise the capital account.

3. Capital Account Liberalisation

3.1. Benefits and risks in theory and practice

The financial crises experienced by many emerging markets in the last two decades have led to an intense debate about the benefits and risks of capital account liberalisation for developing countries. In theory, capital account liberalisation should have unambiguous benefits in terms of promoting more efficient international allocation of capital, boosting growth in developing countries through a variety of channels, and allowing countries to reduce their consumption volatility by offering opportunities for sharing income risk. The reality, however, is far more sobering. There is little conclusive evidence of a strong and robust causal relationship between financial integration and growth. Moreover, there is evidence that financial integration could actually increase the relative volatility of consumption growth for emerging markets (see Prasad *et al.*, 2003).

Opening the capital account while maintaining an inflexible exchange rate regime, especially when domestic macroeconomic policies are not consistent with the requirements of the regime, has proven to be a precursor of crisis in many countries. Recent episodes involving emerging market economies, from the "tequila crisis" of 1995 through the Asian/Russian/Brazilian crises of 1997–98, have added to the evidence that a fixed exchange rate regime with an open capital account provides a fertile ground for crises. By contrast, emerging market economies that maintained greater flexibility in their exchange rate regimes have generally fared much better when faced with external pressures. For example, Chile, Mexico, Peru, South Africa, and Turkey all seem to have benefited from the flexibility of their exchange rates during periods of instability in emerging markets. China and India were less affected by the Asian crisis of 1997–98, and their relatively closed capital account regimes have been credited with helping to limit vulnerability to financial contagion, although other factors may have played a role as well, including comfortable foreign reserves positions (see Krugman, 1998; Fernald and Bobson, 1999).

As noted earlier, capital account liberalisation can also aggravate risks associated with imprudent fiscal policies. Moreover, in the presence of weak and inadequately supervised banking systems and other distortions in domestic capital markets, inflows of foreign capital could be misallocated and create a host of problems, including currency, maturity, and duration mismatches on the balance sheets of financial and corporate sectors, as well as unsustainable levels and maturity structures of external debt (Ishii and Habermeier, 2002).

All of this suggests that China would do well to adopt a cautious approach to capital account liberalisation. Indeed, China's approach of opening up to FDI rather than other types of capital inflows has helped insulate it from many of the risks associated with capital account liberalisation. However, as discussed below, the dominance of FDI in China's total capital inflows has declined markedly in recent years, implying that the composition of inflows is likely to be increasingly driven by market forces rather than the desires of policymakers[11].

---

[11] Prasad and Wei (2005) document changes over time in the relative importance of FDI in China's total capital inflows and discuss various hypotheses about why China's inflows have been largely tilted towards FDI.

3.2. Capital controls and their inevitable erosion over time

Growing awareness about the potential pitfalls of capital account liberalisation has refocused attention on the usefulness of capital controls in managing the process of integration with the global economy. Capital controls do provide a degree of protection from the vagaries of international capital flows and can help in controlling the risks posed by a weak financial sector. However, they can often perpetuate inefficiencies and distortions in domestic financial systems, with consequences for long-term growth and stability.

In countries with weak financial systems, capital controls can prevent the corporate sector, as well as domestic banks whose operations may not entirely be run on a commercial basis, and that may have inadequate risk assessment capacity from excessive external borrowing. In countries with an inflexible exchange rate regime, capital controls are also used to preserve a degree of monetary policy autonomy. Some countries resort to capital controls to reduce both exchange rate volatility generated by swings in short-run capital flows as well as exposure to balance of payments crises. At the same time, capital controls can also support policies of domestic financial repression that can be used to ensure that domestic savings are used to finance the government budget and sectors deemed as priorities by policymakers.

In practice, capital controls tend to be far from watertight. A number of channels can be used to evade capital controls. One of the most frequently used channels has been under-invoicing and over-invoicing of export and import contracts (Gulati, 1987; Kamin, 1988; Patnaik and Vasudevan, 2000). Multinational companies can also use transfer pricing schemes to evade capital controls. Another trade-related channel for unrecorded capital flows is associated with the leads and lags in the settlement of commercial transactions or the variation in the terms offered on short-term trade credits. Remittances of savings by foreign workers in the domestic economy and by domestic nationals working abroad, family remittances, and tourist expenditures—although typically regarded as current account transactions—have also been used as vehicles for the acquisition or repatriation of foreign assets.

There is by now considerable evidence that the effectiveness of capital controls tends to diminish over time, especially when strong exchange rate pressures are resisted by official intervention. Japan's experience in the wake of the collapse of Bretton Woods system in the 1970s and the experiences of Latin American countries during the debt crisis of the 1980s demonstrate that capital controls have generally not been very effective in restricting capital outflows (inflows) when there is strong downward (upward) pressure on the exchange rate.

Capital controls in China are extensive and appear to have been reasonably effective in the past. However, recent experience suggests that their efficiency may be waning. It is widely cited that China's capital controls were one reason the country withstood the Asian financial crisis (e.g., Gruenwald and Aziz, 2003), but it should be noted that the capital flight from China during the Asian crisis was triggered by external shocks, while public confidence in the domestic financial system remained basically intact. In this sense, China's capital controls have not really been tested in a crisis context.

Despite the existence of controls on capital outflows, sizable amounts of financial capital still appear to have flown out of China during the Asian crisis and its aftermath[12]. Since 2001, expectations of an appreciation of the renminbi, coupled with a positive Chinese-US interest rate differential, have resulted in substantial net inflows of non-FDI capital despite the extensive controls on non-FDI inflows (see Prasad and Wei, 2005). Moreover, these expectations have also been reflected in recorded capital account transactions. Foreign currency loans from domestic banks to residents increased by almost 30 percent during 2003, while residents'

---

[12] Gunter (2004) estimates that capital flight from China exceeded US$100 billion a year during 1997–2000. He also notes that, during this period, stricter controls on cross-border currency and investment flows were largely offset by increasing use of trade mis-invoicing.

foreign currency deposits declined slightly. At the same time, anecdotal evidence of early collection of export receipts and increased use of trade credit for imports is also consistent with general expectations of an appreciation of the renminbi.

These experiences, corroborated by more formal empirical work (e.g., Cheung *et al*, 2003), suggest that the capital controls have become less effective over time, increasingly limiting the room for an independent monetary policy. China's continued rapid trade expansion also creates a growing scope for getting around capital account restrictions. As China becomes increasingly integrated into the global economy in the context of its WTO accession, with commitments to further liberalisation of trade and the opening-up of the financial sector, its capital controls are likely to become even more porous.

4. The Foreign Exchange Market

Some commentators have argued that the absence of a well-functioning foreign exchange market will inhibit any move toward greater exchange rate flexibility. Furthermore, it has been argued that, so long as controls on capital account transactions are in place, there will not be a fully functioning foreign exchange market in China, as much of the potential demand for foreign exchange in China is still excluded from the market (e.g., Lau, 2003). The latter is a valid point. However, while liberalising the capital account can expand the sources and uses of foreign exchange, an open capital account is not a necessary condition for deepening the foreign exchange market. Since China has a large volume of trade transactions and few restrictions on convertibility on current account transactions, there is clearly potential for a deep and well-functioning foreign exchange market even without a fully open capital account[13].

---

[13] Duttagupta *et al.* (2004) also discuss the potential to develop the foreign exchange market in these circumstances and show that it is difficult to establish a strong positive relationship between capital account liberalisation and depth of foreign exchange markets.

Furthermore, the notion of needing to first perfect the foreign exchange market before moving towards greater flexibility is, in our view, a red herring. In fact, the functioning of the foreign exchange market can be greatly improved even within the context of the present exchange rate regime[14]. A phased approach toward flexibility should not pose any major risks even if existing financial instruments to hedge foreign exchange risks are limited, and would give economic agents stronger incentives to hedge foreign exchange risks that have so far been borne entirely by the monetary authorities. This would itself be an important factor nurturing the development of a deeper and more sophisticated foreign exchange market.

5. Considerations of Timing

International experiences have varied considerably in terms of the order in which countries have adopted policies to open up to global integration. Some countries have liberalised capital flows without exchange rate flexibility—an approach that entails considerable risks if financial markets are not sufficiently developed—while others have introduced exchange rate flexibility well in advance of capital account liberalisation. In general, countries appear to have better medium-term outcomes if they introduce exchange rate flexibility before fully liberalising their capital account, especially if there are weaknesses in the financial sector[15].

---

[14] For instance, allowing enterprises access to the China Foreign Exchange Trading System through a licensed broker system would increase trading volume and reduce the dominant role of official intervention in the market. Even within a narrow band of a de facto peg, relaxing bid-offer spreads could encourage participants to take positions on both sides. Foreign exchange surrender requirements could also be further reduced. Easing the requirement that enterprises need "real commercial demand" to enter forward contracts would allow them to hedge based on future needs (see Lin, 2004; Luo, 2004; Ma, 2004).

[15] Selected international experiences are discussed in Annex I of the fuller version of this paper (IMF Policy Discussion Paper PDP/05/1; available at www.imf.org/publications). India is one example of a country that has recently introduced some exchange rate flexibility while only gradually easing capital account restrictions.

The Chinese authorities have attempted to alleviate recent appreciation pressures by easing controls on capital as well as current account transactions in order to provide more channels for capital outflows[16]. These measures, while broadly in the direction of the authorities' long-term objective of full capital account convertibility, run the risk of getting the sequencing wrong. As discussed above, an increasingly open capital account without exchange rate flexibility has been the root cause of many recent emerging market financial crises.

Moreover, easing of controls on capital outflows may end up being counter-productive since this could stimulate further inflows. The removal of controls on outflows, by making it easier to take capital out of a country when desired, tends to make investors more willing to invest in a country (Labán and Larraín, 1993). In addition, to the extent that easing of controls on outflows is perceived as a commitment to sound domestic macroeconomic policies, more capital could be induced to flow in (Bartolini and Drazen, 1997). A number of countries (e.g., Italy in 1984, New Zealand in 1984, Spain in 1986, Uruguay in 1970) that have removed controls on outflows have experienced rapid and massive inflows soon after.

While capital controls provide some degree of protection to the domestic financial system, these controls are likely to become less effective over time. It would, therefore, be in China's best interest to consider an early move towards exchange rate flexibility, while the existing capital account controls are still relatively effective and the underlying structural problems manageable. The current strength and stability of the economy, together with existing capital account controls, have contributed to a reasonably high level of confidence in the banking system despite its weak financial position. But domestic banks are likely to come under increasing competitive pressure, especially once foreign

---

[16] See Annex II of the fuller version of this paper (cited in previous footnote) for a detailed description of recent measures taken to ease restrictions on cross-border foreign exchange transactions.

banks are allowed to enter the Chinese market under WTO accession commitments.

In principle, an orderly exit from a fixed exchange rate regime to greater flexibility can best be accomplished during a period of relative tranquility in exchange markets. Since such periods are rare and fleeting, however, experiences of other countries suggest that a next-best set of circumstances is when the domestic economy is strong and pressures are for an appreciation of the currency (Eichengreen and Mussa, 1998; Agénor, 2004). Such circumstances provide a useful window of opportunity that should be taken full advantage of. History is replete with examples of countries that, having passed up such opportunities, had to change their exchange rate regimes in far less ideal circumstances and with much less desirable macroeconomic outcomes during the adjustment to the new regime.

6. Concluding Remarks

China is firmly on the path of greater integration with the global economy—a path that has provided great benefits for China and for the world in general (Prasad (ed.), 2004). The Chinese authorities clearly intend to continue on this path, undertaking more trade integration and a gradual liberalisation of capital controls. In view of these objectives, gaining experience over time with greater flexibility in the exchange rate and achieving a more stable financial system should be prerequisites to fully opening the capital account.

Introducing more flexibility in the exchange rate would help to improve macroeconomic control and reduce vulnerabilities to shocks. Steps toward more flexibility in the exchange rate need not be deferred until all of the prerequisites for full capital account convertibility have been achieved. The exchange rate can be allowed to move in response to the evolution of supply and demand for foreign exchange, even though these forces may be constrained by restrictions on capital flows.

Historical experiences of other countries highlight the risks associated with capital account liberalisation in the absence of exchange rate flexibility. Easing controls on capital outflows in order to alleviate pressures on the exchange rate could, in fact, be counter-productive and induce even larger inflows. Thus, capital account liberalisation should be given a lower priority and should not be regarded as a substitute for greater exchange rate flexibility.

This paper has also argued that greater flexibility can be introduced without creating disruptions in the financial sector. Maintenance of capital controls can, to some degree, support this process by providing protection from potential instability arising from capital flows while institutional arrangements needed to support capital account convertibility, including a stronger domestic banking sector, are allowed to develop. A movement toward more exchange rate flexibility also does not necessarily mean immediate adoption of a free float. In fact, a period of "learning to float" can be useful in overcoming "fear of floating".

However, capital controls will become increasingly ineffective as integration with the global economy continues. Furthermore, historical experiences of other countries clearly show the merits of making a move toward flexibility when the domestic economy is growing rapidly and the external position is strong. All of these factors lead to the conclusions that a relatively early move toward greater exchange rate flexibility would be in China's best interest and that there could be significant costs associated with long delays in making such a move.

Acknowledgements

We are grateful to Ray Brooks, Steven Dunaway, Gauti Eggertsson, Cem Karacadag, and numerous other colleagues for their helpful comments and advice. The analysis in this paper draws extensively upon work by other members of the IMF's China team, whose input and suggestions we gratefully acknowledge. The views expressed in this paper are those of the author(s) and do not necessarily represent those of the IMF or IMF policy.

References

1. Agénor, P.-R., "Orderly Exits from Adjustable Pegs and Exchange Rate Bands: Policy Issues and Role of Capital Flows," *Global Development Finance Report 2004 Background Study*, (World Bank, Washington, 2004).
2. Anderson, J., "How I Learned to Stop Worrying and Forget the Yuan," *Far Eastern Economic Review*, Vol. 168(1), 37-42 (2004).
3. Bank for International Settlements (BIS), "China's Capital Account Liberalisation: International Perspectives," BIS Papers No. 15 (2003).
4. Bartolini, L., and A. Drazen, "Capital Account Liberalisation as a Signal," *American Economic Review*, Vol. 87, 138-154 (1997).
5. Cheung, Y.-W., M. D. Chinn, and E. Fujii, "The Chinese Economies in Global Context: The Integration Process and its Determinants," NBER Working Paper No. 10047, (National Bureau of Economic Research, Cambridge, MA, 2003).
6. Clark, P. B., N. Tamirisa, and S.-J. Wei, "Exchange Rate Volatility and Trade Flows," IMF Occasional Paper No. 235, (International Monetary Fund, Washington, 2004).
7. Dooley, M. P., D. Folkerts-Landau, and P. Garber, "Direct Investment, Rising Real Wages and the Absorption of Excess Labor in the Periphery," NBER Working Paper No. 10626, (National Bureau of Economic Research, Cambridge, MA, 2004).
8. Duttagupta, R., G. Fernandez, and C. Karacadag, "From Fixed to Float: Operational Issues in Moving Towards Exchange Rate Flexibility," IMF Working Paper 04/126, (International Monetary Fund, Washington, 2004).
9. Eichengreen, B., "Chinese Currency Controversies," CEPR Discussion Paper Series No. 4375, (Centre for Economic Policy Research, London, 2004).
10. _____ , and M. Mussa, "Exit Strategies: Policy Options for Countries Seeking Greater Exchange Rate Flexibility," IMF Occasional Paper No. 168, (International Monetary Fund, Washington, 1998).
11. Fernald, J., and O. D. Babson, "Why Has China Survived the Asian Crisis So Well? What Risks Remain?" International Finance Discussion Paper No. 633, (Board of Governors of the Federal Reserve System, Washington, 1999).
12. Frankel, J. A., "On the Renminbi: The Choice between Adjustment under a Fixed Exchange Rate and Adjustment under a Flexible Rate," unpublished, (Kennedy School of Government, Harvard University, Cambridge, MA, 2004).
13. Funke, M., and J. Rahn, "Just How Undervalued is the Chinese Renminbi," *The World Economy*, Vol. 28(4), 465-489 (2005).
14. Goldstein, M., "Adjusting China's Exchange Rate Policies," Institute for International Economics Working Paper 04/1, (2004).

15. _____, and N. Lardy, "Two-Stage Currency Reform for China," *Asian Wall Street Journal*, September 12 (2003).
16. Goodfriend, M., and E. Prasad, "A Framework for Independent Monetary Policy in China," manuscript, (International Monetary Fund, Washington, 2006).
17. Gruenwald, P., and J. Aziz, "China and the Asian Crisis," in *China: Competing in the Global Economy*, (International Monetary Fund, Washington, 2003).
18. Gulati, S., "A Note on Trade Misinvoicing," in *Capital Flight and Third World Debt*, (Institute for International Economics, Washington, 1987).
19. Gunther, F.R., "Capital Flight from China: 1984-2001," *China Economic Review*, Vol. 15, 63–85 (2005).
20. International Monetary Fund, "People's Republic of China: Article IV Consultation—Staff Report," (International Monetary Fund, Washington, 2004).
21. Ip, G., "Greenspan Warns About Yuan Float," *Wall Street Journal*, March 2 (2004).
22. Ishii, S., and K. Habermeier, "Capital Account Liberalisation and Financial Sector Stability," IMF Occasional Paper No. 232, (International Monetary Fund, Washington, 2002).
23. Kamin, S., "Devaluation, Exchange Controls, and Black Markets for Foreign Exchange in Developing Countries," International Finance Discussion Paper No. 334, (Board of Governors of the Federal Reserve System, Washington, 1988).
24. Krugman, P., "Saving Asia: It's Time to Get Radical," *Fortune*, September (1998).
25. Labán, R., and F. Larraín, "Can a Liberalisation of Capital Outflows Increase Net Capital Inflows?" Universidad Catolica de Chile, Working Paper No. 155, (1993).
26. Lau, L., "Is China Playing By the Rules?", Testimony at a hearing of the Congressional Executive Commission on China on September 24 (2003).
27. Lim, E.-G., "The Determinants of, and the Relationship Between, Foreign Direct Investment and Growth: A Summary of the Recent Literature," IMF Working Paper 01/175, (International Monetary Fund, Washington, 2002).
28. Lin, Y., "Welcoming a New Era in the Development of China's FX Market," *China Money*, No. 2, (China Foreign Exchange Trading System, Shanghai, 2004).
29. Luo, X., "Options and Measures for Further Development of China's FX Market," *China Money*, No. 2, (China Foreign Exchange Trading System, Shanghai, 2004).
30. Ma, G., "China's FX Market, An International Perspective," *China Money*, No. 1, (China Foreign Exchange Trading System, Shanghai, 2004).

31. McKinnon, R., and G. Schnabl, "China: A Stabilizing or Deflationary Influence in East Asia? The Problem of Conflicted Virtue," Stanford University Working Paper, (2003).
32. Mundell, R., "Globalization and RMB Exchange Rate," presentation made at Renmin University of China, Beijing, October 31 (2003).
33. Patnaik, I., and D. Vasudevan, "Trade Misinvoicing and Capital Flight from India," *Journal of International Economic Studies*, Vol. 14, 99–108 (2000).
34. Prasad, E., "Growth and Stability in China," Remarks at the Plenary Panel of the Harvard China Review Annual Conference, available on the Web at www.imf.org (2004).
35. _____ , ed., with S. Barnett, N. Blancher, R. Brooks, A. Fedelino, T. Feyzioglu, T. Rumbaugh, R. Jan Singh, and T. Wang, "China's Growth and Integration into the World Economy: Prospects and Challenges," IMF Occasional Paper No. 232, (International Monetary Fund, Washington, 2004).
36. _____ , K. Rogoff, S.-J. Wei, and M. A. Kose, "Effects of Financial Globalization on Developing Countries: Some Empirical Evidence," IMF Occasional Paper No. 220, (International Monetary Fund, Washington, 2003).
37. Prasad, E., and S.-J. Wei, "China's Approach to Capital Inflows: Patterns and Possible Explanations," in Sebastian Edwards ed., *Capital Controls and Capital Flows in Emerging Economies: Policies, Practices and Consequences*, (University of Chicago Press, forthcoming).
38. _____ , and R. Rajan, "China's Financial Sector Challenge," Op-ed article in *Financial Times*, May 10 (2005).
39. Rajan, R., and A. Subramanian, "Exchange Rate Flexibility is in Asia's Interest," *Financial Times*, September 22 (2004).
40. Rogoff, K., A. M. Hussain, A. Mody, R. Brooks, and N. Oomes, "Evolution and Performance of Exchange Rate Regimes," IMF Occasional Paper No. 229, (International Monetary Fund, Washington, 2004).
41. Rosen, D., S. Rozelle, and J. Huang, "Roots of Competitiveness: China's Evolving Agricultural Interests," Policy Analyses in International Economics, No. 72, (Institute for International Economics, Washington, 2004).
42. Standard & Poor's, "Risky Move to Float China's Exchange Rate," September 13 (2003).
43. United Nations, "MNC's Express Site Preferences for Investing," *Development Business*, Vol. 22(502), (1999).
44. Yu, Y., "China's Capital Flow Liberalisation and Reform of Exchange Rate Regime," manuscript, (Chinese Academy of Social Sciences, Beijing, 2004).

CHAPTER 6

CHINA'S COMPETITIVENESS, INTRA-INDUSTRY AND INTRA-REGIONAL TRADE IN ASIA

Linda Yueh

Pembroke College, University of Oxford, and the Centre for Economic Performance, London School of Economics and Political Science

Abstract: This paper examines the widespread perception that China's competitive strength has had a harmful impact on other countries, particularly on its export-led Asian neighbours. Since undertaking its "open door" policy in the early 1990s, China has transformed itself into one of the most open economies in the world with an export-to-GDP ratio of 30% and one that accounts for an impressive 6% of the global manufactured export market. It is a market share that rivals the old and new Asian "tiger" economies, which are known for their export-oriented growth strategy. Using detailed trade data, we find that China's growth in global market share was accompanied by growth in market share by all of the developing Asian nations except for Hong Kong, whose analysis is complicated by its rejoining with China during this period. There is also evidence of a rise in intra-industry trade in the region, which suggests closer trade links through production chains in Asia. We conclude that China may well be a magnet for attracting foreign direct investment (FDI) in the region, and its increased competitiveness has not inflicted harm on its neighbours.

1. Introduction

China's increasing competitiveness has raised concerns in both developed and developing countries alike. The widespread perception that China will undercut production elsewhere in the region is based on its abundant labour supply, low level of wages and a reasonably skilled labour force. Moreover, China has demonstrated an impressive ability to upgrade its technology to produce increasingly complex manufactured goods. China produces not just textiles, but also semiconductors. Indeed, the concerns heard are not only in Asia but throughout the global economy. Its effects on the Asian region, though, are worthy of consideration, particularly as these countries share an export-oriented focus in their growth approach. Also, given the geographic proximity of these countries, there are potential implications for intra-regional trade and indeed, intra-industry trade, in the Asian region.

China's "open door" policy since taking off in the early 1990s, and trade liberalisation measures leading up to membership in the WTO in 2001, have seen the ascendancy of a powerhouse economy which is currently the fourth largest in the world and the third largest exporter, after the U.S. and Germany. China has also been a leading destination for inward FDI, receiving between $50-60 billion per year, falling behind only the US and the UK in terms of stock.

Over the period 1990-2000, Chinese manufactured exports grew by 16.9% per annum, compared with 10.3% for the rest of East Asia, and its world market share almost tripled from 1.7% to 4.4%. China's share of the global export market grew even faster after 2000. By 2005, four years after accession to the WTO, China accounted for around 6% of global market export share and exports grew at over 30% on average per annum. Accession to the WTO is expected to improve market access for Chinese textiles and garments abroad as well as open the domestic market to trade. Further, China's position in the global market will be supported by WTO entry. Reforms consistent with international economic law are expected, which should facilitate inward FDI, reform of the financial and banking sectors, and otherwise liberalise the Chinese economy.

These trends underlie the perception that China's competitiveness will reduce the market share of other countries in Asia. Some of the questions commonly raised are whether China's growth in exports has harmed the region and if there are any areas in which the rest of Asia might still be able to compete in light of China's lower costs, the traditional source of comparative advantage of the Asian "tiger economies." For instance, average real wages in China are estimated to be only 20% of that of Malaysia and Taiwan, and 10% of the average wage in Singapore. Although China's export strength, in particular, will challenge the productive bases of its neighbours, it is unlikely that China will become the sole producer of manufactured goods in the region. It is not surprising that China's ascendancy should cause concern in a region whose development has depended on export-oriented growth. However, there are likely to be complementarities between China and the rest of the Asian region. China's rise, moreover, will likely entail structural changes in the other Asian economies, such as alterations in their respective divisions of production and areas of specialisation. Changing production patterns and specialisation are a natural part of maturing economies. Therefore, the anticipated changes will differ for each nation depending on its progress in the path of development.

The countries in Asia that we will focus on will be the four mature East Asian 'Tigers,' namely, Hong Kong, Taiwan, South Korea and Singapore, and the 'New Tigers,' namely, Malaysia, Thailand, Indonesia and the Philippines. Together with China (and excluding Japan) these nations account for more than 99% of trade of global merchandise in the region. The region's exports in turn account for an impressive 48% of global merchandise trade. The Southeast Asian nations of this group founded the Association of South East Asian Nations (ASEAN), another popular grouping. The Association of South East Asian Nations was founded by Indonesia, Malaysia, the Philippines, Singapore and Thailand. Brunei, Vietnam, Laos, Myanmar and Cambodia were later members. As a developed economy, Japan's declining global market share in manufactured exports might be expected, but reflects a different set of considerations than the rest of the developing countries in the region. We focus on the main industrialising nations in Asia: China, as well as the Old and New Tigers. As our chosen divisions suggest, the Old Tigers require an analysis that accounts for the structural changes in their economies, including increases in real wages that have eroded their original comparative advantage deriving from low cost labour. The New Tigers, in contrast, have burst onto the scene offering lower wages and enticing multinational corporations to relocate production to their emerging industrial sectors.

In turn, we will analyse the theory and evidence to assess whether Chinese exports have harmed the exports of other Asian nations. Then, we examine the possible future sources of comparative advantage for the Asian Tigers and the role of multinational corporations in affecting the patterns of trade in Asia, namely, the development of intra-industry trade. We conclude with some assessments about the patterns of trade in Asia with the 'opening' of China.

2. Competitiveness and Trade Theory

The noted economist and Nobel Laureate Paul Samuelson described comparative advantage as the best example of an economic principle that is undeniably true yet not obvious to intelligent people. The comparative advantage of a nation refers to the concept that countries can gain from trade if they specialise and exchange goods in which each country is relatively more efficient. Therefore, even if a nation, such as China, is the lowest cost producer of every manufactured good and has an absolute advantage in production in every industry, it will still be welfare enhancing for China to trade with other nations to obtain the goods in which it is relatively less efficient.

By this basic tenet of trade theory, we should expect that the rapid expansion of China's exports will not result in detrimental effects on the exports of the rest of the Asian region, as each nation should specialise in the production of goods in which they are less inefficient. Moreover, differences among the national endowments of the Asian nations in terms of resources, skills, technological capabilities, institutions and infrastructure predict different areas of specialisation. The available detailed data on trade in manufacturing goods from 1990-2000 generally, but not perfectly, supports the basic theory of Ricardian comparative advantage.

Manufacturing accounts for the bulk of global merchandise trade, and accounts for around 80% of global trade. Primary products constitute the remainder, split fairly evenly between agricultural and mining products. We further divide the data on manufactured products into four categories to gain a better sense of the nature and dynamics of global trade[1]. The first division is into 'resource based manufacturing' (resource based goods), which, excluding petroleum, comprise of agricultural/timber based products and mineral based products, such as prepared meats and fruits, rubber, cement, glass, cut gems, etc. 'Low technology products' (low tech goods) are textiles and fashion goods, such as textile fabrics, clothing, footwear, leather goods, pottery, furniture, jewellery, toys, and plastic products, amongst others. 'Medium technology products' (medium tech goods) comprise of automotive products and medium technology process industries, including vehicle parts, synthetic fibres, chemical and paints, fertilizers, plastics, iron, engines, industrial machinery, watches, ships, etc. Finally, 'high technology products' (high tech goods) are electronic and sophisticated electrical products, such as telecommunications equipment, televisions, transistors, pharmaceuticals, and cameras, etc.

Although this last category of goods is characterised as high technology goods, there is some debate as to whether these are indeed goods which involve innovation and technological advances. Krugman (1994) has argued that the East Asian 'miracle', which is derived from the Tigers' much acclaimed export-oriented growth strategy and based largely on producing electronics, is not growth based on technological progress. Assembly of electronics should not be akin to producing sophisticated products using new or improved technologies. However, it is still the case that an estimated 50% of the world's PCs are assembled and 85% of all silicon chips are produced in Asia. These exports have fostered the growth of Taiwan, Hong Kong, Singapore and South Korea for the past three decades, and global demand is strong. Whether production of these goods reflects technological advancement is a debate for another day.

---

[1] This follows the classification of Lall and Albaladejo (2004).

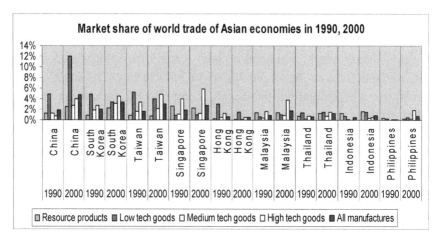

Figure 1. Market Share of World Trade of Asian Economies in 1990 and 2000
Source: WTO.

In terms of market share of global trade in manufactured products as seen in Figure 1, China has grown from having a mere 1.87% share in 1990 to 4.70% in 2000. China has the greatest market share in low technology products, such as textiles and clothing. Also impressive has been its gain of export markets in medium and high technology goods as well as in resource based goods. The rapid growth in market share of high technology goods, which has been the main engine of growth of the Asian Tigers, in particular, is noteworthy. In the span of a decade, China grew from having 0.69% of the world market, a percentage similar to the New Tigers (*e.g.*, Thailand with 0.74%), to 4.06% in 2000, a market share that is threatening the Old Tigers. For instance, South Korea has a market share of 4.48% and Taiwan holds 4.87%, while Singapore has 5.88%. Alone among the New Tigers, Malaysia has achieved a similar share of 3.75% in 2000, although it started with a greater share in 1990 of 1.59% of the market. This adds support to the ability of China to engage in the rapid technological upgrading of its manufacturing base as well as expanding its established labour-intensive products.

In summary, China now has a share of global trade that is comparable to that of the established Tigers. The four New Tigers of Malaysia,

Thailand, Indonesia and the Philippines, who began with less than 1% of global trade in 1990, have grown quickly to each account for more than 1% of the share in the overall manufacturing market in 2000. However, this lags behind China, which started with a slightly larger share of the manufacturing market (mainly in textiles) at the start of the 1990s and has reached an impressive 4.70% of global market share in all manufactured exports by the end of the decade.

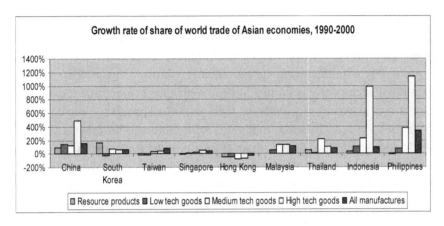

Figure 2. Growth Rate of Share of World Trade of Asian Economies, 1990-2000
Source: WTO.

Examining rates of growth of market share in Figure 2, China's share of world trade in manufacturing goods grew at an impressive rate of 151% between 1990 and 2000. Its production of high tech goods grew 488%, while other sectors of manufacturing goods grew at a brisk pace increasing around 100% over the decade. This rate of growth of export market share eclipses the growth experienced by South Korea, Taiwan, and Singapore, whose manufactured exports grew 66%, 86% and 46%, respectively. The only mature Tiger which experienced a severe contraction of its export market is Hong Kong. Hong Kong's share of global markets shrank by 29% from 1990 to 2000 and at present stands at just 0.45% of global market share in manufacturing. The situation for the New Tigers, in contrast, looks strong. Malaysia's share of global markets grew 109% whereas Thailand and Indonesia saw their exports grow by 79% and 89% respectively in 2000, as compared with 1990. The most rapid growth in share of global trade is the Philippines, which grew 341% over this period. The export growth rates for the New Tigers, though, reflect their low starting points in terms of global market share. This is in contrast to China, which started with a market share similar to the new Tigers in 1990 but has since attained a share of global markets more akin to the mature Tigers.

Analysing the evidence on exports, it appears that China's share of global trade has not come at the expense of the rest of the region. Aside from Hong Kong, which is somewhat unique, the rest of Asia's overall exports of manufacturing grew rapidly during the 1990s. When individual sectors are examined, it becomes more evident that the mature Tigers are experiencing shifts in their export capacities, causing them to begin to recede in some industries while advance in others. For the newly industrialising Tigers, their strong growth in nearly every sector reflects their comparative advantage as lower cost producers of manufacturing goods in contrast to the mature Tigers, which are characterised by rising real wages, other operating costs and real estate, to name a few factors.

As noted earlier, although China has grown rapidly in global market share in all sectors of manufacturing ranging from resource based goods to low and medium tech goods, its fastest growing sector is in the production of high technology goods. These include electronics and other sophisticated telecommunications equipment, such as televisions and transistors. This has not adversely affected most of the Old Tigers. For Taiwan and Singapore, high technology goods remain their most important export sector and both have gained in terms of global market share in these goods between 1990 and 2000. In fact, Singapore retained its position from the start of the decade as the largest exporter of high tech goods in the region.

Unlike the other Tigers, Singapore does not have a strong base of production in low and medium technology goods. It has had, and continues to have, about 1% of global market share in these two categories of goods. Interestingly, Singapore's strongest bases for export are resource based products and high technology goods. Starting with a relatively large market share, Singapore experienced a slight decrease in its exports of resource based goods, while its low and medium tech goods increased slightly during the period from 1990 to 2000. This is complementary to China's surge in exports in the same sectors, with its strong growth in resource based goods possibly affecting Singapore's exports in the same category.

In contrast, Taiwan's sources of export seem to have shifted from low technology or labour-intensive goods to medium and high technology goods that are more capital-intensive. Their share of trade in resource based goods has also fallen, but this has been a rather small sector for Taiwan. Low technology goods, though, appear to be losing market share while medium and high technology goods are growing. Even though high technology goods have been the mainstay of Taiwan's export-oriented growth strategy, China's ascendancy in the same sector appears not to have affected Taiwan's position. China's strength in textiles and labour-intensive products, though, may have contributed to this shift in Taiwan's comparative advantage.

South Korea poses an interesting case. High technology products continue to constitute its main comparative advantage in exports, similar to Taiwan and Singapore. However, South Korea has had a significant amount of growth in resource based products. For South Korea, exports of resource based products grew the fastest over the period from 1990 to 2000, eclipsing the growth of medium and high tech goods. On the whole, all sectors, except for low tech goods, have gained global market share in 2000. Given the rapid rise in the production of low technology goods in China, primarily textiles and clothing on the back of lower labour costs, South Korea's shifting comparative advantage most likely reflects the strength of its neighbour.

Hong Kong's economy is an illustration of the importance of domestic structural factors which can compound and confound a nation's comparative advantage. Hong Kong witnessed across-the-board decreases in global market share in all sectors, resulting in a 28% fall in all manufactured exports from 1990 to 2000. By 2000, Hong Kong had the smallest global market share among any of the Old or New Tigers, about less than half of one percent. Significant changes in the Hong Kong economy, including rejoining China in 1996, make it difficult to determine the precise effect of the surge of China's exports on its economy. Roughly speaking, however, the increased openness of the Chinese economy reduced the importance of Hong Kong as the gateway to mainland China. For instance, much of Hong Kong's production facilities are located in the New Territories near the Chinese border and are often located in Shenzhen. Thus, Hong Kong has seemingly lost its unique position. Its bases of comparative advantage appear to have been eroded by China's increased trade liberalisation. Furthermore, a lack of natural resources does not suggest a future in primary product exports. Instead, Hong Kong's path will more likely follow those of other post-industrial nations into the service sector. However, its normally robust financial services sector will come under increasing pressure with China's growing financial liberalisation expected after WTO membership. In the past, financial transactions tended to take place in Hong Kong rather than Shanghai. Whether this will continue remains to be seen. Coupled with domestic socio-political challenges, Hong Kong's economic outlook is somewhat uncertain.

The mature Asian economies exhibit shifting patterns of comparative advantage that would be expected with economic development. The might of China, though, has played a catalytic role in the resulting pattern of trade. In contrast, the New Tigers of Malaysia, Indonesia, Thailand and the Philippines have had rapid and impressive export growth over the past decade. For these countries, there does not appear to be a large impact from China's growing manufacturing strength. As the Old Tigers are increasingly characterised by rising factor (labour, land and capital) costs which normally accompany economic development, the New Tigers appear more attractive as centres of production with their lower wages and operating costs. The shift from the older to the newly industrialising nations is most apparent in the Philippines and Malaysia.

These countries are producing less or the same amount of resource based manufacturing goods, but more high technology goods. The global market share of Malaysia's high tech exports was 3.75% in 2000, a share which is not much less than the shares of the Old Tigers. Similarly, Thailand and Indonesia have both had rapid growth in and across export sectors, ranging from resource based to low/medium/high technology products. Indonesia, in particular, witnessed tremendous growth of exports of high tech goods starting from a base of having only 0.05% of the global market share in 1990 rising more than ten-fold to 0.54% by 2000.

In conclusion, the uniformly strong growth in high technology manufactured exports of the new Tigers contrasts with the usual prediction of comparative advantage of developing countries. At the initial stages of development, the expected comparative advantage of a less industrialised nation is that it will possess minimal technology and produce mainly labour-intensive, low technology goods, such as clothing and toys. The Old Tigers, like Taiwan, grew primarily by exporting low technology goods and then upgrading to electronics and other high technology products. The situation of the New Tigers may reflect the strength of China's comparative advantage in low technology goods. Even in 1990 prior to WTO entry, China had an impressive 4.90% of the global share of low tech goods. By 2000, its share had grown into an unrivalled 12%, easily eclipsing the other Asian nations. The specialisation of the New Tigers is consistent with the basic theory of comparative advantage, and their rapid growth in all export sectors largely supports the complementarities of trading nations.

The situation of the Old Tigers, though, suggests a more mixed picture. South Korea has lost market share in low tech exports; Taiwan in resource based and low tech goods; and Singapore in resource based products. Hong Kong has lost global market share across all export sectors. The erosion of traditional bases of comparative advantage for these nations may be due in part to China, but also could be a result of the natural progression of trade specialisation with the development process. In other words, economic development will necessarily be accompanied by increases in standards of living brought about through rising real wages and incomes. The development of more complex economic organisations will require rules, regulations and institutions to govern transactions. The combination of these factors, even aside from rising rents and diminishing returns to capital, will result in higher costs of production and overall operational costs. Through the process of economic growth, a nation's source of comparative advantage will likely shift as it has throughout history when newly industrialising nations open their economies to investment and production. Just as Japan's manufacturing advantage was superseded by the Old Tigers, the New Tigers are growing rapidly to erode the market shares of the Old Tigers. China's growth has appeared to be largely complementary to this process. The concern with China's accession to the WTO is whether this will continue to be the case.

3. Intra-Industry Trade in Asia

The evidence since the 1990s suggests that China's strength in producing low technology goods such as clothing and textiles may have facilitated the shift in comparative advantage of the New Tigers into high and medium technology goods. South Korea has even increased its production of resource based goods, perhaps on account of the slower growth of its low tech exports. With accession to the WTO in 2001, China is expected to gain from increased overseas market access and will undergo further trade liberalisation. The pattern of trade in manufacturing goods in Asia will likely depend on a number of factors, such as vertical specialisation by multinational corporations and the growth of intra-industry trade.

Standard trade theories are based on a set of assumptions, one of the most important of which is the assumption relating to constant returns to scale. If there are, however, economies of scale and increasing returns to factor inputs, then firms can gain market share through size and product differentiation (Krugman, 1980). With such monopolistically competitive industries, the patterns of trade will reflect some but not complete specialisation contrary to the predictions of standard trade models. Also, nations will become more similar in their levels of technology, the availability of capital and the skills of their labour force over time. Many of the developing Asian nations aim to attract foreign investment in order to produce similar types of high technology products, which are attractive as technological advancement lies at the heart of long-run growth and is the key link between trade and economic development. The outcome is that there is often no clear comparative advantage within an industry. However, with differentiated products, it is likely that there will be two-way trade within an industry. International trade then takes the form of two-way exchanges within industries rather than inter-industry specialisation derived from comparative advantage. Comparative advantage is thus established through first mover advantage and other sources of market power. This type of trade is thought to account for a quarter of world trade. It is clearly seen in the case of industrial nations whose major trading partners have been other industrial nations, such as the US and the EU.

Table 1. Intra-Industry Trade as a Percentage of Total Trade Growth, 5 Year Averages

	1986-1990	1991-1995	1996-2000
East Asia	42.5%	46.9%	75.0%
South Asia	31.2%	21.8%	34.5%

Source: IMF.

A similar scenario is possible for Asia. Intra-industry has grown significantly over the past decade, particularly in the second half of the 1990s, as seen in Table 1. Intra-industry trade accounts for three-quarters of total trade growth from 1996-2000 in East Asia, rising rapidly from under 50% in the previous decade. South Asia has also seen increases in the extent of intra-industry trade. The prominence of multinational corporations plays a significant role in generating such trade, including those in Asia such as *chaebols* or conglomerates in South Korea.

Multinational corporations are important players in the export sectors of Asia's developing nations. Over half of China's manufacturing exports are produced by foreign (part) owned firms and have been since the mid 1990s. Granting tax and other concessions aimed at encouraging foreign investment characterises the general growth strategy of industrialising Asian nations. Taiwan, Hong Kong and even New Tigers like Malaysia have focused on attracting foreign investment in their export sectors.

The literature on how multinational corporations affect patterns of trade has been developed with similar assumptions of imperfectly competitive markets (Navaretti and Venables 2004). It is thought that the desire for vertical integration frequently results in upstream and downstream acquisitions, outsourcing and development of global supply chains. A multinational firm will likely have production facilities located in different countries to both diversify risk and utilise various national strengths to fortify their production chain. Multinationals will be reluctant to locate all of their facilities in one country given possible potential for socio-economic and political instability. Moreover, China may have low wages, but South Korea could be operationally cheaper. Producing intermediate goods in another country is a sound strategy for multinationals and would predict significant intra-industry trade for Asia.

The nature of Asian trade is also seemingly driven by vertical specialisation, in contrast to horizontal specialisation which can be seen in Europe. Horizontal specialisation occurs when a firm locates an entire new facility in a country, duplicating an existing one. Vertical specialisation refers to production chains.

A measure of the extent of vertical specialisation is the ratio of merchandise trade to merchandise value-added, as presented in Table 2. Increasing numbers of parts and components that travel across borders for further processing would result in a higher trade-to-value-added ratio. In spite of the difficulty of distinguishing final from intermediate goods, the rising ratios of total merchandise to value-added indicate the growing presence of cross-border production chains in Asia. This evidence is also consistent with the export-oriented growth strategy undertaken by Asian nations. Local capacity building would be much slower than plugging

Table 2. Ratio of Merchandise Trade to Merchandise Value-Added in Percentages

	1980	1990	2000
Asian region	93.8	115.6	168.5
China	12.1	23.7	32.9
Old Tigers: Taiwan, Singapore, Hong Kong, South Korea	216.5	259.3	365.5
New Tigers (also Pakistan and Bangladesh): Malaysia, the Philippines, Thailand, Indonesia	39.4	52.4	84.3

Source: IMF.

into an existing global production chain of a multinational firm. Therefore, the nature of FDI and trade in Asia suggests that investment in China would have positive spill-over effects on the region. So long as multinationals are attracted to China and view it as a production base, then the region has the potential to benefit from supply chains and integrated intra-industry trade.

Finally, imperfect competition also means that there are likely to be external economies. External economies refer to the clustering of firms in a specific location that can take advantage of specialised suppliers, specifically the skilled labour pool and knowledge transfer activities. Firms can benefit from these external factors. The localisation of industries centred in specific centres, such as Hollywood, Silicon Valley and the Pearl River Delta, are some examples. These centres also raise the possibility that countries can develop these centres to improve their bases of comparative advantage. Theories of international trade based on fixed resource endowments have had inconclusive empirical support. Thus, nations with a low cost advantage based on cheap labour might prefer not to compete solely on that basis but on the more attractive premise of higher technology products. The attractiveness derives from the link between technological advances and economic development whereby developing countries are thought to be able to "catch up" with developed nations through imitation of established technology. This is not an easy path to follow and there are numerous instances of countries which have failed in directing private economic activity.

In Asia, there are examples of success but also of failure in pursuing such policies. Malaysia started with the assembly of semiconductors and then quickly developed industries in producer and consumer electronics. In contrast, Bangladesh was unsuccessful in developing industries other than garments and clothing. Irrespective of China's production advantage in low technology goods as evidenced by its remarkable global market share in textiles and similar goods, it has spent significant resources in building a high technology centre in areas such as Pudong. The development of these technology-oriented Special Economic Zones throughout China indicate a FDI policy aimed at attracting more technologically-oriented foreign direct investment, including research and development. Although the evidence is limited, the active policies shaping comparative advantage for China and other countries in the region suggest that future trade patterns may well be affected, not only by endowments and multinational corporations, but also by the localisation of industry effects.

Finally, China's accession to the WTO means not only access to overseas markets, but also an eventual opening up of its domestic markets. The attractiveness of China as the world's largest consumer market with one-fifth of the global population will be apparent to multinational corporations. As the newly opened sectors will increasingly include consumer goods and services, more foreign direct investment in the retail and wholesale sectors should follow. These firms will require supply chains, such as transport of goods and distribution networks. It is again possible to see China as a part of a supply chain in Asia, where some parts and sales will be cross-border. Moreover, given the small domestic markets of most of developing Asia, China itself could potentially become an increasingly important final goods market along the lines of the US and EU. However, it will still be some time before China will have opened its markets fully, as it is estimated that approximately 80% of China's imports are capital goods while only 20% are consumer products (Zebregs, 2004).

4. Conclusion

The evidence since China's "open door" policy took off indicates that China's rapid growth in manufactured exports has not inflicted the widely perceived harmful effects on its neighbours. The Old Tigers have matured and experienced structural changes in their economies usually associated with development, particularly in the case of Hong Kong. Chinese economic policy aimed at attracting FDI in specifically designated export sectors has been largely successful in shifting their comparative advantage from low tech products to medium and high technology goods. This is partly the nature of development and perhaps partly the result of specialisation in response to China's large market share in textiles and low technology goods. It is also complementary to China's rapid growth of medium and high technology exports. This scenario is perhaps surprisingly mirrored in the position of the New Tigers.

Malaysia, Thailand, Indonesia and the Philippines have promoted the development of high tech goods export sectors through attracting foreign investment. Using economic policy to upgrade domestic enterprises and improve local capacity has significant benefits for economic development if successful. Again, this strategy may also be a reaction to China's large market share in textiles, which would pressure the newly industrialising countries to specialise in other manufacturing sectors. Growth in manufacturing exports across the board for the new Tigers further suggests complementarities with China. China's own efforts at developing the high tech sector through the attraction of foreign direct investment have been seemingly successful thus far. Starting from a position of possessing a minimal global market share, China's exports of high tech goods now rival the volume of the Old Tigers while efforts continue in promoting the development of a high technology centre near Shanghai and other areas.

Despite China's impressive gains in all export sectors, the global market shares of its neighbours have mostly grown as well. Aside from Hong Kong, the mature Asian economies still experienced notable increases in global market share of manufacturing exports. There are changing areas of specialisation though. South Korea has surprisingly exported more resource based goods, whereas Taiwan and Singapore lost out in low tech and resource based goods but gained in medium and high tech goods. The evidence of both complementarities and specialisation predicted by trade theory is best seen in the remarkable gains in global market share of the newly industrialising Asian countries. The gains of Indonesia in market shares of low tech goods exceeds that of China over the period 1990-2000, and all four New Tigers experienced substantial surges in the manufacturing exports of medium and high technology goods. These complementarities derive not only from the usual prescriptions of trade theory, but also from the behaviour of multinational corporations and foreign direct investment or in other words, intra-industry trade.

When economies of scale and global production chains are considered, the needs of risk diversification and utilisation of national capacities would predict increasing intra-industry trade among the Asian nations. There is indeed evidence of growing trade integration in the region, including movement to formalise ties between China and ASEAN. Given the nature of intra-regional trade and investment patterns in Asia, intra-industry trade should increase in importance. Looking ahead, the division of production among Asian nations will likely be affected by the existing market positions of domestic and foreign corporations, as well as the success of targeted industrial policies.

Therefore, rather than being perceived as a threat, China should prove to be a strong centre for attracting FDI and multinational production facilities that could have positive spill-over effects for its neighbours. China's competitiveness has seemingly stimulated the competitiveness of its neighbours and the region as a whole has also grown well. The increase in intra-industry trade, which accounts for the bulk of intra-regional trade growth, suggests that China's growth and attractiveness as a manufacturing base will enhance the position of the rest of Asia in the global supply chain. In particular, the evidence that vertical specialisation characterises Asian trade implies that China's growth will be beneficial to the region. Finally, China's size offers considerable prospects for imports from Asia, increasing the potential for economies of scale for Asian Tiger economies that do not have sizeable domestic markets.

References

1. International Monetary Fund, *World Economic Outlook*, (International Monetary Fund, Washington, 2002).
2. Krugman, P., "Scale Economies, Product Differentiation and the Pattern of Trade," *American Economic Review,* 70(5), 950-959 (1980).
3. Krugman, P., "The Myth of Asia's Miracle," *Foreign Affairs*, 73(6), 63-78 (1994).
4. Lall, S., and M. Albaladejo, "China's Manufactured Export Surge: The Competitive Implications for East Asia," *World Development*, 32, 1441-1466 (2004).
5. Navaretti, B., A.J. Venables, *et al.*, *Multinational Firms in the World Economy*, (Princeton University Press, Princeton, 2004).
6. World Trade Organization, *Annual Report,* various years, (World Trade Organization, Washington, various years).
7. Zebregs, H., "Intraregional Trade in Emerging Asia," IMF Policy Discussion Paper PDP/04/01, pp. 1-24, (International Monetary Fund, Washington, 2004).

CHAPTER 7

THE ECONOMIC IMPACT OF GLOBALISATION IN ASIA-PACIFIC: THE CASE OF THE FLYING GEESE MODEL

Christer Ljungwall* & Örjan Sjöberg**[1]

*China Center for Economic Research, Beijing University,
and Stockholm School of Economics

**Department of Economics and the School of Asian Studies/EIJS,
Stockholm School of Economics

Abstract: In Pacific Asia, globalisation has resulted in rapidly growing international flows of goods, portfolio capital, and direct investment. At the same time, several countries have shifted from a command to a market economy. Against this background, we analyse perhaps the most popular model used to depict the process of economic integration and development in Pacific Asia, commonly known as the "flying geese" pattern of shifting comparative advantage. Our point of departure is that economic and other social processes are best understood in relation to one another. We confine ourselves to intra-regional patterns of trade and investment but locate them within the broader framework of global trends.

1. Introduction

Globalisation is a catchword of our times. Capital flows across national borders are greater than ever before, as is the overall movement of goods and people. Piggy-backing on a revolution in communication and transport technologies, globalisation sets a new historical agenda affecting all spheres of life and requiring new solutions around the globe.

---

[1] *Corresponding author. Visiting Research Fellow, China Center for Economic Research at Beijing University, Beijing 100871, P.R. China. chrlju@ccer.edu.cn **Dept. of Economics and the School of Asian Studies/EIJS, Stockholm School of Economics.

Globalisation has been defined as the closer integration of countries and the people of the world, brought about by the enormous reduction in the costs in transportation and communication technologies, which have in turn led to the break down of man-made barriers to the flow of goods, services, capital, knowledge, ideas, and to a lesser extent, people, across borders (Stiglitz, 2002). These new technologies also imply that people move and communicate at an unprecedented scale and at an unsurpassed speed. Mobile financial and industrial capacity defy borders in a manner seldom (if ever) experienced in the past, and power, interests, and life-styles are increasingly shared across continents (e.g. Giddens, 1999; Bauman, 1998; Beck, 2000).

However, the empirical record is not quite as straightforward as statements such as these would lead us to expect. Firstly, the statistics that are available are difficult to reconcile with the fact that today's "runaway world" (Giddens 1999) has worthy predecessors as far as openness to trade and factor endowments are concerned, at least as measured in relative terms (e.g. Hirst and Thompson, 1999; O'Rourke and Williamson 1999). Secondly, as Held *et al.* (1999) point out, there are three broad ways of perceiving globalisation. The "hyperglobalisers" claim that we have entered a completely new era in human history with the "denationalisation" of national economies and the demise of the nation-state (cf. Ohmae 1990; 1995). The sceptics, on the other hand, claim that globalisation is a myth that obscures other forms of economic relationships and suggest that the world has simply become organised into different trading blocs, which has resulted in new cultural and economic enclaves as opposed to an increasingly interconnected world. Positioned between these two, the "transformationalists" hold that the contemporary globalisation process is unprecedented and that states and societies must adapt to this changing world. Held *et al.* (1999) put it as follows:

> In comparison with the sceptical and hyper-globalist accounts, the transformationalists make no claims about the future trajectory of globalisation; nor do they seek to evaluate the present in relation to some single, fixed ideal-type 'globalised world', whether a global market or a

global civilization. Rather, transformationalists accounts emphasise globalisation as a long-term historical process which is inscribed with contradictions and which is significantly shaped by conjectural factors.

If this is the case, the process of cross-border integration could be expected to be subject to various shifts and reversals. This would presumably be true across a variety of different levels: at a truly global level; at a regional level; in the bilateral relations between two countries; and at the sub-national level. Indeed, it is likely that processes of integration and disintegration, just as processes of convergence and divergence (e.g. Boldrin and Canova 2001), may critically depend on the scale of analysis adopted.

Against this background, we set out to analyse what is perhaps the most popular model or metaphor used to depict the process of economic integration and development in East and South-east Asia, namely, the "flying geese" pattern of shifting comparative advantage. We argue that the model, for all its pedagogical virtues, is likely to conceal as much as it reveals about the inexorable process of economic integration within the region.

Without necessarily giving up the economist's traditional concern for the universal and preference for generalisation, through the adoption of a transformationalist view, this paper highlights the unevenness, open-endedness and diversity engendered by globalisation when applied to different geographical and social contexts. Put differently, while particular processes under scrutiny may or may not be truly universal, we acknowledge the possibility that the outcome of similar processes and structures of incentives etc. may well result in different outcomes simply because they are played out in different contexts. States, economies and societies respond in a number of ways to the large-scale forces that are affecting the contemporary world. As Hefner (1998) and Wee (2002) point out with regard to modern capitalism in Asia, the responses must be understood in relation to particular contextual factors. In addition, rather than strictly highlighting economic processes, our point of departure is that economic and other societal processes are best understood in relation to one another.

Our focus is on the changing pattern of regional integration. While this is clearly part of a wider, global process of increasing interaction in all spheres of economic life, this is a process that may, or may not, have distinctly Asian traits. Thus, while our focus is on East and South-east Asia, we are not implying that the Asian experience is necessarily exceptional. We are striving to locate the typical, and how it changes over time, rather than the singular or unique.

For the purpose of this chapter, we confine ourselves to intra-regional patterns of trade and investment and try to locate them within a broader framework of global trends. We adopt a broad-brush approach, and for now do not attempt the detailed empirical work necessary to either verify or disprove the overall patterns (and potential explanations) that we tentatively identify. As such, our picture is painted with a view to generating debate. By explicitly addressing the broader patterns of intra-regional flows and structural change, we hope to encourage others to consider the empirical patterns that are all too often neglected.

2. Most Favoured Metaphor: The Flying Geese

In a slightly ironic twist, the favoured metaphor these days used in describing the East and South-east Asian pattern of development is the "flying geese". Originating some four decades ago in an environment of Japanese expansionism and colonial onslaught, it has since been provided with a more polished appearance by Akamatsu (1961; 1962). Since then it has engendered a substantial literature, both in its adoption as the metaphor used to describe the model of economic development in the region (Blomqvist, 1997; Kojima, 2000) and as a factor behind other societal phenomena, such as metropolitan growth (Smith, 2001). However, as is true of any successful intellectual construct, the flying geese model has also attracted criticism on grounds ranging from logical, indeed at times ideological flaws (Hart-Landsberg and Burkett, 1998) to empirical oversights (Ozawa, 2001; 2003). Other, possibly more detached, observers have tried to substantiate the claims of the model by subjecting it to empirical tests (Dowling and Chia, 2000).

The flying geese model suggests that following the successful establishment of an industry based on an economy's comparative advantage, subsequent factor depletion leads to the erosion of current advantages, thereby inducing a search for the ways and means to up-grade production *in situ* as well as a search for and eventual relocation to a new production environment, preferably one which still enjoys the original comparative advantage. Thus, while individual plants, firms and industries may strive to increase productivity, it is often in the long run less taxing (and sometimes the only feasible option) to move to a different location. At a higher level of aggregation, and over a period of time, the economy will eventually have to shift towards sectors based on more intensive use of skills, capital and technology, as the comparative advantage in labour intensive production enjoyed initially is undermined. Combining this with a production cycle perspective, as did Cumings (1984), it readily provides for a model that can accommodate a number of different ways of looking at intra-regional trade and investment.

This is essentially compatible with one of the most important notions ever to originate within the "dismal science", that of comparative advantages. In fact, the existence of and actions based on comparative advantage is a necessary condition for it to work. However, it also adds two further elements. The first is that comparative advantage, based on factor proportion, is not carved in stone. Rather, they change over time and it is these changes that induce industries to shift from one country to another. The other element that the flying geese model adds to the traditional Ricardian story is that shifts are subject to the friction of distance. All other factors held constant, industries selecting a new location, whether it takes the form of relocation of plants or simply a relative shift in the sources of origin of a given product, are likely to choose to relocate to the economy which is closest in distance to their original location. In the case of relocation of plants by individual firms, this is perhaps not at all surprising, but it may also be natural to expect this to happen when and where the shift merely takes the form of a shift in a set of countries' respective index of specialisation. For many types of goods the distance to the market is still of consequence and although a more developed economy may lose their advantage in the production of a given good, it is likely to remain an important market for that product.

What is often overlooked, however, is that the form, extent and general thrust of economic integration in the region change over time. Although the driving forces behind a process of integration may be the same, at least insofar as they are located within the general sphere of globalisation, the 1997 Asian crisis appears to mark an important watershed in the pattern of regional economic integration and interaction. Thus, while the flying geese model indeed postulates shifts along a given trajectory, with one layer of economies replacing another as the more developed economies experience a change in their comparative advantage, it is neither capable of accommodating leapfrogging economies nor instances where shifts in trade and investment do not adhere to the basic properties of the model. This may include: changing properties of product cycles; political changes at the national level (for example, China's opening up to the world economy 25 years ago); and international trade agreements.

3. Beyond the Flying Geese

Sympathetic critics have been quick to point out that there are a number of deviations from the basic model that may well be of some importance and it is only to be expected that there will be instances where the model is not entirely correct, or that its predictive capacity is not quite as good as we would like it to be. As any intellectual construct that aspires to identify how things work, the flying geese model both generalises and isolates critical ingredients. However, other discrepancies are more serious, in the sense that they do not merely reflect reasonable deviations from the norm, but in fact represent a challenge to the very idea the model tries to capture. In the following section we identify some instances where the model falls short.

3.1. Driving economies and the lead goose

The first instance is the illusion created by the notion of a lead goose, a role generally understood to have been assumed by Japan. Following the Plaza agreement in the mid-1980s, Japanese firms, in particular, have been instrumental in keeping the process in motion through their search for lower production costs. However, Ozawa (2003) argues that this type of outward foreign investment tends to be trade creating rather than trade diverting, and that it is therefore too easy to overlook the importance of a non-goose within the flying geese pattern. Ozawa forcefully makes the point that the majority of activity is generated on the demand side, and that while Japan is of course important in this regard, it is in fact the U.S. that is the most important player in maintaining overall demand.

3.2. Global processes, external shocks and other extra-regional factors

Above we note the concern that the model does not take into account non-regional actors. A second concern it that it does not give due consideration to the wider effects of globalisation. Product cycles, inward foreign direct investment (FDI), demand generated by, technological and structural changes and finally shifting comparative advantages elsewhere should not be overlooked (e.g. Grosser and Bridges 1990, Bernard and Ravenhill 1995). In addition, the outside world may be the source of shocks that, from the point of view of economic agents based in the region itself, are best viewed as external or exogenous. If Ozawa is correct in identifying the US as wielding considerable influence, any dramatic shift for the better or worse there is likely to create a ripple effect (if not a shock wave) in East and South-east Asia. Indeed this was seen in the late 1990s with the bursting of the IT-bubble and the subsequent realignment of currencies. While this was neither a surprise nor a lightening-like event, the affect on the flying geese of Asia was pronounced.

3.3. The importance of political contingency

More serious perhaps is the realisation that not all countries are equally open to the process at the heart of the flying geese pattern. The obvious examples are the socialist economies of the region, the majority of which have now entered the world market. However, this process has been neither self-evident nor straightforward, and trade and investment in the region has been substantially affected by their decision to give up their autocratic and extreme import substitution policies. Indeed, precisely because countries like China previously tried to shield its economy from the perceived adverse effects of the world market, factor price differentials were all the more dramatic and hence the on-going attraction.

3.4. The "distorting" effects of development policies and business systems

The argument that development policies may have a distortionary effect is not a prerogative of former centrally planned economies. Consider South Korea, which has been very reluctant to accept inward foreign direct investment, and which for a long time was just as reluctant to accept domestic firms engaging in outward investment. It simply did not fit the flying geese model of development (Castley, 1997). However, its position further down the value added ladder, meant that this mattered less than it has done over the past few years. In other countries a reluctance to accept the rules of the model are perhaps less pronounced. For example, in Taiwan, the influence of the local economy meant that its manufacturing sector, which is dominated by small and medium sized firms (SMEs), faced greater obstacles to relocation and outsourcing than firms of a larger size. This is due to the fact that SMEs have a transaction cost disadvantage resulting from their relatively small size. Hence, what is sometimes referred to as "business systems" (e.g. Whitley, 1992; Orrù et al., 1997) may have an impact on the order, the direction and the speed with which the geese fly.

3.5. Trade arrangements

East and South-east Asian economies are largely export oriented and, while not always as open as is often suggested (e.g. IBRD, 1993), are committed to the potentially welfare enhancing effects of foreign trade and, at least at a theoretical level, to free trade. Although, or perhaps because, the region is less experienced than other regions in establishing and managing free trade areas - the ASEAN Free Trade Area (AFTA) being the only prominent, yet not entirely successful, example to date - it has largely supported a policy of open regionalism. As free trade areas and other similar arrangements discriminate against non-participants, this has proven an obstacle both to export oriented development strategies and the provisions under the World Trade Organization. In response, open regionalism was adopted in 1989 as a fundamental principle of the Asia-Pacific Economic Cooperation (APEC) and in 1994 APEC members at their meeting in Bogor committed themselves to achieving full openness in trade and investment for its industrialised members by the year 2020.

In addition, APEC has also made a commitment to achieve openness for non-member countries within a decade of this date. The fact that they have been able to do this without establishing a formal trade arrangement has, as Bergsten (1997) noted, potentially far-reaching consequences, not least because APEC weighs heavily in the world economy. However, others have claimed that this 'regionalism is 'soft' and 'open', that is, it is un-institutionalised and discriminates less against non-participant economies (Cai, 1999). From the perspective of the flying geese model, such open regionalism is more likely to reinforce the pattern that it attempts to limit rather than the opposite, however, it may influence the speed and direction of change in the region, not least because a substantial part of the APEC region is made up of the economies of the Western hemisphere rather than Pacific Asia.

Whether this is enough to throw the flying geese formation off course is an open question. What we shall argue is that the above factors have in fact made a difference. These factors include, critically, the opening up of China, which with dramatic and with immediate effect, altered the set-up of relative prices in the region. The so called open door policy launched in the late 1970s, combined with a process of internal economic liberalisation has been instrumental in changing the economic landscape of the region. The opening up of China also proves that political and economic policies, and not only the impersonal and inexorable forces of economic change, can make a difference.

To illustrate our point, we have to turn elsewhere within the region. While the move to a unified currency and a more modern tax system in 1994 irreversibly transformed China's economy (Qian, 2000), it also provided a catalyst for change in terms of the pre-existing system of trade and investment. However, we believe that other factors should be taken into account. What we have in mind is not only the ultimate and proximate causes of the Asian crisis of 1997, but also other changes, the impact of which have been brought to the fore in the wake of that event.

4. Trade and Investment on Either Side of the 1997 Watershed

If external shocks matter, internal ones do too. Between 1994 and 1997, and in some cases earlier than this, the position of the ASEAN economies weakened. Although growth remained high, this was accompanied by deteriorating current account and trade balances (e.g., Baer *et al.*, 1999). However, in spite of these warning signs, the South-east Asian economies were not prepared for the lightening that struck on 2 July 1997. The causes of this event need not detain us here. It is enough to note that this date marked something of a watershed as it was after this date that China truly made its entry onto the scene. In fact, we shall tentatively argue, while the flying geese pattern of intraregional trade and investment may well be valid for the period up to 1997 (see Blomqvist (1997), Alvstam (1995), Das (1998), and Murshed (2001)), subsequent developments have served to distort it beyond recognition.

At the heart of this process we find the reasons for the wave of FDI into the ASEAN region 'receding into history', to use Petri's (1995) apt phrase, while at the same time we can see the consequences of investment made under the Chinese investment boom of the mid-1990s (Lin 2004). As a result both of high levels of inward FDI (see Table 1), and substantial investment provided by the authorities at the provincial level, the industrial capacity of mainland China has surged in leaps and bounds. Considerable overcapacity within many manufacturing industries was created first in 1992, with the firm commitment to reform marked by Deng Xiaoping's tour of south-eastern China in 1992 and thereafter by the 1994 economic reforms. Thus, the ground was well prepared. As Petri (1995) observed,

> [t]he concurrence of the Chinese investment surge and the ASEAN investment collapse may be an example of a new kind of intraregional competition for FDI, fuelled by improved capital mobility. Chinese reforms and progress toward economic and political stability, together with low labour costs and a huge market, have made investment in China very attractive to other East Asian sites....Investors are flooding to China simply to acquire the option of expanding there later.

Table 1. Foreign Direct Investment Inflow to ASEAN and China (USD 100 million)

Region	1996	1997	1998	1999	2000	2001	2002	2003
ASEAN	299.1	339.3	221.6	272.5	234.1	193.5	134.6	193.5
China	417.2	452.7	454.6	403.2	407.2	468.8	527.4	535.5

Source: *China Statistical Yearbook 2004*, and *ASEAN Statistical Yearbook 2004*. Mainland China excluding Hong Kong.

This helped China maintain growth and contain inflation during the crisis of 1997 and its immediate aftermath. As such it provided a valuable source of stability in the region. Furthermore, China has increasingly come to be viewed as the region in which to locate; with the consequence that capacity has further expanded.

This is also reflected in regional trade and investment patterns. Prior to 1997, the East Asian economies were well integrated. This integration increasingly included China, if still at rather low levels. The proportion of total foreign trade within the region had increased to the point where, just prior to the crisis, almost half of all trade generated was intraregional in nature. This is illustrated in Table 2.

Table 2. Intra-ASEAN Trade, 1995-2003 (USD 100 million)

Country	1995	1996	1997	1998	1999	2000	2001	2002	2003
Brunei									
Exp	5.3	4.5	4.9	2.2	3.7	6.4	7.7	6.8	6.3
Imp	10.1	28.5	9.8	5.9	8.9	5.4	5.5	6.3	6.2
Cambodia									
Exp	--	--	--	--	--	0.8	0.7	0.9	1.0
Imp						5.5	10.9	6.0	16.9
Indonesia									
Exp	64.8	83.1	88.5	93.4	82.8	108.8	95.1	99.3	107.2
Imp	42.2	55.5	54.1	45.6	47.8	67.8	57.2	69.9	80.3
Malaysia									
Exp	184.3	226.9	232.5	216.1	218.8	244.1	210.2	221.3	266.3
Imp	125.2	146.8	148.4	129.4	124.1	159.3	152.5	172.4	143.3
Myanmar									
Exp	--	--	--	--	2.1	3.9	9.5	12.2	30.6
Imp					9.9	11.1	13.2	11.9	9.7
Philippines									
Exp	23.6	29.7	34.4	38.2	49.9	59.8	49.9	55.3	65.8
Imp	24.6	40.1	48.7	44.3	44.6	49.5	46.6	55.4	64.0
Singapore									
Exp	317.7	344.4	357.9	259.9	292.7	377.8	328.2	339.6	358.4
Imp	245.5	273.6	303.9	236.5	262.4	332.9	289.9	304.4	310.8
Thailand									
Exp	106.1	121.1	135.2	83.1	99.1	127.1	121.9	128.4	161.4
Imp	88.2	97.6	81.2	54.4	79.9	100.5	92.4	96.8	117.0

Source: *ASEAN Statistical Yearbook 2004.*

This pattern of trade closely resembled the flying geese pattern of economic development. This could be clearly seen in South-east Asia, where intra-ASEAN trade, for the most part, was bilateral trade between individual members and Singapore, the only truly industrialised country in their midst. As the model suggests there was relatively little trade between the less developed members of the ASEAN, although over time such trade began to make an impact, primarily because countries such as Malaysia and Thailand found that their poorer neighbours in Indochina were useful for outsourcing purposes (Grosser and Bridges, 1990). The fact that these countries were also to become members of the ASEAN itself probably helped, while at the same time they induced a measure of streamlining in the poorer countries' foreign trade arrangements.

The events of 1997 changed this. The crisis affected both demand for and the value of local currencies and as such intraregional trade as a proportion of all foreign trade dropped. Since then most countries have managed to engineer a recovery, but typically not to the same high levels of growth as existed prior to the crisis. More importantly, the pattern of trade and investment appears to have changed. As suggested by the quote from Petri above, competition for inward investment has increased, a competition in which China appears to hold its own.

Trade flows have also been affected. For, although the flying geese pattern can easily accommodate a newcomer like China, it cannot accommodate the way in which China currently trades with the rest of the world (see Table 3). Today, China runs a substantial surplus in its trade with the US, and to a lesser extent with Europe and Japan. However, it also runs a deficit with most other countries in the region, including developed economies like Taiwan. Other industrialised countries within the region have responded to China's seemingly insatiable hunger for imports and as such have seen their exports to China increase at higher rates than their imports, thereby contributing to the closing of the gap.

A further indication of what is afoot is the fact that Chinese exports have a very high import content, and that a high proportion of imported inputs are of a high-tech nature. At the same time, many economies enjoying a surplus in their trade with China are also substantial suppliers of raw materials. Taken together this suggests that China has become a specialist in assembling activities and, as is often claimed, is something of the "factory of the world" (Lemonie and Ünal-Kesenci, 2002).

Table 3. China's Trade with Other Regions (USD 100 million)

Region	1996	1997	1998	1999	2000	2001	2002	2003
Total Exports	1 510.5	1 827.9	1 837.1	1 949.3	2 492.0	2 661.0	3 256.0	4 382.3
N. America	282.9	346.1	401.1	443.9	552.7	576.4	742.7	981.3
Europe	238.6	289.6	334.3	354.8	454.8	492.4	582.7	881.7
Asia	912.4	1 089.2	981.8	1 025.6	1 323.2	1 409.6	1 713.0	2 225.8
Japan	308.8	318.2	296.9	324.1	416.5	449.6	484.3	594.1
Taiwan	28.1	33.9	38.7	39.5	50.4	50.0	65.8	90.0
ASEAN	88.3	110.3	94.62	108.8	152.7	163.9	206.4	267.4
Total Imports	1 388.3	1 423.7	1 402.4	1 657.0	2 250.9	2 435.5	2 951.7	4 127.6
N. America	187.3	183.1	191.9	218.2	261.2	302.4	308.8	382.6
Europe	276.5	257.5	263.1	326.5	407.8	484.0	519.7	696.9
Asia	834.4	883.9	870.5	1 016.8	1 413.4	1 471.8	1 917.3	2 728.9
Japan	291.8	289.9	282.1	337.6	415.1	427.9	534.7	741.5
Taiwan	161.8	164.4	166.3	195.3	254.9	273.4	380.6	493.6
ASEAN	104.1	120.2	123.2	144.6	211.2	221.8	299.2	456.9

Source: *China Statistical Yearbook* (1997-2004). Mainland China excluding Hong Kong. Cambodia included in ASEAN.

On the other hand, China can also be observed entering the value added ladder at higher levels, with an almost inexhaustible source of not only unskilled labour but also of engineers. Put differently, it combines the virtues captured by traditional (or static) comparative advantages with the ability to avail itself of the dynamics of regional integration. It cannot be denied that China is capable of holding its own in certain industries, both in respect of high-tech inputs and the quality of output. What it does suggest is that China has become the main staging point for exports from both developing and developed economies in Asia, as they make their way onto the rest of the world market. Rather than, for example, the US running large trade deficits with the majority of countries in the region, it has now become concentrated in the statistics of bilateral trade with China.

5. Concluding Remarks

In Pacific Asia, globalisation has resulted in a rapidly growing international flow of goods, portfolio capital and direct investment. This has taken place at the same time as the transformation of several countries from command to market economies. Both processes have had a profound impact on the institutional and business environment in the region. When we apply classical trade theory, or a version of it sensitive to the dynamism and geographical character of shifting comparative advantage, we can see that resource allocation and trade are determined by factor endowments and technology, and that processes such as relative resource depletion and distance should be given their due. This paper has sought to apply these insights in an analysis of the so-called *flying geese* model of shifting comparative advantage. Although still very tentative in character – its testable implications have to be tested – and indications are that it may be worthwhile pursuing this train of thought more systematically.

This is especially the case as recent theories also let comparative advantage be determined by the scale of operations and agglomeration economies. The location of firms depends on factor endowments, but access to markets for intermediate and final goods also matter (Crafts and Venables 2002). As Petri (1995) noted – and which more recent studies on the location of industry in China itself bear witness to (Wen 2004) – China has a huge advantage with respect to the vantage point of clusters and agglomeration, to which home market effects are also critical. The vast scale of operations, combined with the potential size of the market and its near inexhaustible supply of labour allow it certain privileges. The emerging pattern of trade and investment suggests as much and, by doing so, it also starts to realign the flying geese pattern of regional economic integration along a different path than that which has prevailed during most of the post-war period. This is not to deny the usefulness of a dynamic and regional perspective on comparative advantage, only that the shift in such advantages may not always be driven by factors endogenous to the model. Globalisation, political change and markets beyond the confines of the model are all important to the picture, but do not get the attention they deserve.

At a more general level, we may note that there is an abundance of work showing that openness to trade and economic growth are interrelated (Edwards, 1998). This has been criticised due to difficulties in determining the direction of causality (Rodrigues and Rodrik, 2001), but recent studies give further support to the notion that there is a causal effect from trade to growth (Frankel and Romer, 1999; Irwin and Terviö, 2002) and that trade liberalisation supports growth (Greenaway *et al.* 2002). Against this background, the extent to which successful Pacific Asian countries have pursued an open and liberal economic policy has been debated (IBRD, 1993). Economic policies have certainly differed between countries, but generally they have all moved in a liberal and outward oriented direction. In the course of the establishment of this pattern, the flying geese model has increasingly been embraced as a useful way of depicting the process of regional integration. As this happened, traits typical of yet not necessarily unique to Asia, intervene in such a fashion to make the story both a richer one, but also one that may enlighten theory – precisely because they deviate from the universal. In this sense the process of regional integration can help further the call of Yeung and Lin (2003) to take 'the situatedness of theories' seriously, yet doing so without losing the sight of universals where relevant.

References

1. Akamatsu, K., 'A theory of unbalanced growth in the world economy', *Weltwirtschaftliches Archiv*, vol.86: 196-217 (1961).
2. Akamatsu, K., 'A historical pattern of economic growth in developing countries', *The Developing Economies*, vol. 1(1): 3-25 (1962).
3. Alvstam, C., 'Integration through trade and investment: Asian Pacific patterns', in R. Le Heron and S.O. Park, eds, *The Asian Pacific Rim and Globalisation* (Aldershot: Avebury, 1995): 107-128.
4. Baer, W., W.R. Miles and A.B. Moran, 'The end of the Asian myth: why were the experts fooled?', *World Development*, vol. 27(10): 1735-1747 (1999).
5. Bauman, Z., *Globalisation: The Human Consequences* (Cambridge: Polity Press, 1998).
6. Beck, U., *What is Globalisation?* (Cambridge: Polity Press, 2000).
7. Bergsten, C.F., *Open Regionalism* (Working paper, 97-3. Washington, DC: Institute for International Economics, 1997).

8. Bernard, M. and J. Ravenhill, 'Beyond product cycles and flying geese: regionalization, hierarchy, and the industrialization of East Asia', *World Politics*, vol. 47(2): 171-209 (1995).
9. Blomqvist, H.C., *Economic Interdependence and Development in East Asia* (Westport, CT: Praeger, 1997).
10. Boldrin, M. and F. Canova, 'Inequality and convergence: reconsidering European regional policies', *Economic Policy*, no. 32: 205-245 (2001).
11. Cai, K.G., 'The political economy of economic regionalism in Northeast Asia: a unique and dynamic pattern', *East Asia*, vol. 17(2): 6-46 (1999).
12. Castley, R., *Korea's Economic Miracle: The Crucial Role of Japan* (Basingstoke: Macmillan, 1997).
13. Crafts, N. and A. Venables, *Globalisation in History: a Geographical Perspective* (Discussion paper 3079. London: Centre for Economic Policy Research, 2002).
14. Cumings, B., 'The origins and development of the Northeast Asian political economy: industrial sectors, product cycles and political consequences', *International Organization*, vol. 38(1): 1-40 (1984).
15. Das, D.K., 'Changing comparative advantage and the changing composition of Asian exports', *The World Economy*, vol. 21(1): 121-140 (1998).
16. Dowling, M. and T.C. China, 'Shifting comparative advantage in Asia: new tests of the "flying geese" model', *Journal of Asian Economics*, vol. 11(4): 443-463 (2000).
17. Edwards, S., 'Openness, productivity and growth: what do we really know?', *Economic Journal*, vol. 108(447): 383-398 (1998).
18. Frankel, J.A. and D. Romer, 'Does trade cause growth?', *American Economic Review*, vol. 89(3): 379-399 (1999).
19. Giddens, A., *Runaway World: How Globalisation is Reshaping our Lives* (London: Profile Books, 1999).
20. Greenaway, D., C.W. Morgan and P. Wright, 'Trade liberalization and growth in developing countries', *Journal of Development Economics*, vol. 67(1): 229-244 (2002).
21. Grosser, K. and B. Bridges, 'Economic interdependence in east Asia: the global context', *Pacific Review*, vol. 3(1): 1-14 (1990).
22. Hart-Landsberg, M. and P. Burkett, 'Contradictions of capitalist industrialization in East Asia: a critique of "flying geese" theories of development', *Economic Geography*, vol. 74(2): 87-110 (1998).
23. Hefner, R.W., 'Introduction: society and morality in the new Asian capitalisms', in R.W. Hefner, ed., *Market Cultures: Society and Morality in the New Asian Capitalisms* (Boulder, CO: Westview, 1998).
24. Held, D. *et al.*, *Global Transformations, Politics, Economics, and Culture* (Cambridge: Polity Press, 1999).

25. Hirst, P. and G. Thompson, *Globalisation in Question: The International Economy and the Possibilities of Governance* (Cambridge: Polity Press, 2nd ed., 1999).
26. IBRD, *The East Asian Miracle* (Washington, DC: World Bank, 1993).
27. Irwin, D.A. and M. Terviö, 'Does trade raise income? Evidence from the twentieth century', *Journal of International Economics*, vol. 58(1): 1-18 (2002).
28. Kojima, K., 'The "flying geese" model of Asian economic development: origins, theoretical extensions, and regional policy implications', *Journal of Asian Economics*, vol. 11(4): 375-401 (2000).
29. Lemonie, F. and D. Unal-Kesenci, *China in the International Segmentation of Production Processes* (CEPII Working paper, 2002:2. Paris: Centre d'Etudes Prospectives et d'Informations Internationales, 2002).
30. Lin, J.Y., 'Is China's growth real and sustainable?', *Asian Perspective*, vol. 28(3): 5-29 (2004).
31. Murshed, S.M., 'Patterns of East Asian trade and intra-industry trade in manufactures', *Journal of the Asia Pacific Economy*, vol. 6(1): 99-123 (2001).
32. Ohmae, K., *The Borderless World: Power and Strategy in the Interlinked Economy* (New York: Harper Business, 1990).
33. Ohmae, K., *The End of the Nation State: The Rise of Regional Economies* (New York: Free Press, 1995).
34. O'Rourke, K. and J.G. Williamson, *Globalisation and History: The Evolution of a Nineteenth-Century Atlantic Economy* (Cambridge, MA: MIT Press, 1999).
35. Orrù, M., N.W. Biggart and C.G. Hamilton, *The Economic Organization of East Asian Capitalism* (Thousand Oaks, CA: SAGE, 1997).
36. Ozawa, T., 'The "hidden" side of the "flying-geese" catch-up model: Japan's *dirigiste* institutional setup and a deepening financial morass', *Journal of Asian Economics*, vol. 12(4): 471-491 (2001).
37. Ozawa, T., 'Pax Americana-led macro-clustering and flying-geese style catch-up in East Asia: mechanisms of regionalized endogenous growth', *Journal of Asian Economies*, vol. 13(6): 699-713 (2003).
38. Petri, P.A., 'The interdependence of trade and investment in the Pacific', in E.K.Y. Chen and P. Drysdale, eds, *Corporate Links and Foreign Direct Investment in Asia and the Pacific* (Prymble, NSW: HarperEducational, 1995): 29-55.
39. Qian, Y., 'The process of China's market transition (1978-1998): the evolutionary, historical and comparative perspectives', *Journal of Institutional and Theoretical Economics*, vol. 156(1): 151-174 (2000).

40. Rodrigues, F. and D. Rodrik, 'Trade policy and economic growth: a sceptics guide to the cross-national evidence', in B. Bernanke and K.S. Rogoff, eds, *Macroeconomic Annual 2000* (Cambridge, MA: MIT Press, 2001).
41. Smith, D.W., 'Cities in Pacific Asia', in R. Paddison, ed., *Handbook of Urban Studies* (London: SAGE, 2001): 419-450.
42. Stiglitz, J., *Globalisation and its Discontents* (New York: W.W. Norton, 2002).
43. Wee, C.J.W., 'Introduction: local cultures, economic development, and Southeast Asia', in *Local Cultures and the 'New Asia': The State, Culture, and Capitalism in Southeast Asia* (Singapore: Institute of Southeast Asian Studies, 2002).
44. Wen, M., 'Relocation and agglomeration of Chinese industry', *Journal of Development Economics*, vol. 73(1): 329-347 (2004).
45. Whitley, R., *Business Systems in East Asia: Firms, Markets and Societies* (London: SAGE, 1992).
46. Yeung, H.W. and G.C.S. Lin, 'Theorizing economic geographies of Asia', *Economic Geography*, vol. 79(2): 107-128 (2003).

CHAPTER 8

CHINA'S TRADE POLICIES IN WIDER ASIAN PERSPECTIVE

Razeen Sally

International Relations Department, London School of Economics and Political Science

Abstract: This paper looks at China's trade-policy developments compared with related trends in India and southeast Asian nations. First it sets China, India and southeast Asia in the context of economic globalisation and policy reforms around the world. Then it looks at their trade-policy frameworks. It summarises recent reforms, links them down to domestic economic policies, and up to foreign policy and trade diplomacy. The next sections focus first on China, India and southeast Asia in the WTO, and then on FTAs. The central argument is that trade *policy* matters more than trade *negotiations.* There has been huge trade-and-investment liberalisation; but this has happened *unilaterally* for the most part, not through trade negotiations, whether in the WTO or in FTAs. Trade negotiations have distinct and perhaps increasing limitations, and their effects should not be exaggerated. All the more reason, therefore, to rely on the unilateral engine of freer trade, with China setting the late 20th/early 21st-century example much as Britain did in the second half of the 19th century. That will have powerful *emulatory* effects elsewhere, particularly in Asia. A combined China-and-India effect, with India accelerating liberalisation in response to China, will send even stronger liberalisation signals.

1. Introduction

This paper looks at China's trade-policy developments compared with related trends in India and southeast Asia (the ASEAN countries). The larger backdrop is the historic – but very recent – integration of first China and then India into the global economy; but in between also lies the longer history of southeast-Asian integration into the global economy, which accelerated after the 1970s. Such preliminary observations also raise the question of economic integration *between and among* these different parts of Asia – or the lack thereof – and how that relates to trade policies. Time and space prohibit an even wider comparison with Japan, South Korea and Taiwan, the more developed countries of northeast Asia.

Consider the following questions. How far has economic opening come in China, India and southeast Asia, and how much farther is it likely to go? Where does trade policy in these regions fit in the spectrum between liberalism and intervention? How does it relate to broad trends in domestic and foreign policies? What is China's place in the World Trade Organisation, just four years into accession? What are its negotiating positions and strategies in the Doha Round? How does it interact with other WTO members, particularly the major players? What of China's future in the WTO? How does that compare with India's and the ASEAN countries' longer history in the GATT/WTO and their Doha-Round negotiating positions? What is China's Free-Trade-Agreement (FTA) strategy? How does that compare with FTA developments in India and the ASEAN countries?

Making a stab at answering these questions will proceed as follows. The first section sets China, India and southeast Asia in the context of economic globalisation and policy reforms around the world. The second section looks at their trade-policy frameworks. It summarises recent reforms, links them down to domestic economic policies, and up to foreign policy and trade diplomacy.

The next sections focus first on China, India and southeast Asia in the WTO, and then on FTAs.

The concluding argument of the paper, worth flagging at the outset, is that trade *policy* matters more than trade *negotiations*. There has been huge trade-and-investment liberalisation; but this has happened *unilaterally* for the most part, not through trade negotiations, whether in the WTO or in FTAs. Trade negotiations have distinct and perhaps increasing limitations, and their effects should not be exaggerated. All the more reason, therefore, to rely on the unilateral engine of freer trade, with China setting the late 20th/early 21st-century example much as Britain did in the second half of the 19th century. That will have powerful emulatory effects elsewhere, particularly in Asia. A combined China-and-India effect, with India accelerating liberalisation in response to China, will send even stronger liberalisation signals, not least to southeast Asia.

2. China, India and Southeast Asia in the World Economy: Globalisation and Policy Reform

2.1. China, India and southeast Asia in economic globalisation

What makes the crucial difference to economic globalisation today, and probably for next half century, is the dramatic opening of first China and then India. They are the world's second- and fourth-largest economies respectively (at purchasing-power parity): China accounted for 12.5 per cent, and India about 6 per cent, of global GDP in 2003. Together they are home to 40 per cent of humanity (China with a population of 1.37 billion, and India 1.07 billion). With still low levels of per-capita income (China's being 15 per cent, and India's 7 per cent, of US levels, measured at PPP), and huge supplies of cheap, productive labour, they have the potential for stellar catch-up growth rates for decades ahead. Their integration into the world economy, still in its early stages, promises to be more momentous than that of Japan and the east-Asian Tigers, and perhaps on a par with the rise of the US as a global economic power in the late nineteenth century.

Asia was conspicuously absent from the world economy from early modernity to relatively recent times. International economic integration spread from Britain to Western Europe and the British offshoots of Empire, notably north America and Australasia, plus a handful of other lands of recent settlement (such as Argentina). Mostly, Asia came into the fold only in the second half of the 20th century: first with the emergence of Japan in the 1950s (rather its re-emergence after its late nineteenth century rise and then wartime destruction); followed by Hong Kong, Singapore, Taiwan and South Korea; and then the second-generation Tigers of southeast Asia. China and India remained closed during most of this period. Only come the 1980s and 1990s did they wake up and join the fray.[1]

Southeast Asia has a longer history of global economic integration than China or India. This is particularly the case with Singapore and Malaysia: both were tightly integrated into the commercial networks of the British Empire. Notwithstanding vast differences among countries in the region, the older ASEAN members (Singapore, Malaysia, Thailand, Indonesia and Philippines) have integrated further into the world economy since the 1970s, especially through trade and foreign direct investment (FDI) in manufactures. In terms of headline indicators, the ASEAN countries have a combined GDP well below that of China but still ahead of India (at market prices, though below the Indian level in terms of PPP comparisons); a combined population less than half that of China or India; and an average per-capita GDP that is higher than China's or India's. (See Table 1 for such China, India and ASEAN comparisons.)

Now turn to China specifically.[2] Between 1980 and 2003, its real income per head rose by over 300 per cent. Its export and import volumes grew by 11-13 per cent in the same period, and by 35-40 per cent annually in the last few years. Manufactures account for 90 per cent of merchandise exports. China's ratio of trade in goods to GDP, at market prices, now

---

[1] See Maddison (2001).

[2] The following account draws on Martin Wolf's excellent columns on the China phenomenon in the *Financial Times*. See "Why Europe was the past, the US is the present and a China-dominated Asia the future of the global economy," September 22 2003; "China must adapt if it is to lead the world economy," November 19 2003; "Three reasons to be cheerful about the world economy," June 30 2004; "The long march to prosperity: why China can maintain its explosive rate of growth for another two decades," December 9 2003. Also see his equally excellent Wolf (2004), pp. 144-145; Hale and Hale (2003) pp. 36-53; Rumbaugh and Blancher (2004).

stands at about 70 per cent. This is truly exceptional. The most-peopled country in the world has, in quick time, acquired the trade openness of a much smaller country (such as South Korea). It is far more open than roughly equivalent large countries like the US, India and Japan, with trade-to-GDP ratios of about 20 per cent. China's share of world

Table 1. Important Economic Indicators of ASEAN-6, China and India in 2003

	GDP	GDP Growth	Population	Per Capita GDP	PPP GDP	Merchandise Exports
	(US$ bn)	(%)	(mn)	(US$)	(US$ bn)	(US$ bn)
China	1409.0	9.1	1372.1	1026.9	6449.0	438.2
Indonesia	208.3	4.1	215.0	968.6	758.8	70.3
Malaysia	103.2	5.2	25.0	4118.5	207.8	117.9
Philippines	79.2	4.5	81.1	977.2	390.7	41.9
Singapore	91.3	1.1	4.2	21748	109.4	144.1
Thailand	143.2	6.7	64.0	2238.4	477.5	80.5
Vietnam	36.7	7.2	80.9	453.3	203.7	20.7
ASEAN-6	661.9	5.4	470.2	1407.5	2147.9	475.4
India	575.3	8.1	1073.0	536.2	3033.0	60.0
World	36252	3.8	6,379	5683.0	51480.0	7502.9
TOTAL	2646.2		2915.3	5627.3	11629.9	973.6

	Service Exports	Total Merchandise Trade	Services Trade	Trade/ GDP	FDI Inflow	FDI/ GDP
	(US$ bn)	(US$ bn)	(US$ bn)	(%)	(US$ bn)	(%)
China	46.4	851.0	101.2	60.4	53.5	3.8
Indonesia	NA	112.4	NA	54.0	-0.6	-0.3
Malaysia	13.5	217.0	30.8	210.4	2.5	2.4
Philippines	3.0	86.8	7.4	109.6	0.3	0.4
Singapore	30.4	272.1	57.6	297.9	11.4	12.5
Thailand	15.7	156.3	34.0	109.2	1.8	1.3
Vietnam	NA	45.7	NA	124.6	1.4	3.8
ASEAN-6	62.5	890.3	129.8	134.5	16.8	2.5
India	25.0	137.4	46.6	23.9	4.3	0.7
World	1796.5	15281.0	3578.9	42.2	560.0	1.5
TOTAL	133.9	1878.7	277.7		74.6	

Source: Computed from ADB (2004); WTO (2004); in Sally and Sen (2005), p. 94.

merchandise exports was 6 per cent in 2003, up from 1.2 per cent in 1980. China overtook Japan as the world's third-largest trading nation in 2004.

China's trade openness is intimately bound up with its openness to inward investment. The stock of FDI in China was over $550 billion in 2004 from $25 billion in 1990. It was about 40 per cent of Chinese GDP, compared with 1.5 per cent for Japan, just over 5 per cent for India and 13 per cent for the US. FDI inflows in 2004, at $60 billion, were over one-third of the total going to all developing countries. The bulk of FDI stock is in manufacturing, and it is estimated that China is home to about 7 per cent of global manufacturing production. Foreign-owned firms generate over 50 per cent of exports (on a par with small, highly open economies like Estonia, Costa Rica and Malaysia) and 60 per cent of imports. The latter figures are especially striking, and bear repetition: *foreign affiliates generate one-half of total exports and an even greater share of imports.*

This astounding combination of trade-and-FDI penetration means that China is already well integrated into the world economy, indeed more so than other developing countries (except highly open, small-to-medium economies, most of them in east Asia), and much more so than the giant rival on its eastern flank, Japan.

China's global integration dwarfs that of India, but the latter has come far by its own standards, especially since the early 1990s. Real incomes have increased by 125 per cent since 1980 (less than half the increase in China). Exports and imports have picked up since the early 1990s, albeit from a very low base. India accounts for less than 1 per cent of world manufacturing exports, putting it in 30th position globally. It has a 1.4-per-cent share of world commercial-services exports, in 19th position globally (though Chinese commercial-services exports are about double the Indian level). FDI has increased from a low base, with an inward investment stock of about $36 billion by 2004. FDI inflows were $6 billion in 2004 – about 10 per cent of Chinese levels.[3]

---

[3] WTO 2004 figures; World Trade Atlas.

What about southeast Asia? Its figures mirror China's but not India's. Its trade levels in 2003 were a little ahead of China's but well ahead of India's. Basically, China has been catching up fast with southeast-Asian trade shares (Figures 1a & 1b); and, with higher growth in trade volumes, it will rapidly overtake southeast Asia. ASEAN countries are highly open to the world economy, with an average trade/GDP ratio of 134.5 per cent, about double that of China. This masks differences within the

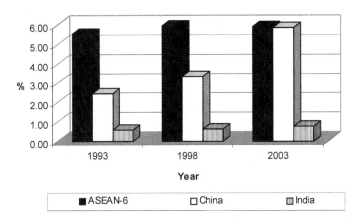

Figure 1a. Shares in World Merchandise Exports, 1993-2003

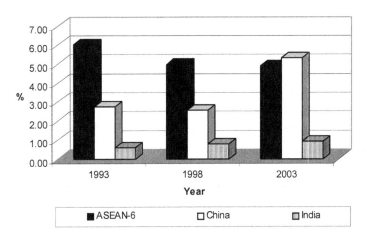

Figure 1b. Share in World Merchandise Imports, 1993-2003
Source: WTO (2004).

region: Singapore is at one extreme; Malaysia is also extremely trade dependent; and even Thailand, Philippines and Vietnam have trade/GDP ratios of over 100 per cent. FDI inflows, which have not maintained their pre-Asian-crisis rate of increase, pale in comparison with inflows to China but are still some way ahead of Indian levels. (See Table 1 and Figure 2 for these comparisons.)

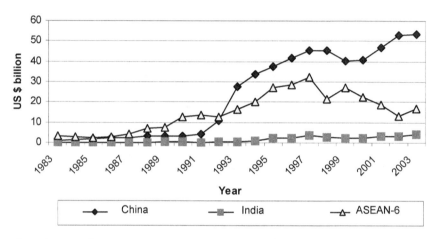

Figure 2. FDI Inflows in ASEAN-6, China and India, 1980-2003
Source: UNCTAD (2004).

There are increasing economic links between China, India and southeast Asia, though from a low base. The main link is between China and southeast Asia. China's share in ASEAN exports nearly tripled, and its share of ASEAN imports more than quadrupled, between 1993 and 2003. Trade in manufactures accounted for most of this increase. ASEAN trade with India, though increasing, is about 20-25 per cent of ASEAN-China trade levels (Figure 3).

What do these comparisons tell us about relative specialisation in the current and emerging international division of labour? The main point is that China has clear-cut comparative advantage in labour-intensive manufactured exports; and this will remain the case for some time ahead, given a huge pool of cheap labour pouring from the countryside into the

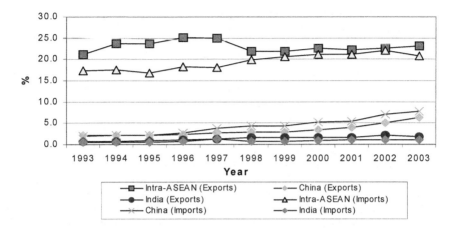

Figure 3. Share of ASEAN's Exports and Imports with Selected Countries: 1993-2003
Source: ASEAN Secretariat (2004).

cities, particularly on the coast. Less often mentioned is China's growing exploitation of comparative advantage in labour-intensive agricultural exports such as fruits and vegetables. At the same time, it is sucking in ever-increasing land-intensive agricultural imports as domestic resources shift further to industrial production. It has recently become a net importer of farm produce. [4] Such rapid specialisation is forging complementary trade relationships with agricultural and other commodity producers in Australasia, Latin America and Africa. In manufactures, as China integrates into global supply chains, it is forging very strong links with the USA, EU and other east-Asian countries, including ASEAN. Much of this is in the form of vertically-integrated, intra-industry trade: China imports capital-intensive components for labour-intensive processing and export to the rest of the world. Finally, rising real incomes are driving domestic demand for sophisticated foreign consumer products and services.

The net effect of China's insertion into the global economy is to intensify competition, and with it the need for mutual adjustment and adaptation.

---

[4] "China fears food crisis as imports hit $14bn," *Financial Times.* August 23, 2004.

More pressure will bear down on low-value, low-wage industries in the West that compete directly with Chinese exports. More pressure is already being felt in developing countries that compete directly with Chinese manufactured exports for third-country export markets. Competition is particularly keen in the global market for clothing.

Now turn to India. China should be the shadow of India's future. With an abundance of cheap labour, India should become a powerhouse for manufacturing exports, occupying low-wage niches (e.g. in textiles and clothing) vacated by China as real incomes rise there. This should apply to labour-intensive agricultural exports too. That is the story of fast-paced, catch-up growth in developing countries in the last half-century.

But this is not happening in India. Its major problem is that only 10 million people are employed in the formal manufacturing sector, out of a total employable population that is rising to 450 million. Industry has a less than 30 per-cent share of GDP, compared with a figure of 50 per cent or more in China and other east-Asian developing countries. External protection, strangulating domestic labour-market regulation, poor infrastructure and other bad business-climate conditions are to blame. Agriculture accounts for 60 per cent of employment but only 20 per cent of GDP. Growth and employment generation are hindered by high external protection, poor infrastructure, other barriers to internal trade, small plots of land, and otherwise pervasive government intervention.

That leaves services, with a share of 50 per cent of GDP (high by developing-country standards and much higher than the share of services in China's GDP). India does have comparative advantage in labour-intensive areas of services, which it is exploiting in business-process outsourcing and software exports. But this is not the panacea often advertised. IT-related services will generate an extra 1 million jobs and account for 1 per cent of GDP by 2010, according to the most optimistic projections. The jobs created require relatively high qualifications and are well paid by Indian standards. But they are a drop in the ocean compared with the wealth-creation and employment-generation potential in manufacturing and, to a lesser extent, in agriculture.[5]

Where does southeast Asia fit into this comparative-advantage picture? It will maintain strong trade-and-FDI links with the USA and Europe. But its future also seems to lie in complementary trade, especially of the intra-industry manufacturing variety, with China and other parts of northeast Asia (Japan, Korea and Taiwan). This will bring in associated FDI. Production-sharing arrangements in IT-related sectors figure prominently, with different parts of the value chain in different locations. But, to exploit these niches fully, the older ASEAN countries need to improve infrastructure, education, skills and governance in order to compensate for eroded advantage in cheap labour. They also need to liberalise highly protected markets in agriculture and services. The newer and much poorer ASEAN countries (Cambodia, Vietnam, Laos and Myanmar) can exploit comparative advantage in cheap labour, especially as relative incomes rise in China. However, for some ASEAN countries with an eroding labour-cost advantage, there are areas where trade with China is more frictional than complementary, e.g. in agriculture, textiles and clothing. Finally, the older ASEAN countries should be able to export more commercial services to an opening and expanding Chinese market, gain from expanding travel and tourism, and invest in large Chinese infrastructure projects.

ASEAN trade with India is much less developed. Trade-and-FDI links are increasing in services and pockets of manufacturing (e.g. cars and car parts). However, for bilateral trade to really take off, India will have to burst its self-imposed chains in manufacturing. That would lead to much stronger, complementary trade and associated FDI between China, India and southeast Asia in goods and services, and with it a more rational, integrated Asian division of labour. But that appears to be on the distant horizon.[6]

---

[5] Vijay Joshi, "Myth of India's outsourcing boom", *Financial Times* 16 November 2004.
[6] On ASEAN-China and ASEAN-India trade links, see Sally and Sen, (2005), pp. 99-101.

In all, China's, India's and southeast Asia's integration into the world economy creates vast opportunities. In China and southeast Asia, catch-up growth based on inward investment and manufactured exports, underpinned by trade-and-investment liberalisation, has massively benefited the poor. That has happened to a lesser extent in India because it has been far less successful in exploiting comparative advantage.[7] The task for public policy is to grasp these opportunities by keeping borders open, or opening them where they are closed, while managing the necessary adjustments. The emerging complementary commercial relationships between China, India and southeast Asia, and between them and other countries, in both developed and developing worlds, will hopefully make this political task realistic and manageable. But protectionist danger lurks behind every free-trade opportunity. These dangers are bound to increase as China's advance gathers pace; and they will increase further if India accelerates its pace of global integration. They will come from declining industries in rich countries and directly-competing industries in other poor countries.

2.2. China, India, southeast Asia and global policy reform

The opening wide of China's door to trade and FDI has not occurred in isolation. Trade policy around the world has become progressively more liberal as part of wider packages of market-based reforms. A veritable trade policy revolution has spread across the developing world, especially since the early 1980s, though it has been patchy and uneven.[8] The Asian financial crisis, followed by crises in Russia, Brazil and Argentina, raised strong doubts about further liberalisation. This has centred on financial liberalisation, especially of short-term capital flows, but it has had a knock-on effect on trade and FDI. Broadly speaking, previous liberalisation has not been reversed, but its forward momentum has slowed.

---

[7] Links between trade policy, openness, growth, poverty reduction and improvements in human-welfare indicators are a separate but related subject. Unfortunately they cannot be dealt with here.

[8] On trade and other economic policy reforms since the 1970s, see Henderson (1998). On developing countries' trade policy reforms, see Michalopoulos (2001), pp. 45-88.

Southeast Asia fits this pattern. The real burst of trade-and-investment liberalisation took place in the 1980s and first half of the 1990s, particularly in Malaysia, Thailand and Indonesia. Singapore and the Philippines were exceptions: in the former, export-led industrialisation and the return to liberal trade policies took place earlier; in the latter, substantial trade-and-investment liberalisation had to wait until the 1990s. Vietnam started opening its borders as part of its transition from Plan to Market from the late 1980s. Cambodia has seen liberalising reforms only more recently. Laos remains largely closed; and Myanmar even more so. Tiny Brunei is a largely unreformed economy and polity based on oil-revenue windfalls.

The Asian crisis changed matters somewhat. True, trade, FDI and other liberalisation measures were not reversed. Indeed, Singapore, Thailand and Indonesia went further in a liberalising direction – in the latter two countries induced by IMF structural-adjustment programmes. But, with the exception of Singapore, government enthusiasm for further liberalisation declined markedly. This was reinforced by powerful interests keen to protect their markets against foreign competition, and a populist backlash of sorts against globalisation in general.[9]

How does China fit in? Its first decade of reforms centred on internal liberalisation, especially in agriculture. Then followed a brief period of uncertainty and suspense after the Tienanmen massacre. The last decade, however, has seen the biggest trade-and-investment liberalisation programme the world has ever seen. In short time, China has swung from extreme protection to rather liberal trade policies, indeed very liberal by developing-country standards. This was crowned by its accession to the WTO, with by far the strongest commitments of any developing country. The pace of internal and external liberalisation has not let up since.

This recent episode is all the more remarkable in that it has happened in the world's most populous country. In contrast, most episodes of radical

---

[9] Sally and Sen, (2005), pp. 101-102. On recent and historical economic-policy developments in southeast Asia, see Hill (2002), especially Hall Hill, "Introduction".

external liberalisation have occurred in quite small countries (e.g. most of the east-Asian Tigers, Chile, and the east- European transition economies). While many others slowed down after the Asian crisis, China continued to race ahead.

India has had a rather different trajectory. Its retreat from the "licence raj" – its equivalent of Soviet-style central planning – began half-heartedly in the 1980s; but it was a foreign-exchange crisis in 1991 that provided the window of opportunity for more thoroughgoing market-based reforms. These were radical by Indian standards, though less so compared with policy reforms elsewhere. They covered macroeconomic stabilisation, trade liberalisation, relaxation of FDI restrictions, privatisation and, not least, the dismantling of domestic licensing arrangements that had governed most formal economic activity. Since the initial burst in 1991-93, reforms have proceeded in a stop-go manner. They have not been reversed; but they have moved ahead more slowly and fitfully compared with southeast Asia (pre-Asian crisis) and China (pre- and post-Asian crisis). Democratic politics, including the complications of multi-party governing coalitions and the federal division of powers between the Union government and the states, has made faster, more decisive reforms elusive.[10]

3. China's, India's and Southeast Asia's Trade-Policy Frameworks

3.1. Trade-policy reforms

In China, since 1978, economic-policy reform has been incremental and ultra-pragmatic.

The more comprehensive transformation of the Chinese economy and society belongs to the post-Tienanmen phase. A headline reform package was introduced in 1994, covering banking, finance, taxation, investment, foreign exchange and foreign trade. It included the unification of the

---

[10] Agarwal (1997).

exchange rate and a new Foreign Trade Law. Currency convertibility, privatisation, the formal recognition of private-property rights and a host of other market-based reforms have followed.

China's integration into the world economy, particularly through its trade reforms, is also more a product of the latter phase, following more gradual opening in earlier phases.[11] Liberalisation has whittled down licensing coverage (down to 5 per cent of imports in 2000 from two-thirds of the total in 1988), and the use of plan prices (to less than 5 per cent of retail commodities by 2000). Even in agriculture, where state pricing is more important, over 80 per cent of sales are at market prices. The overall coverage of non-tariff barriers (NTBs) (licenses, quotas, tendering requirements, state trading and designated trading) had come down to 21.6 per cent of imports and less than 10 per cent of tariff lines by 2001. NTBs fell by about 80 per cent during the 1990s. At a rough estimate, the protective impact of NTBs has fallen from 9.3 per cent in the mid 1990s to 5 per cent today (Table 2).

Table 2. Changes in the Import Coverage of Non-Tariff Barriers from 1996 to 2001

	Licences & Quotas %	Licensing Tendering %	State Only %	Designated Trading %	Trading %	Any NTB %	No NTBs %	Total %
2001	12.8	2.7	0.5	9.5	6.2	21.6	78.4	100
1996	18.5	7.4	2.2	11.0	7.3	32.5	67.5	100

Note: Calculations for 2001 performed by Mei Zhen of MOFTEC during an internship at the World Bank.
Source: Ianchovichina and Martin (2003).

---

[11] Probably the best English-language source on China's trade reforms up to WTO accession is Lardy (2002). Also see Ianchovichina and Martin (2003); Ianchovichina and Martin (2001); Martin (2001), pp. 717-742; Kong (2000), pp. 655-690; *Report of the Working Party on the Accession of China*, Ministerial Conference, Fourth Session, Doha, 9-13th November 2001, WT/MIN(01)/3, November 10th 2001, www.wto.org; *2004 National Trade Estimate Report on Foreign Trade Barriers: China*, Office of the US Trade Representative, www.ustr.gov.

Table 3. Changes in Average Statutory Tariff Rates in China (%)

	All products		Primary products		Manufactures	
	Simple	Weighted	Simple	Weighted	Simple	Weighted
1992	42.9	40.6	36.2	22.3	44.9	46.5
1993	39.9	38.4	33.3	20.9	41.8	44.0
1994	36.3	35.5	32.1	19.6	37.6	40.6
1996	23.6	22.6	25.4	20.0	23.1	23.2
1997	17.6	18.2	17.9	20.0	17.5	17.8
1998	17.5	18.7	17.9	20.0	17.4	18.5
1999	17.2	14.2	21.8	21.8	16.8	13.4
2000	17.0	14.1	22.4	19.5	16.6	13.3
2001	16.6	12.0	21.6	17.7	16.2	13.0
Post-Accession	9.8	6.8	13.2	3.6	9.5	6.9

*Source: World Bank (1999, p340) to 1998. Ianchovichina and Martin's calculations for tariff lines with imports from 1999 and China's final WTO offer. CDS Consulting Co. provided applied tariffs for 2001. Trade data comes from COMTRADE.

Source: Ianchovichina and Martin (2003).

Tariffs have come down sharply in tandem with the decline in NTBs. The simple average statutory tariff was 43 per cent in 1992. Waves of tariff reform, particularly one in 1996, had brought it down to 17.5 per cent by 1998 and 16.6 per cent by 2001 (Table 3). Extensive duty exemptions almost completely liberalised imports of intermediate inputs and of investment goods used for export processing.

In sum, as Nicholas Lardy argues, China had undertaken enormous unilateral liberalisation of trade and FDI, and with it sweeping industrial and agricultural restructuring, in the decade *before* WTO accession.[12] That still left significant knots of up-front protection: declining state-run industries; oil and sensitive agricultural commodities subject to monopolistic state-trading arrangements; high-tech industries targeted for industrial-policy promotion; and, most important, services sectors.

---

[12] Lardy (2002).

China's accession to the WTO and subsequent initiatives have taken reforms even further. That will be discussed later. But it is now clear that the main obstacles to doing business in China have less to do with formal border barriers and more with (formal and informal) non-border barriers. These concern the unpredictability and arbitrariness that come with large regulatory discretion; the lack of a rule of law in terms of impartial judicial oversight and enforcement of property rights and contracts; and the anti-competitive drag of state-owned industrial enterprises and state-owned banks. All this gets deep into domestic economic policies and institutions. It concerns the long-term restructuring of the Chinese state, away from pervasive interference and in the direction of a smaller, more limited operation that can perform fewer functions better. This is a vast trade-related reform agenda; but it has as much to do with the liberalisation of internal trade and the integration of domestic markets as with further external liberalisation. Growth and more widely shared prosperity can only improve if there is a better interaction between external openness and the internal market, mediated by market-supporting institutions.[13]

Indian trade-policy reforms have not been as dramatic or breathtaking, but still considerable by Indian standards. In 1991, the average unweighted tariff was 125 per cent, with peak tariffs on agricultural products going up to 300 per cent. The tariff structure was extremely complicated, with high tariff escalation (higher tariffs on processed goods compared with semi-processed and unprocessed production inputs). This was accompanied by extremely high NTBs (quotas, licensing arrangements and outright bans). Inward investment was either banned or severely restricted. Exchange controls and the internal restrictions of the licence raj (almost) completed the picture.

---

[13] This linkage of internal trade, external trade and domestic institutions is one of Lord Bauer's favourite themes, though one much neglected in post-war development economics. See Bauer (2000).

Much has changed almost fifteen years on. Most border NTBs have been removed, as have internal licensing restrictions. Applied tariffs have come down to an average of about 20 per cent. The maximum tariff on manufactures was lowered to 20 per cent in 2004, and then to 15 per cent in the 2005 budget. Manufacturing tariffs will be rationalised into three bands (0-5-15 per cent); and the intention is to bring average tariffs down to ASEAN levels (around 10 per cent) soon. However, agricultural tariffs remain very high, averaging over 50 per cent. Most restrictions on manufacturing FDI have been removed. Executive orders are being used to relax FDI restrictions in services (given the difficulty of securing a parliamentary majority for such measures).[14]

Hence Indian trade-policy reforms have come far, especially in manufactures. This leaves much to do on tariffs and NTBs in agriculture; and on FDI as well as domestic-regulatory restrictions on foreign services providers. These are much tougher nuts to crack, as are domestic labour-market regulations, privatisation of SOEs, domestic agricultural policies, and a bloated public administration.

What about southeast Asia?[15] Overall, largely as a result of reforms in the 1980s and 90s (earlier in Singapore), the old ASEAN members have average tariffs in the 10-per-cent range or lower, with correspondingly low NTBs (Table 4). FDI restrictions have been progressively lowered. Tariffs, NTBs and FDI restrictions are particularly low in manufacturing – hence in large part the integration of the region into east-Asian and global manufacturing supply chains, especially in IT products. But agricultural protection is much higher; tariff escalation is not insignificant; and services markets are subject to high FDI and domestic-regulatory restrictions. Dual-economy structures have resulted: relatively open and efficient manufacturing sectors driven

---

[14] On these Indian trade-policy developments, see Hoda (2005); *Trade Policy Review: India 2002* (Geneva: WTO, 2002). www.wto.org

[15] On the following developments, see Sally and Sen (2005), pp. 102-107. Also see the articles on Singapore, Malaysia, Thailand, Indonesia, Philippines and Vietnam in the same volume.

by FDI and exposed to global competition coexist with protected, inefficient domestic sectors. The new ASEAN members, either stuck with planned economies or in transition from Plan to Market, have much higher tariff and especially non-tariff barriers.

Table 4. Tariff Levels in ASEAN

Country	Applied	Bound	% Unbound
Singapore*	0	9.7	29.5
Malaysia**	10.2	19	35
Thailand***	12	28.4	28
Indonesia****	8.4	30.4	7
Philippines*****	7.6	28	40
Developing countries			
Latin America/Caribbean	13	38	
Asia	21	37	
Sub-Saharan Africa	20	74	
Middle-East/Mediterranean	23	46	
Developing countries average******	19	49	

Notes: Applied = Simple average applied rate. Bound = Simple average bound rate at the end of implementation of Uruguay Round Agreements. % Unbound = proportion of total tariff lines unbound.

*WTO Singapore Trade Policy Review (TPR) 2000; USTR National Trade Estimate Report on Foreign Trade Barriers: Singapore 2005.

**WTO Malaysia TPRs 1997, 2001; USTR National Trade Estimate Report on Foreign Trade Barriers: Malaysia 2005 (Athukorala *et al.*, 2004).

***WTO Thailand TPR 1998; USTR National Trade Estimate Report on Foreign Trade Barriers: Thailand 2005; (Athukorala *et al.*, 2004).

****WTO Indonesia TPRs 2003, 1998; USTR National Trade Estimate Report on Foreign Trade Barriers: Indonesia 2005; (Athukorala *et al.*, 2004).

*****WTO Philippines TPRs 1995,1999; USTR National Trade Estimate Report on Foreign Trade Barriers: Philippines 2005; (Athukorala *et al.*, 2004).

******Average for 42 developing countries having had WTO TPRs.

Sources: WTO Trade Policy Reviews; USTR National Trade Estimate Report on Foreign Trade Barriers, Michalopoulos (2001), pp. 48, 52 (Tables 4.1 and 4.3).

4. China, India and Southeast Asia in the WTO

4.1. China in the WTO

4.1.1. WTO accession, commitments, effects and implementation

China's WTO-accession negotiations lasted 14 arduous years before full membership was achieved in 2001. China joined the WTO for reasons common to developing countries and countries in transition switching from high command-and-control protectionism to relatively open, market-based commerce with the outside world.[16] When trade, and associated inward investment, move closer to the heart of national economic activity and growth prospects, WTO membership becomes a higher priority. It guarantees access to export markets through unconditional and non-discriminatory Most-Favoured-Nation (MFN) status. Its rules provide members with rights against the arbitrary protection of more powerful countries. A strong dispute settlement mechanism gives these rights legal force, and allows members to work out conflicts in an orderly, containable manner. Membership also confers a seat at the negotiating table, with a better chance to bargain for more export market access and participate in strengthening rules.

China, exceptionally, gave WTO membership top, overriding priority. Crucially, the Chinese leadership consciously and strategically used the WTO accession process as a pillar to bolster domestic reforms: it used entry to the WTO and binding WTO commitments as a device to speed up the transition to a market economy. WTO membership is the most concrete expression and powerful symbol to date of China's transformation, of its engagement with the outside world and its integration into the global economy. It is also the crowning point of over two decades of market-oriented policy reforms across the developing world.

---

[16] See Hoekman and Kostecki (2001), pp. 25-36; Bacchetta and Drabek (2002).

China's WTO commitments are very strong.[17] They exceed those of other developing countries by a wide margin. Indeed, they are almost as strong as they are for developed countries; they are much stronger than those of other large developing countries such as India, Brazil, Egypt and Nigeria; and they are stronger than those of smaller, open economies in southeast Asia. These comparisons hold not only for tariff ceilings on goods (including agriculture), but also for border and behind-the-border non-tariff barriers in goods *and* services. Very strong commitments are not just of the first-generation-reform type (border barriers), but also go deep into second-generation institutional reforms. Notably, there are detailed commitments on judicial and administrative review, and other transparency procedures, on all manner of domestic regulation (e.g. on services, intellectual property and product standards).

On *tariffs*, China's simple-average level of protection comes down to 9.8 per cent. This breaks down into 9.5 per cent on manufactures and 13.2 per cent on agricultural goods (Table 3). Once these averages are weighted by the volume of imports, the overall average tariff on merchandise trade comes down to 6.8 per cent (6.9 per cent on manufactures and 3.6 per cent on agriculture). This is a massive reduction from 40.6 per cent in 1992 and 22.6 per cent in 1996; and it almost halves the 12 per-cent average tariff at the time of accession (Table 3). These figures are for statutory tariffs. The actual level of tariff protection is even lower when duty exemptions (e.g. to attract FDI for export reprocessing) are taken into account. With that in mind, the weighted-average tariff on manufactured imports fell to less than 6 per cent by 2003.

---

[17] See in particular *Report of the Working Party on the Accession of China*, the *Draft Protocol on the Accession of the People's Republic of China*, and attached Annexes with schedules of concessions on goods and services, all in WT/MIN(01)/3 at www.wto.org . Also see *China's Accession to the WTO*, USTR/World Regions, Office of the US Trade Representative www.ustr.gov/regions/china-hk-mongolia-taiwan/accession.shtml; Ianchovichina and Martin, (2001); Ianchovichina and Martin, (2003); Aaditya Mattoo (2003), pp. 299-339; Anderson *et al* (2003); Martin, (2001); Messerlin (2004), pp. 104-130. Some of the World Bank Working Papers on China and the WTO have appeared in Bhattasali *et al.* (2004).

These are astounding numbers – even more so when compared with other countries. China's weighted-average tariffs, overall and on manufactures, are approaching *developed-country* levels (in the region of 3 per cent for the US, EU and Japan). They are significantly below developing-country levels (an average-applied rate of 13 per cent, GATT-bound at a 25 per-cent average after implementation of the Uruguay Round agreements). On agriculture, China's average-weighted tariff is below the developed- country level, and way below the developing-country average. (See Tables 5 & 6 for these comparisons).

The comparison with other developing countries is stark. Not only are China's overall figures lower, but also its bound rates essentially reflect applied (actual) rates, with 100 per cent of tariff lines bound in the WTO[18]. Nearly all other developing countries have large gaps between applied and bound rates, with many tariff lines unbound. Taking simple-average applied tariffs, China has come down to southeast-Asian levels (10 per cent or less), and it is way below Indian levels. China's bound tariffs are well below those of India and the ASEAN countries.

Table 5. Post Uruguay Round Tariff Rates — Developed and Developing Economies (Percent ad valorem)

	Bound		Applied	
	Developed economies	Developing economies	Developed economies	Developing economies
All merchandise	4	25	3	13
Industrial products	4	20	3	13
Textiles and clothing	11	24	8	21
Agricultural products [a]	15	60	14	18

[a] Includes tariffied and not-tariffied products.
Source: J. Michael Finger and L. Schuknecht: "Market Access Advances and Retreats: The Uruguay Round and Beyond", World Bank Working Paper, September, 1999.

---

[18] Bound tariffs are ceiling rates that cannot be exceeded, except under narrowly specified conditions. They are contractual obligations in the WTO. Applied tariffs are actual rates WTO members are free to vary up or down, providing they do not exceed bound tariffs.

Table 6. Post-Uruguay Round Import Weighted Applied and Bound Tariff Rates (%)

Country group or region	Applied	Bound
World	4.3	6.5
High income economies	2.5	3.5
Latin America	11.7	32.7
East Asia & Pacific	11.9	21.0
South Asia	30.4	50.8
Eastern Europe	6.7	13.3
Rest of Europe	24.2	16.3
North Africa	24.8	48.7
Saharan Africa	9.0	19.4

Note: Weighted averages, excluding trade within FTAs. The applied rates are those for the base period, while the bound rates are those applying after the implementation. The data on developing countries was based on 26 out of 93 developing country participants in the Round, representing 80 percent of merchandise trade and 30 percent of tariff lines. Source: J. Michael Finger and L. Schuknecht: "Market Access Advances and Retreats: The Uruguay Round and Beyond", World Bank Working Paper, September, 1999.

In *agriculture,* apart from tariff reductions, there are disciplines on state-trading enterprises, and tight disciplines on trade-distorting domestic subsidies. Export subsidies are banned. Commitments on other *non-tariff barriers* on goods are equally strong. Nearly all import and export quotas and licenses, as well as specific tendering arrangements (377 specific items in all), are to be eliminated by 2005, with disciplines on remaining NTBs. Most remaining price controls are also eliminated. Remaining restrictions on trading rights are to be phased out. By 2005, all firms, domestic and foreign-owned, with or without production facilities in China, will have the right to import and export goods.

There are strict disciplines on industrial subsidies. State-trading and other state-owned enterprises are subject to WTO disciplines. China agreed to fully implement the WTO agreement on trade-related investment measures (TRIMS), without exemptions. All export-performance, local-content and forex-balancing requirements on foreign-owned firms are banned. Imports can no longer be made conditional on these requirements.

A transformation in China's *intellectual-property* regime is another consequence of its WTO accession. It has adopted the WTO's trade-related intellectual-property-rights (TRIPS) agreement in full, and without a transition period. Legislation on patents, trademarks, copyrights, trade secrets and integrated circuits has been amended in conformity with TRIPS.

In *services*, the impact of WTO accession is, roughly, to cut protection by half. With a 6-year phase-in period, this is the most radical services-liberalisation programme ever seen. At least on paper, China's commitments in the General Agreement on Trade in Services (GATS) will transform a highly protected market into one of the most open in the developing world. This massive *net* liberalisation contrasts with developed countries' and other developing countries' weak GATS commitments: at best they bound existing practice; and in most cases fell well short of that. As Table 7 shows, China's GATS market-access coverage on two indicators ("unweighted average count" and "average coverage") is higher than the developed-country average, only falling below the latter on the complete liberalisation ("no restrictions") indicators. Most indicators show China with much higher coverage than other developing countries. Furthermore, its national- treatment commitments, across sectors and modes of supply, are more substantial than all other country groups. The most extensive commitments are in banking, insurance, telecommunications, professional, transport and distribution services.

China's commitments go beyond up-front liberalisation: *transparency* in implementing trade-related laws and regulations are strongly built in too. New trade-related laws and regulations have to be translated into English and published regularly in designated official journals. Enquiry points have to be established so that foreign firms and governments can request information. Normally, responses should be forthcoming within 30 days. A reasonable period of time should be allowed for comment before new laws and regulations come into force. Laws and regulations relating to WTO obligations have to be applied uniformly throughout China –

Table 7. Coverage of Specific Commitments (%)

	High-income countries	Low-and middle-income countries	Large developing nations	China
Market access				
Unweighted average count (sectors-modes listed as a share of maximum possible)	47.3	16.2	38.6	57.4
Average coverage (sectors-modes listed as a share of maximum possible, weighted by openness or binding factors)	35.9	10.3	22.9	38.1
Coverage/count (average coverage as a share of the average count)	75.9	63.6	59.3	66.4
No restrictions as a share of total offer (unweighted count)	57.3	45.5	38.7	40.2
No restrictions as a share of maximum possible	27.1	7.3	14.9	23.1
National treatment				
Unweighted average count (sectors-modes listed as a share of maximum possible)	47.3	16.2	38.8	57.4
Average coverage (sectors-modes listed as a share of maximum possible, weighted by openness or binding factors)	37.2	11.2	25.5	45.0
Coverage/count (average coverage as a share of average count)	78.6	69.1	66.1	78.4
No restrictions as a share of total offer (unweighted count)	65.1	58.0	52.3	63.5
No restrictions as a share of maximum possible	30.8	9.4	20.2	36.5
Memo item				
No restrictions on market access and national treatment as a share of maximum possible	24.8	6.9	14.3	29.8
Number of sectors committed	293.0	100.0	239.0	356.0

Source: Mattoo (2003), p. 303. The breadth and depth of commitments by other countries are understated because their more recent commitments in telecommunications and financial services have not been taken fully into account.

vertically (at sub-national as well as central levels of government) and horizontally (in all cities and regions). Individuals and firms have recourse to a new internal review mechanism to investigate instances of non-uniform application. Finally, new independent and impartial tribunals are to review administrative acts relating to implementation of WTO commitments. Individuals and firms can bring problems to the attention of tribunals, with the right of appeal to higher judicial bodies. This is nothing short of fundamental legal innovation in China – one major step in the direction of the rule of law.

Trade remedies are another feature of China's accession to the WTO. China has adopted new anti-dumping legislation in conformity with GATT provisions – with the protectionist bias of similar legislation in other developed and developing countries. However, the innovation here is extra-generous allowance for *other* WTO members to protect their markets *against* Chinese exports. First, WTO members can use special anti-dumping measures against China until the end of 2015. They can continue to designate China a "non-market economy" and apply a special methodology for determining dumping margins. This involves using "shadow" reference prices in other countries, going well beyond the (fairly generous) provisions in GATT Article VI. In essence, this makes dumping even easier to find (or, more accurately, "construct"). Second, there is a new China- and product-specific safeguard instrument to restrain a surge of imports. This will be in force until the end of 2012. Its "material-injury" definition and related procedures will make it easier to use than the safeguard provisions in GATT Article XIX. Third, a safeguard instrument specific to textiles and clothing will be in force until the end of 2007.

Finally, the WTO has set up an annual Transitional Review Mechanism to scrutinise China's implementation record. It will run annually for 8 years, with a final review in the 10th year.

The main short-term effect of WTO accession is to accelerate the restructuring of the Chinese economy away from agriculture and towards manufacturing.[19] The surge in garments exports, especially after the phase-out of quotas (covered by the Multifibre Agreement, which expired at the end of 2003), is but one symptom of a broader surge in labour-intensive manufactured exports. China's WTO membership is, of course, a powerful signal to attract more FDI in manufacturing, as well as FDI in newly-opened services sectors. Finally, as a result of previous liberalisation locked in by WTO commitments, China will have a relatively open agricultural market. It will not be able to follow the east-Asian Tigers' path of ever-increasing agricultural protection to accompany industrialisation. That is good news: manufacturing efficiency will not be held back; rural and urban poverty can be tackled through better-targeted instruments than high agricultural prices (which tend to benefit the relatively well off and hurt the poor); and consumers will have access to cheap food and other imports from all over the world.

China has a gigantic burden to implement all its WTO commitments in timely fashion. It has passed or revised 190,000 laws, regulations and other measures in preparation for WTO accession and to comply with commitments post-accession. Chinese officials argue that they are on track. Hardened cynics – mostly in the US – aver that there has been a slowdown of momentum and some backtracking. Broadly speaking, China's implementation record has been reasonably good, notwithstanding inevitable hiccups and teething problems. That is the consensus of the last three annual WTO Transitional Reviews of China's implementation record. The major exception is intellectual-property protection: China's enforcement of TRIPS obligations has been inadequate – a recurring source of tension with the USA.

However, complaints about China's implementation record pale in comparison with those that should be directed at the USA and EU. Both have refused China market-economy status and have resorted to extra-generous trade remedies to limit Chinese exports, notably transitional safeguards against garment exports. The intention seems to be to force

---

[19] On the effects of WTO accession, see Ianchovichina and Martin, (2001) and (2003); Mattoo, (2003); Anderson *et al.* (2003); Martin (2001).

China into "voluntary export restraints" along the lines of those with Japan in the 1980s.

4.1.2. Participation in the Doha Round

China's accession to the WTO coincided with the launch of the Doha Round (the Doha Development Agenda in official parlance). Its participation in the round is a good indication of how it is shaping up as a WTO member. So far the signals are very encouraging.[20]

In the end-phase of China's accession negotiations, many players and observers (this author included) feared that China might playcontrarily sillybuggers once inside the WTO. Would it, like India, use the WTO as a foreign policy football? Would it indulge in power plays and provocative rhetoric? Would it undermine the rules-based multilateral system? Based on four years' evidence, the answer is a convincing No. China has exceeded all optimistic expectations: it has been an exemplary WTO citizen. Why? How?

China's unilateral reforms and WTO commitments, its integration into the global economy, and its clear-cut comparative advantage in cheap manufactured exports, give it a strong market-access focus in the WTO. Paradoxically, this puts it in select company with small, open economies like Hong Kong, Singapore, Australia, New Zealand and Chile -- all strong unilateral liberalisers that have big stakes in open markets worldwide, underpinned by well-functioning, non-discriminatory rules. China has not spent 14 years negotiating its way into the WTO to try to wreck it once inside. It is not in the business of militantly defending inflexible positions, endlessly griping about injustices perpetrated by the North, or waxing lyrical about Third-World solidarity. Rather it is in the business of doing serious business – on market access and rules to facilitate market access.

---

[20] The views expressed in this section rely primarily on my discussions with Chinese and non-Chinese trade officials, in Geneva and elsewhere.

Therefore, in contrast to most developing countries, and indeed to other developed- and developing-country majors, China's commitment during the Doha Round has never been in doubt. It has the biggest stake in the success of this round. It has made the biggest down payment, in terms of its accession commitments, even before the round started. But these were one-way concessions. Now it is time for others to open up to Chinese exports; and the Doha Round is the chief vehicle of delivery.

China has gone about its Doha Round business quietly and unobtrusively. Unlike India and Brazil, and indeed unlike the US and EU, it has avoided polarising rhetoric and confrontational posturing. It has been particularly careful not to antagonise the USA – plainly evident in the charged atmosphere of Cancun. Rather it has advanced its positions patiently and flexibly, without rocking the boat, in a spirit of all-round compromise. It tries to be on good terms with all major constituencies, and to build bridges across developed-developing country divides. Thus it does its best to support the WTO process and spread its spirit of all-round compromise – so sorely lacking in Geneva since Seattle.

China's overall negotiating position is that, having already made such extensive liberalisation commitments, and with a sizeable implementation burden, it is not willing to concede much more in this round. It argues that newly-acceded members of the WTO should be given special consideration in multilateral liberalisation formulas. This is alluded to in the Doha mandate; and it is specifically recognised in the Annexes on agricultural goods and non-agricultural goods in the July-2004 framework for future negotiations.[21]

---

[21] See "Proposal on flexible provisions for recently acceded members," WT/MIN(03)W/8, September 4 2003; "Ministerial Declaration," WT/MIN(01)/DEC/W/1, November 14 2001; "Doha Work Programme: Decision Adopted by the General Council on 1 August 2004," WT/L/579, all at www.wto.org . In the latter document, Annex A ("Framework for Establishing Modalities in Agriculture") para. 47 states that: "The particular concerns of recently acceded members will be effectively addressed through specific flexibility provisions;";and Annex B ("Framework for Establishing Modalities in Market Access for Non-Agricultural Products) para. 11 states that: "We recognise that newly acceded members shall have recourse to special provisions for tariff reductions in

China's negotiating positions on specific issues are mixed: offensive here, defensive there, and in between here-and-there. That reflects a big, complicated country with a large spectrum of interests and preferences internally. On all major issues, many shades of opinion within government and in business have to be reconciled before agreeing a negotiating position in the WTO. Also, China is still in listening-and-learning mode as a new member of the club. That is one reason why it does not appear as publicly proactive and assured as India and Brazil. But, to repeat, all-round flexibility and compromise appear to be China's defining characteristics in the WTO.

4.1.3. Addressing China's Doha-Round priorities individually[22]

In the *non-agricultural market-access* negotiations, China's interests are manifestly offensive: it needs greater access for its manufactured exports. This is by far the main area where it is looking for multilateral liberalisation by developed *and* developing countries.

China has mixed positions on *agriculture*. Domestic sensitivities make it loath to commit to substantial extra liberalisation. On the offensive side, it needs lower developed- and developing-country tariff and non-tariff barriers to its agricultural exports. It also has a strong interest in banning developed countries' export subsidies and significantly reducing their production-related domestic subsidies. Hence it joined the G20[23] to put extra pressure on developed countries. Its G20 participation, however, has been low key, and certainly not belligerent.

China is defensive in *services*. It has few export interests; and domestic political sensitivities make it reluctant to concede significantly stronger GATS commitments (though this would still leave it free to liberalise

---

order to take account their extensive market access commitments undertaken as part of their accession and that staged tariff reductions are still being implemented in many cases. We instruct the Negotiating Group to further elaborate on such provisions."

[22] Also see Michalopoulos (2003); Messerlin (2004).

[23] The G20 is a coalition of developing countries that aims for developed-country liberalisation of agricultural markets in the Doha Round. It is led by Brazil and India.

unilaterally). However, as in goods, China is exceptional: in some cases its existing GATS commitments even exceed those of developed countries (e.g. in maritime and audiovisual services, transparency obligations, and cross-border movement of business personnel).

One of China's biggest priorities concerns *anti-dumping*. It is active in the anti-dumping component of the rules negotiations and has tabled proposals, mainly with a view to removing, or at least diluting, its non-market-economy status (covered by GATT Article VI:I second para.).

China is flexible on *Special and Differential Treatment* (S&D) for developing countries, and on the *Singapore issues* (investment, competition, transparency in government procurement, and trade facilitation).

Fairly soon, China should graduate from its post-accession listening-and-learning phase, emerge from the background, and take its rightful place in the foreground of WTO negotiations and ongoing day-to-day business. It should then be more proactive in tabling proposals, cooperating with other majors, participating in large and small coalitions (such as the G20 and issue-based Friends Groups), helping to overcome inter-member differences and breaking logjams, and coming up with creative solutions. Its practical, diplomatic, problem-solving, system-supporting skills should be used more vigorously. Stronger US-China collaboration in the WTO would be particularly welcome. This would reflect closer bilateral relations and emerging political and economic realities on the broader canvas. All this will be needed if the WTO is to get back on track. For that to materialise, China has to be centre-stage.

4.2. India in the WTO

WTO disciplines impinge more on Indian trade policy than was the case in the old GATT. India can no longer impose quantitative restrictions (QRs) on balance-of-payments grounds (which used to be possible under GATT Article XVIII[b]). Many other QRs have been abolished in line with GATT 1994 commitments. And, in 2005, Indian legislation on patent protection was strengthened in line with the TRIPS agreement.

That said, India remains the most protectionist of the three developing-country majors (i.e. China, India and Brazil) in the WTO. Though it has come down considerably, India's average-applied tariff of about 20 per cent is more than double China's figure, and it has much higher levels of tariff dispersion and escalation. Its WTO bound-average tariff is 50 per cent (much higher on agriculture), with many tariff lines unbound. China's commitments on NTBs, trading rights, state-owned enterprises and state-trading enterprises, industrial and agricultural subsidies, are all stronger than India's. China's GATS commitments are very strong compared with India's weak commitments. Equally strong are China's transparency obligations, buttressed by administrative- and judicial-review mechanisms. In addition, other WTO members – including India – can apply extra-generous trade remedies against China's exports for several years ahead.[24]

Traditionally, India has been by far the most defensive of the developing-country majors in the GATT and the WTO. In the Doha Round, China is generally pragmatic and flexible, balancing offensive and defensive positions, but with discrete market-access priorities to advance. India, on the other hand, is defensive almost across the board. Its main offensive position – on GATS Mode One (cross-border service delivery) and Mode Four (cross-border movement of skilled personnel) – is clouded by inflexible, defensive positions on market access, implementation, S&D and the Singapore issues. It is perhaps the chief obstacle to meaningful South-South negotiations on market access. It is the main reason why the G20 has a one-sided mercantilist negotiating position on agriculture, insisting on developed-country liberalisation but offering little or no reciprocal developing-country liberalisation. Overall, India has been widely seen as a polarising force. It has had the dubious reputation of

---

[24] See Trade Policy Review: India 2002, op cit., for India's WTO commitments.

being the developing world's mirror image of France: an eternal spoiler in the WTO.

There are signs that this unflattering state of affairs is gradually changing. Indeed, some of India's negotiating positions have budged a little. It has not taken an especially hard line on exempting "special products" (staples like rice and sugar) from overall agricultural liberalisation in developing countries. It supported the "Girard formula" for tariff cuts on non-industrial goods (though largely because the coefficient does not make big cuts in high developing-country bound tariffs). And it has crafted bold offensive positions in the GATS negotiations, on the back of new comparative advantage in services such as software and outsourced business-processing operations.[25]

An optimist would argue that India is gradually shedding its traditional scepticism of multilateral liberalisation (at least for developing countries) to join the liberalisation bandwagon. This would fit logically with the progressive opening of the Indian economy since 1991, and the recent acceleration of trade, FDI and related economic reforms.

One hopes that accelerating unilateral reforms will, in the not-too-distant future, lead to a decisive shift of positions in the WTO, bringing India closer to the flexibility and pragmatism displayed by China. This would send powerful signals to other WTO members. It has the potential to change coalition dynamics between developing countries and across the developed-developing country divide. And it could significantly improve the prospects for successfully concluding the Doha Round. But India has much further to go.

4.3. Southeast Asia in the WTO[26]

By developing country standards, the ASEAN-5 – Singapore, Thailand, Malaysia, Indonesia and the Philippines – are relatively well integrated

---

[25] See Hoda (2005), on India's Doha-Round positions.
[26] On the following, see Sally and Sen (2005), pp. 101-107, 110-112; Sally (2004a).

into the WTO. They are among a score or so of developing countries with reasonably well-staffed missions in Geneva, who take an active part in WTO committees and working groups, are actively involved in formal and informal coalitions on particular issues, and have initiated anti-dumping actions and dispute settlement complaints (both complex tasks). All this presupposes a critical minimum of trade-policy capacity, which the overwhelming majority of developing countries do not possess. Of course trade-policy capacity among the ASEAN-5 varies with levels of development, ranging from Singapore at one end to Indonesia and the Philippines at the other.

The other three ASEAN members of the WTO are hardly active. Myanmar and Brunei have never been active; and Cambodia joined the WTO as a least-developed member only in 2004.

ASEAN cooperation worked quite well during the Uruguay Round, but has broken down since. Intra-ASEAN differences have become more pronounced, making consensus on nearly all substantive issues very difficult to achieve. Go-it-alone bilateral FTA initiatives are one response to intra-ASEAN divisions; going separate ways in the WTO is another.

Intra-ASEAN divisions on launching a new round and on the substance of its negotiating agenda were evident before Seattle and persisted into the Doha Round. Singapore and Thailand retained broadly pragmatic stances. They had offensive (export market access) positions, and, in Thailand's case, defensive (domestic protectionist) positions (hardly any for Singapore); but were generally willing to compromise and trade-off in order to ensure overall progress in the round. Malaysia, Indonesia and the Philippines, on the other hand, became increasingly defensive in critical areas such as agriculture, Special and Differential Treatment, and the Singapore issues (see Table 8 for country positions in the Doha Round).

Table 8. The Doha Development Agenda: National Positions on the Issues

Country	Market Access	Rules	Developing Country Issues	Singapore Issues	Trade and Environment
Singapore	Top priority: industrial goods and services	Stronger disciplines on anti-dumping	No problems	Comfortable. Trade facilitation a priority	—
Malaysia	Top priority: industrial goods + palm oil exports. Defensive on services	Stronger disciplines on anti-dumping	Few implementation/ SDT/TRIPs problems but promotes LMG positions. However, more flexible than LMG hardliners	Defensive, especially on investment. More flexible on trade facilitation	—
Thailand	Top priority: agriculture. Mixed on industrial goods. Defensive on services	Stronger disciplines on anti-dumping	No major concerns. Flexible	Reasonably flexible	Concerns about SPS+TBT barriers to agriculture and fisheries exports
Indonesia	Defensive, particularly on agriculture, but also on services. Wants access for industrial and tropical product exports	Stronger disciplines on anti-dumping	Promotes LMG positions. But more flexible than hardliners	Defensive but not hardline	—
Philippines	Defensive on agriculture. Also on services. Mixed on industrial goods. Wants market access for industrial and tropical product exports	Stronger disciplines on anti-dumping and fisheries subsidies	Defensive but not hardline	Defensive but not hardline	Concerns about SPS and TBT barriers to agriculture and fisheries exports

Source: Sally (2004a), pp. 94-95.

4.4. China, India, southeast Asia and the future of the WTO

China's entry into the fold is just about the only good news the WTO has had since the late 1990s.[27] Otherwise it has been almost totally crippled. Its agenda has been overloaded with multiple and contradictory objectives; and the hyperinflation of membership has virtually destroyed effective decision-making. Most leading WTO players are distracted by FTA negotiations. The Doha Round remains stuck. If short-term and longer-term problems are not resolved, the WTO will be overwhelmed on two fronts: by politically explosive dispute-settlement cases on the inside; and by a messy patchwork of unbalanced, power-driven, discriminatory bilateral and regional trade arrangements on the outside.

To get the WTO out of its rut, its members need to do two things: restore focus on the core market-access agenda, i.e. progressive liberalisation; and revive effective decision making. The latter depends less on reforming formal procedures than on intergovernmental political will and informal decision making. This requires recognition of hard-boiled realities outside Geneva. About 50 countries account for well over 80 per cent of international trade and foreign investment. This comprises the OECD plus 20-25 developing countries that have been globalising rapidly and successfully. These are the ones with workable governments, sufficient appreciation of own interests, negotiating capacity and bargaining power. They must take the lead.

China, India and some of the ASEAN countries (especially Singapore, Malaysia and Thailand) are in this basket. ASEAN collectively will not be important; but individual ASEAN countries should be active and forge like-minded coalitions, especially with the USA and China, but possibly with India too if it becomes less defensive.

Within this outer core, there is an inner core of "big beasts": the USA and EU, of course, but now joined by the increasingly influential

---

[27] This section relies on my previous writing on the WTO. See especially Sally (2004b), pp. 1-14.

developing-country majors, India, China and Brazil. Without their leadership, nothing will move.

Poorer and weaker developing countries – the vast majority of the membership – must of course be consulted and will exercise influence through the African, LDC (least-developed countries), ACP (African, Caribbean and Pacific) and G90 groupings. But the plain fact is that their very marginal involvement in the world economy, bad-to-terrible governance and scarce negotiating resources make them unable to play more than a secondary and reactive role.

Even with the right dose of realism, there are, in my view, *increasing* limits to WTO-style multilateralism. The GATT was successful because it had (with hindsight) a slimline, relatively simple agenda, and small, club-like decision making, glued together by Cold-War alliance politics. Now, the WTO agenda is technically more complicated, administratively more burdensome and politically much more controversial; decision making is unwieldy in a general assembly with near-universal membership; and the unifying glue of the Cold War has dissolved.

This does not bode well for the Doha Round. For the WTO to work after the Doha Round, I think it needs to scale back ambitions and expectations. Market-access and rule-making negotiations should be more modest and incremental; and maybe trade rounds should become a thing of the past. There should be more emphasis on the unsexy, everyday tasks of improving policy transparency and administering existing rules better. Dispute settlement should not degenerate into backdoor lawmaking. Finally, core decision making should remain intergovernmental. Opening it to non-governmental actors would result in an agenda hijacked by organised minorities pursuing a plethora of conflicting objectives.

In sum, with more modest goals and proportionate means in a restricted intergovernmental setting, the WTO might best be able to serve what should be its core purpose: to be, at the margin, a helpful auxiliary to market-based reforms, especially in the developing world.

5. China, India, Southeast Asia and FTAs

FTA initiatives have spread like wildfire through Asia-Pacific in the past five years (see Table 9 for the state of play in China, India and ASEAN). Before that the region tended to rely more on unilateral measures and non-discriminatory multilateral liberalisation, whereas other regions, such as eastern Europe, Africa and Latin America, have long been involved in (discriminatory) FTA activity. In recent years Asia-Pacific has been playing FTA catch-up. All the major regional powers – China, India and Japan – are involved, as are Korea, Australia, New Zealand, Hong Kong, other south-Asian countries and the ASEAN countries. The USA is involved with individual countries in Asia-Pacific, as are some Latin American countries (notably Mexico, Chile and more recently Brazil). Of the major powers, only the EU has so far remained outside the fray of FTA activity in Asia-Pacific.[28]

Why this rush of FTA activity?[29] Foreign-policy considerations loom large. FTAs are viewed as a means of cementing stronger political (as well as economic) links with favoured partners. On the economic front, FTAs are a response to stalled multilateral liberalisation and a weak WTO. Indeed, they are seen as insurance policies against continuing WTO weakness: they secure *preferential* access to major markets; and are a means of managing and defusing trade tensions with powerful players.

Not surprisingly, governments in the region and elsewhere present FTAs in a positive light. They are seen as part of a benign "competitive-liberalisation" process, a building block of multilateral liberalisation.

---

[28] For an overview and assessment of RTAs in developing-country regions, see World Bank, *Global Economic Prospects 2005: Trade, Regionalism and Development* (Washington DC: World Bank/OUP, 2004); World Bank, *Regional Integration and Development* (Washington DC: World Bank/OUP, 2004).

[29] The following account on FTA motives, advantages and disadvantages draws on World Bank, *Trade Blocs* (Washington DC: World Bank/OUP, 2000); Bhagwati in de Melo and Panagariya (1993); *Global Economic Prospects 2005, op cit.*, chapter 6 ("Making regionalism complementary to multilateralism"), pp. 125-151.

Table 9. Recently Established or Proposed RTAs/CEPAs in ASEAN, China and India, 2000-2005

Country/ Grouping	Partners	Nature of Agreement	Status of Agreement, 2005
ASEAN	China	EPA	EHP in force
	India	EPA	EHP in force
	Japan	EPA	Framework
	Korea	EPA	Agreement signed
	USA (TIFA)	TIFA	Joint Declaration signed
	CER	EPA	Under Negotiation
	EU	TREATI*	Under Study
			Proposed
China	ASEAN	EPA	EHP in force
	Thailand	PTA	Agreement signed
	Australia	EPA	Under negotiation
	India	BIPA	Under study
	Hong Kong	EPA	Agreement signed
	Macau	EPA	Agreement signed
	New Zealand	EPA	Under Negotiation
	Chile	EPA	Under Negotiation
	SACU	FTA	Proposed
Malaysia	Japan	EPA	Under Negotiation
	USA	TIFA	Signed
	Australia	EPA	Under Negotiation
	NZ	EPA	Under Negotiation
	EU	FTA	Under Study
	Korea	EPA	Proposed
	India	EPA	Under Study
	Pakistan	FTA	Proposed
Philippines	Japan	EPA	Agreement signed
	USA	EPA	Under Study

Table 9. (*Continued*)

Country/Grouping	Partners	Nature of Agreement	Status of Agreement, 2005	Country/Grouping	Partners	Nature of Agreement	Status of Agreement, 2005
India	ASEAN	EPA	Framework	Singapore	Australia	EPA	Agreement in force
	China	BIPA**	Agreement signed		Canada	EPA	Under Negotiation
	Korea	FTA	Proposed		Egypt	EPA	Proposed
	Singapore	EPA	Agreement signed		EFTA	EPA	Agreement in force
	Sri Lanka	EPA	Agreement signed		EU	EPA	Proposed (rejected by EU)
	Thailand	PTA	FTA in force		India	EPA	Agreement signed
	BIMSTEC	FTA	Framework		Japan	EPA	Agreement in force
	SACU	FTA	Agreement signed		Jordan	EPA	Agreement in force
	COMESA	FTA	Framework		Korea	EPA	Agreement signed
	MERCOSUR	FTA	Agreement signed		Mexico	EPA	Under negotiations
	Mauritius	EPA	Framework		New Zealand	EPA	Agreement in force
	Japan	EPA	Agreement signed		Sri Lanka	EPA	Under negotiations
	Malaysia	EPA	Framework		USA	EPA	Agreement in force
	Brazil/RSA	FTA	Agreement signed		Qatar	EPA	Agreement signed
	GCC	EPA	Framework		Peru	EPA	Under negotiations
	Chile	PTA	Agreement signed		Panama	EPA	Under negotiations
	Egypt	PTA	Under negotiation		Kuwait	EPA	Under negotiations
			Proposed		Bahrain	EPA	Proposed
			Under Study		Brunei	EPA	Under negotiations
			Proposed		Chile/NZ	EPA	
			Framework				
			Agreement signed				
			Under Negotiation				
			Under Negotiation				

Table 9. (*Continued*)

Country/ Grouping	Partners	Nature of Agreement	Status of Agreement, 2005	Country/ Grouping	Partners	Nature of Agreement	Status of Agreement, 2005
Vietnam	US	BTA***	Agreement signed	Thailand	Australia	FTA	Agreement signed
	Japan	FTA	Under negotiation		Bahrain	FTA	Agreement signed
	Sri Lanka	EPA	Agreement signed		China	PTA	Agreement signed
	Korea	FTA	Proposed		India	EPA	PTA in force
					Japan	EPA	Under negotiation
Brunei	Singapore/NZ/ Chile	EPA	Negotiations completed		Korea	EPA	Under Study
					New Zealand	EPA	Under Study
					Peru	PTA	Agreement signed
					South Africa	PTA	Under study
					USA	EPA	Under negotiation Framework
					BIMSTEC	FTA	Agreement signed

Source: Compiled by author from various government and news sources.

Notes: Nature of Agreement is dependent on the stated objectives of these agreements while being proposed. EPA: Economic Partnership Agreement; FTA: Free Trade Agreement (aims for complete liberalization of trade in goods and in some cases, services); PTA: Preferential Trade Agreement: (aims for preferential tariff reduction only for a few goods traded); TIFA: Trade and Investment Facilitation Agreement (as a precursor to a possible PTA/FTA in future); BIPA: Bilateral Investment Promotion Agreement (precursor to a possible PTA/FTA); BTA: Bilateral Trade Agreement (since Vietnam is not yet a WTO member).

Bay of Bengal Initiative for Muti-Sectoral Technical and Economic Cooperation (BIMSTEC) members: Bangladesh, India, Myanmar, Sri Lanka, Thailand, Nepal and Bhutan.

South American Common Market (MERCOSUR) members: Brazil, Argentina, Uruguay, Paraguay.

European Free Trade Association (EFTA) members: Switzerland, Liechtenstein, Norway, Iceland.

South African Customs Union (SACU) members: South Africa, Botswana, Lesotho, Namibia and Swaziland.

Common Market of Eastern and Southern Africa (COMESA) members: Angola, Burundi, Comoros, Congo. D.R, Djibouti, Egypt, Eritrea, Ethiopia, Kenya, Madagascar, Malawi, Mauritius, Namibia, Rwanda, Seychelles, Sudan, Swaziland, Uganda, Zambia, and Zimbabwe.

Gulf Cooperation Council (GCC) members: Saudi Arabia, Kuwait, Bahrain, Qatar, the United Arab Emirates, and the Sultanate of Oman.

Sen (2005), p. 8.

FTAs among small clubs of like-minded countries can, they argue, take liberalisation and regulatory reform further than would be the case in a large, heterogeneous and unwieldy WTO. This can in turn stimulate multilateral liberalisation.

For FTAs to make economic sense, they should have comprehensive sectoral coverage, be consistent with relevant WTO provisions (in Article XXIV GATT and Article V GATS), and preferably go beyond both WTO commitments and applied practice at home. In other words, they should involve genuine and tangible, not bogus, liberalisation. There should be strong provisions for non-border regulatory cooperation, especially to improve transparency in domestic laws and regulations in order to facilitate market access and boost competition. Rules-of-origin (ROO) requirements should be as simple, generous and harmonised as possible to minimise trade diversion and red tape. Finally, strong, clean "WTO-plus" FTAs should reinforce domestic economic and institutional reforms to remove market distortions and extend competition.

All this presupposes a sense of economic strategy when entering into FTA negotiations – on choosing negotiating partners, assessing the costs and benefits of negotiating positions, and how they relate to the WTO and to the national economic-policy framework.

Unfortunately, the above characterisation is the exception, not the rule, of FTAs in practice. The EU, NAFTA and Australia-New Zealand CER are the exceptions. Most other FTAs and customs unions are weak, often falling short of WTO provisions. This is particularly true of South-South FTAs (i.e. between developing countries), but also holds for many North-South FTAs. Such FTAs tend to be driven by foreign-policy aspirations, but with justifications that are all too often vague, muddled and trivial, having little relevance to commercial realities and the economic nuts and bolts of trade agreements. This can amount to little more than symbolic copycatting of other countries' FTA activity and otherwise empty gesture politics. In such cases economic strategy is conspicuous by its absence.

The predictable results of foreign-policy-driven FTA negotiations light on economic strategy are bitty, quick-fix sectoral deals. Politically sensitive sectors are carved out, as are crucial areas where progress in the WTO is elusive (especially disciplines on anti-dumping duties and agricultural subsidies). Little progress is usually made on domestic regulatory transparency. These FTAs hardly go beyond WTO commitments, deliver little, if any, net liberalisation and pro-competitive regulatory reform, and get tied up in knots of restrictive, overlapping rules of origin. Especially for developing countries with limited negotiating capacity, resource-intensive FTA negotiations risk diverting political and bureaucratic attention from the WTO and from necessary domestic reforms. Finally, the sway of power politics can result in highly asymmetrical deals, especially when one of the negotiating parties is a major player.

Going about FTAs the wrong way – negotiating weak agreements with ROO complications that deflect attention from sensible unilateral reforms and the WTO – could easily lead to a world where most international trade would be governed by arbitrary market-distorting preferences. Then the cornerstone of the multilateral trading system, the principle of non-discrimination embodied in the GATT's Most-Favoured-Nation clause, would become more an abstraction than concrete reality. MFN would end up as LFN – Least-Favoured-Nation treatment. This would make a mockery of comparative cost advantages, the foundation of sensible and mutually advantageous globalisation.[30]

5.1. China and FTAs

China's FTA strategy is directed at its northeast and southeast-Asian neighbourhood. Politically, China would like to use FTAs to reinforce its weight and establish its leadership credentials in east Asia. Economically, it wants extra export market access as well as secure access to energy and other commodity imports. Overall, China clearly

---

[30] Sutherland *et al.* (2004).

aims to be the political and economic driving force in the region. China-driven FTAs are a means to that end.[31]

Ever-closer intra-industry trade-and-investment linkages in east Asia inform the economic logic of region-wide FTAs. Comprehensive, clean, WTO-consistent FTAs with China, and preferably a pan-east Asian FTA, might make sense for the region. Complementary intra-industry trade is broadly consistent with shifting comparative advantages. A region-wide FTA, *on the right terms*, should be trade creating, not trade diverting.

The problem is that the region subsumes a diverse array of economies with big pockets of protection here and there. Opening to trade with China would leave several sheltered sectors exposed: agriculture in Japan and South Korea; and agriculture, textiles and clothing in the lesser developed ASEAN countries (Indonesia, the Philippines, Cambodia, Laos, Vietnam and Myanmar). Extreme agricultural protection in Japan and South Korea will make comprehensive China-Japan and China-Korea FTAs almost impossible to negotiate. Also, ambitious FTAs between developing countries with similar resource and production structures, and therefore with competing products, are extremely difficult to negotiate. That is the major problem for a China-ASEAN FTA. The risk is that, like inter-developing-country FTAs in the past, it will end up as a bitty deal covering some sectors but with large areas excluded and with restrictive rules-of-origin requirements. This would minimise mutual gains and increase the risk of trade diversion. A regional patchwork quilt of overlapping hub-and-spoke FTAs, many or all with partial coverage and differing, complicated and restrictive rules of origin, would make matters worse.

The China-ASEAN set of negotiations, more than any other FTA initiative, is the one to watch in the region. The aim is to have an FTA in place by 2010. It would be the largest FTA ever negotiated, covering 11 diverse economies with a population of 1.7 billion and a GDP of US$2 trillion. An "early harvest" programme is supposed to cut or eliminate

---

[31] See "Everybody's doing it," *The Economist*, February 28th 2004.

about 10 per cent of tariff lines, mainly in agricultural products, by January 2006. Other tariffs are to be cut or eliminated on a "normal track" between 2005 and 2010. Ninety-five per cent of tariff lines should be covered by 2010, with the rest to be dealt with later. The new ASEAN members have an extension to 2015 to comply with obligations. Negotiations will also begin on services and investment, with economic cooperation planned in other areas.[32]

Revealingly, the initiative, overarching strategy and negotiating motor come from Beijing, not the ASEAN capitals. ASEAN collectively is weak, divided and lacks a common negotiating machinery. Its weaker members, especially Indonesia, the Philippines and the new ASEAN members, are reluctant to open protected agricultural sectors. No wonder that tariff negotiations have been tortuous, and hardly any progress has been made in other areas. It looks unlikely that the FTA, as envisaged, will be in place by 2010.

China has a separate mini-FTA with Thailand – basically a preferential sectoral deal on some agricultural products. It has an FTA (called a Closer Economic Partnership Agreement – CEPA) with Hong Kong. It is about to start FTA negotiations with Australia and New Zealand. There are exploratory talks with Japan, South Korea and others. China has announced its preference for a pan-east Asian FTA encompassing "ASEAN plus Three" (the three being China, Japan and South Korea). It may only be a matter of time before China launches FTA initiatives outside the region, say with some Latin American countries and South Africa.

A key component of China's FTA strategy is to get wider acceptance of market-economy status, especially with anti-dumping actions in mind. As mentioned earlier, China is pushing hard for removal of non-market economy status in the WTO, and bilaterally with the EU and US. Singapore, Malaysia, Thailand, New Zealand and Australia have already accorded China market-economy status. The other ASEAN countries did

---

[32] Sen (2004), 75-84.

the same in a joint statement.[33] It is not accidental that China is in or talking about FTA negotiations with the countries that have conceded market-economy status. This is bound to be a central Chinese demand if FTA talks begin with countries outside the region.

The contrast between China's FTA strategy and those of other powers in the region is instructive. Japan seems to be reacting to China's advance, but without a real strategy. Unlike China, it is defensive on agriculture and appears not to be interested in ambitious market-access coverage. Also in contrast to China, it seems to prefer bilateral deals with ASEAN countries individually to something more challenging with ASEAN collectively. The latter is, of course, much more difficult to negotiate but holds out the prospect of commensurately greater gains. South Korea's profile is similar to Japan's.

In all, China is making the running on FTAs in Asia. How this will pan out, and how it will relate to domestic reforms, its WTO commitments and participation, and its foreign- policy goals, remains to be seen.

In the WTO, China's approach is clearly linked to national economic policies that have a single-minded focus on growth. Commercial realities are front and centre in what China does in the WTO. This stands in contrast to most other players, including the USA, EU, India and Brazil, who sometimes let extraneous political considerations distract attention from the commercial facts on the ground.

The danger is that China might have a more blurred focus in FTAs than it has in the WTO; that it will allow other political factors (such as competition with Japan to establish leadership credentials in east Asia) to crowd out sensible, grounded economic strategy. That would be the fast track to weak, partial FTAs that create little trade but a lot more political and economic complications. That is what other players, big and small, are doing. But it would be a serious mistake for China to copy them.

---

[33] "China full market economy: ASEAN," *Straits Times* September 7 2004.

FTAs, rather, should fit into the mould set by economic policies at home and in the WTO.

5.2. India and FTAs

India is also newly active with FTAs, in its south-Asian backyard, across to southeast Asia, and, in the opposite direction, to Africa and Latin America. In south Asia it has an FTA with Sri Lanka, a much weaker one with Nepal, and one that might be negotiated with Bangladesh. Hitherto loose regional cooperation is supposed to be transformed into the South Asian FTA (SAFTA) by 2010, leading to a customs union by 2015 and economic union (whatever that means) by 2020.[34] But this looks very much like ASEAN Vision statements: rhetorically ambitious but unachievable in practice. Planned negotiations are only on goods; they do not cover services, investment and other non-border market access issues. There are bound to be plenty of exemptions on goods, given similar trade structures with competing products (especially in agriculture). There will be serious ROO complications. Finally, severe political problems in the region (the Indo-Pakistani conflict over Kashmir, and the fact that India is completely surrounded by weak, failing or failed states) will make progress very difficult.

India's approach to FTAs outside south Asia resembles that of Japan and South Korea: it is mostly about foreign policy, with little economic sense or strategy. An FTA with ASEAN is planned for completion by 2011; and bilateral FTA frameworks are also in place with Thailand and Singapore. But so far India has been niggardly on market access, insisting on exempting swathes of economic activity and on very restrictive rules of origin for products covered. India is part of the BIMSTEC group (the other members being Bangladesh, Sri Lanka, Nepal, Bhutan, Thailand and Myanmar) that plans an FTA by 2017. India, South Africa and Brazil are planning a very partial three-way FTA that would cover certain goods. India is exploring the possibility of an

---

[34] Dubey (2004).

FTA with China. All signs are that India is spinning a web of weak and partial FTAs around it.

5.3. Southeast Asia and FTAs

Turning to southeast Asia, Singapore blazed the FTA trail, with Thailand next to follow, and now Malaysia, Indonesia and the Philippines trying to catch up. Singapore has agreements in force with Australia, New Zealand, Japan, USA, Jordan and EFTA; agreements recently signed with Korea and India; and several others proposed or under negotiation with countries in the Americas, the Middle East and south Asia, including a four-way FTA with Brunei, Chile and New Zealand. Thailand has agreements in force with Australia, New Zealand, Bahrain, China and India; it is part of the BIMSTEC framework agreement; it is in negotiations with the USA, Japan, Peru and EFTA; and is considering yet more FTAs, e.g. with Chile, South Africa and Pakistan. Malaysia has an agreement with Japan, is negotiating with Australia, New Zealand, India, Pakistan and Korea, and considering other initiatives. Indonesia is negotiating with Japan and may soon start negotiations with Australia and New Zealand. The Philippines is negotiating with Japan and wants an FTA with the USA. Vietnam has an FTA with the USA, is negotiating with Japan and considering other negotiations. In addition, ASEAN collectively has negotiations with China, India and Japan, and negotiations are about to start with Australia-New Zealand CER and Korea. As of 2005, it is estimated that ASEAN as a regional grouping, China and India are involved in 7, 9 and 15 FTA agreements or negotiations respectively.[35]

Singapore does have reasonably strong, WTO-plus FTAs with developed countries, and an especially strong FTA with the USA. This fits well with the Singapore context of free trade in goods, accelerated unilateral liberalisation of services and a strong regulatory infrastructure. Bilateral FTAs envisaged or being negotiated by other ASEAN countries, as well as those involving ASEAN collectively, also go well beyond old-style

---

[35] Sen (2005), p. 8.

FTAs covering goods alone. They are intended to be WTO-consistent, and notified under Article XXIV GATT and Article V GATS. Their scope extends to services, investment, trade facilitation, regulatory cooperation and dispute settlement.[36]

However, Singapore is a misleading indicator for other ASEAN countries. They have a fuzzier idea of what FTAs entail, weaker negotiating capacity, and more protectionist interests to defend, especially in agriculture and services. Thus far most signs point to ASEAN countries becoming entangled in a web of weak and partial FTAs. Some product areas, especially in agriculture, are likely to be excluded from goods liberalisation; and non-tariff and other regulatory barriers on goods, services and investment are unlikely to be tackled with disciplines that go much deeper than existing WTO commitments. Finally, it is already apparent that agreements in force and those being negotiated are creating a mess of complex and restrictive ROO requirements that differ between agreements and will prove cumbersome and costly for businesses to implement.

The heart of the matter is that within and across south, southeast and northeast Asia, cross-border commerce is throttled by the protectionist barriers that developing countries erect against each other. The type of FTAs that are being negotiated are highly unlikely to make a big dent in these barriers and thereby spur regional economic integration. These have the hallmarks of trade-light agreements. Some might even come close to being "trade-free" agreements. A blunt, uncharitable Texan would say that they are "all hat and no cattle". This characterises much of Indian and ASEAN activity on FTAs. One hopes China will be different, but one fears that short-term political temptations will overwhelm long-term economic logic.

---

[36] See Sen (2004); Sen (2005).

6. Conclusion: What Prospects for Trade Policy in China, India and Southeast Asia?

China's integration into the world economy has come a long way, but it has much further to go. It has even further to go in India and the new ASEAN members, though less so in the more developed parts of southeast Asia. This Asian transformation of the global economy holds out huge opportunities for growth, poverty reduction, improvements in human welfare, and for the extension of economic freedoms. Not least, it will contribute to peaceful international relations as nations and peoples come closer together through commercial ties. However, the magnitude of these changes is bound to increase protectionist pressures, in developed and developing countries.

Asia's belated integration into the world economy is very welcome. But it is not pre-programmed. The future will be full of unforeseen twists and turns. Governments have to manage internal problems such as rising regional disparities, rotting public sectors, environmental pollution, corruption, and anxiety about health, education and pensions systems among the most vulnerable. Then there is the problematic link between a spreading market economy and authoritarian politics, particularly in China. Finally, there are international security flashpoints, such as China-Taiwan relations, China's growing military power in east Asia, and the big-power scramble for global energy supplies. All these could slow down or even halt the onward march of global economic integration.

China's, India's and southeast Asia's challenge is to go further with economic reforms: more trade-and-investment liberalisation; much more internal liberalisation to integrate the domestic market; and more second-generation institutional reforms to support a complex market economy, especially legal and administrative reforms to restructure the state. The external corollary of economic-policy reforms at home is to anchor "constructive engagement" abroad and make it permanent, not hostage to the vagaries of a few personalities and stray events. That means closer, long-term relations with other powers and more active, constructive participation in international institutions, not least the WTO. But constructive engagement is not a one-way street: others have to be willing too – especially the USA. The USA remains the indispensable anchor of global prosperity, security and freedom – far more important than any international organisation or international treaty. Much depends on the right sort of US leadership in relations with other powers, and in international institutions like the IMF, World Bank and WTO.

Trade policy and trade diplomacy are an important part of this larger picture. It is customary to look first to the WTO, or now to FTAs, or to a combination of the two, to advance the liberalisation of international commerce. The conventional wisdom is that unilateral liberalisation is politically very difficult in 20th and 21st-century conditions of democratic politics and collective action by organised interests. This is what trade negotiations, i.e. reciprocal bargaining over export concessions, are supposed to overcome.

This "liberalism from above" overlooks fundamental lessons from theory, history and the world around us today. Compelling political and economic arguments favour unilateral liberalisation, with governments freeing up international trade and flows of capital and labour independently, not via international negotiations. As any student of trade economics knows, welfare gains result directly from *import* liberalisation, which replaces comparatively costly domestic production and reallocates resources more efficiently. Such gains come quicker through own personal, unconditional liberalisation than through protracted, politicised and bureaucratically cumbersome international negotiations. This Nike strategy ("Just Do It!") makes political sense too. Rather than relying on one-size-fits-all international blueprints, governments have the flexibility to initiate policies and emulate better practice abroad in experimental, trial-and-error fashion, tailored to specific local conditions.

Admittedly, unilateral liberalisation now is more difficult than it was for the British in the 19th century. But my point is that trade negotiations have increasing limitations. They do not deliver nearly as much as they did in the first few decades after the Second World War, and are subject to diminishing returns. The transition from GATT to WTO has narrowed the possibilities for multilateral liberalisation and rule strengthening. Most FTAs are weak and partial. Their discriminatory nature creates political and economic complications. Over the last half-century, trade negotiations have dealt reasonably well with relatively simple border barriers (tariffs and quotas). But they are not very good at tackling complex non-border regulatory barriers that do deep into the particularities of domestic institutions. In other words, trade negotiations are worse at second-generation than at first-generation reforms. Finally, trade negotiations are too often hostage to power politics and foreign-policy whims, thus distracting attention from ground-level commercial realities.

Observers often forget that the recent trade-policy revolution in the developing world has come more "from below" than "from above". The World Bank estimates that, since the 1980s, about two-thirds of developing-country trade liberalisation has come about unilaterally. Most of the remaining third has come from the Uruguay-Round agreements, and only a small fraction from FTAs. [37] True, many governments liberalised reluctantly as part of IMF and World Bank structural adjustment programmes. But the strong and sustained liberalisers have gone ahead under their own steam, without the need for much external pressure.

This is especially true of east Asia, and now applies to south Asia too. The bulk of southeast-Asian trade-and-investment liberalisation was done unilaterally in the 1980s and 90s. China's massive external liberalisation programme over the past decade is the biggest the world has ever seen. Most of this was done unilaterally, not through international negotiations, and *before* WTO accession. China's extremely strong WTO commitments, and its very pragmatic and businesslike participation in the WTO post-accession, are more the consequence than the cause of its sweeping unilateral reforms.

---

[37] World Bank, Global Economic Prospects 2005: Trade, Regionalism and Development (2004).

China is in many ways today what Britain was in the second half of the nineteenth century: the unilateral engine of freer trade. It is probably spurring a pickup in trade-and-FDI liberalisation elsewhere in east and south Asia – notably in India. Would all this have happened, or happened as fast, if China had not concentrated minds? Probably not. The southeast-Asian countries in between have slowed down the momentum of liberalisation and regulatory reform since the Asian crisis while China and India have speeded up. The policy gap with China in particular has narrowed. For southeast Asia to take advantage of the opportunities offered by China's and India's global integration, and overcome more-exposed weaknesses caused by protectionist policies and weak institutions, there has to be further liberalisation and regulatory reform. This is less likely to come about through the WTO, FTAs and ASEAN regional cooperation, and more likely to result from unilateral measures by individual governments in response to internal and external conditions. China and India should concentrate minds within ASEAN countries; and it is up to them to follow the liberalisation train through competitive emulation.

Freer trade in the early twenty-first century, and modern globalisation more generally, are happening more "from below" than "from above". Their engine, now to be found in Asia, particularly in China, is bottom-up liberalisation and regulatory reform that spreads through competitive emulation, like ripples and waves across seas and oceans. This process is not driven by international institutions. At best the WTO and FTAs can be helpful auxiliaries to national market-based reforms. But their importance should not be exaggerated.

References

1. Agarwal, M., "India," in P. Desai ed., *Going Global: Transition from Plan to Market in the World Economy* (MIT Press, Cambridge, MA, 1997).
2. Anderson, K., J. Huang and E. Ianchovichina, "Long-run impacts of China's WTO accession on farm-nonfarm income inequality and rural poverty," World Bank Policy Research Working Paper 3052 (The World Bank, Washington, DC, 2003).

3. Athukorala, P. *et al.*, "Tariff reform and the Structure of Protection in Thailand," mimeo (World Bank Thailand, Bangkok, 2004).
4. Bacchetta, M., and Z. Drabek, "Effects of WTO Accession on Policy-making in Sovereign States: Preliminary Lessons from the Recent Experience
of Transition Countries," Staff Working Paper DERD-2002-02 (WTO Development and Economic Research Division, Washington, DC, 2002).
5. Bauer, P., *From Subsistence to Exchange and Other Essays* (Princeton University Press, Princeton, NJ, 2000).
6. Bhagwati, J., "Regionalism and multilateralism: an overview," in J. de Melo and A. Panagariya eds., *New Dimensions in Regional Integration* (Cambridge University Press, Cambridge, 1993).
7. Bhattasali, D., L. Shantong and W. Martin, *China's Accession to the World Trade Organisation, Policy Reform and Poverty Reduction* (World Bank, Washington, DC, 2004).
8. Boekman, B. H., and M. Kostecki, *The Political Economy of the World Trading System: The WTO and Beyond* (Oxford University Press, Oxford, 2001).
9. Dubey, M., "SAFTA: problems and prospects," Paper for the Roundtable Dialogue on Achieving SAFTA Public-Private Partnership, New Delhi, India (2004).
10. Hale, D., and L.H. Hale, "China takes off," *Foreign Affairs*, November/December (2003).
11. Henderson, D., *The Changing Fortunes of Economic Liberalism: Yesterday, Today and Tomorrow* (Institute of Economic Affairs, London, 1998).
12. Hill, H. ed., *The Economic Development of Southeast Asia,* Vols. 1&2 (Edward Elgar, Cheltenham, 2002).
13. Hoda, A., "India in the WTO", in M. Asher, N. Kumar and R. Sen eds., *India-ASEAN Economic Relations: Meeting the Challenges of Globalisation* (ISEAS/RIS, Singapore/India, 2005).
14. Ianchovichina, E., and W. Martin, "Trade liberalisation in China's accession to the World Trade Organisation," World Bank Policy Research Working Paper 2623 (June 2001).
15. Ianchovichina, E., and W. Martin, "Economic impacts of China's accession to the World Trade Organisation," World Bank Policy Research Working Paper 3053 (The World Bank, Washington, DC, 2003).
16. Kong, Q., "China's WTO accession: commitments and implications," *Journal of International Economic Law*, 3(4), pp. 655-690 (2000).
17. Lardy, N., *Integrating China into the Global Economy* (Brookings, Washington, DC, 2002).
18. Maddison, A., "The World Economy: A Millennial Perspective," (OECD, Paris, 2001).

19. Martin, W., "Implications of reform and WTO accession for China's agricultural policies," *Economics of Transition*, 9(3), pp. 717-742 (2001).

20. Mattoo, A., "China's accession to the WTO: the services dimension," *Journal of International Economic Law*, 6(2), pp. 299-339 (2003).

21. Messerlin, P., "China in the World Trade Organisation: antidumping and safeguards," *The World Bank Economic Review*, 18(1), pp. 104-130 (2004).

22. Michalopoulos, C., *Developing Countries in the WTO* (Palgrave, London, 2001).

23. Michalopoulos, C., "China in the WTO: challenges and opportunities," presented for the closing conference of the EU-China WTO Programme for China's Accession to the WTO, Beijing, mimeo (2003).

24. Rumbaugh, T., and N. Blancher, "China: international trade and WTO accession," IMF Working Paper WP/04/36 (2004).

25. Sally, R., *Southeast Asia in the WTO* (ISEAS, Singapore, 2004a).

26. Sally, R., "The end of the road for the WTO? A snapshot of international trade policy after Cancun," *World Economics*, 5(1), pp. 1-14, January-March 2004, www.world-economics-journal.com (2004b).

27. Sally, R., and R. Sen, "Whither trade policies in southeast Asia? The wider Asian and global context," *ASEAN Economic Bulletin*, 22(1), pp. 92-115, 2005, Special Issue: Revisiting Trade Policies in Southeast Asia (2005).

28. Sen, R., *Free Trade Agreements in Southeast Asia* (Institute of Southeast Asian Studies, Singapore, 2004).

29. Sen, R., "'New Regionalism' in Asia: a comparative analysis of emerging regional trading agreements (RTAs) involving ASEAN, China and India," Paper for the Workshop on Global Economic Negotiations, Venice International University, San Servolo (2005).

30. Sutherland, P., *et al.*, *The Future of the WTO* (WTO, Geneva, 2004).

31. Wolf, M., *Why Globalisation Works* (Yale University Press, New Haven, 2004).

CHAPTER 9

AFTER THE CMI: THE FUTURE OF ASIAN MONETARY COOPERATION AND CHINA'S ROLE

He Fan, Zhang Bin & Zhang Ming[1]

Chinese Academy of Social Sciences

Abstract: Following the Asian financial crisis, the pace of regional monetary cooperation in Asia picked up. Notwithstanding this new phase of co-operation, Asian economies are now facing new external risks and without coordinated efforts these risks may develop into financial crises. The Chiang Mai Initiative (CMI) is a stepping-stone for launching fully-fledged Asian monetary cooperation, but it also has problems. This paper reviews the development of the CMI and suggests that multilateralisation of the CMI can both enhance its function as a liquidity provider and pave the way for future regional common monetary arrangement. We believe that exchange rate coordination should also be added to the agenda, however, we realise that the proposals we have examined in this paper are not realistic while individual countries are unwilling to give up their autonomy over domestic policy making. We argue that multilateralisation of the CMI may help to bridge the gap and eliminate some of these obstacles. Finally, we examine the role of China in Asian monetary cooperation and its attitude toward the multilateralisation of the CMI.

[1] He Fan is the Assistant Director of the Institute of World Economics and Politics, Chinese Academy of Social Sciences; Zhang Bin is a Research Fellow at the Institute of World Economics and Politics, Chinese Academy of Social Sciences; Zhang Ming is a Ph.D student at the Graduate School, Chinese Academy of Social Sciences. Corresponding author: hefancass@gmail.com

1. Introduction

Since the Asian financial crisis, the pace of regional monetary cooperation in Asia has picked up. The crisis fostered the belief that Asian countries need to band together to protect themselves from the spread of further financial crises. In May 2000, the Financial Ministers of the ASEAN countries, plus China, Japan and Korea (ASEAN+3), met in Chiang Mai, Thailand, and launched the Chiang Mai Initiative (CMI). This involves an expanded ASEAN swap arrangement and a network of bilateral swap arrangements among the ASEAN+3. The development of the CMI has been the subject of much attention not only because it is the first significant regional financial arrangement in Asia but also because it may be a stepping-stone to fully-fledged regional financial cooperation.

With the recovery of the Asian economy, however, the momentum for regional financial cooperation may be on the wane. The original design of the CMI was to provide liquidity support to member economies at a time when they were facing external disequilibrium. Since there is unlikely to be a repeat of an equivalent Asian financial crisis, the question arises as to why a "war-time" crisis rescue arrangement should be established during "peace-time" (Sangsubhan, 2005)? However, we believe that it would be presumptuous to assume that there will not be any crises in the region in the future. On the contrary, we believe that regional financial cooperation becomes even more relevant at a time when Asian economies are facing new external risks such as the depreciation of the US dollar, US interest rate hikes, and a surge in oil prices. Without coordinated efforts these risks may readily develop into financial crises. In order to solve these problems, the CMI needs to be reformed and transformed from the "fire fighting" mode of liquidity provider to a more restrictive form of regional arrangement. The idea of multilateralisation of the CMI, we believe, can help to enhance its function as a simple liquidity provider, while also providing the opportunity to explore the feasibility and desirability of an efficient regional monetary arrangement capable of addressing more important issues such as exchange rate coordination. Without further integration in this region, Asian economies will lose disproportionately from excessive fluctuations of bilateral exchange rates or currency crises. Many proposals have been put on hold and we have examined the most significant ones in this paper. Currently, authorities in East Asian countries have no plans for establishing a monetary union; however, we believe that the CMI can provide a mechanism for policy dialogue and coordination in this field.

This paper has been structured into four parts. In the first section, we outline the potential external risks faced by Asian economies. The second section provides a review of the CMI and a proposal for the multilateralisation of the CMI. A road map is outlined with the aim of transforming the CMI into a regional common monetary arrangement. In the third section, we discuss several of the most popular proposals for exchange rate coordination in East Asia. Our discussion in this area focuses on how best to link the multilateralisation of the CMI with exchange rate coordination. The fourth and final section explores China's role in Asian monetary cooperation.

2. New External Risks and the Desirability of Enhancing Asian Monetary Cooperation

The lessons of the Asian financial crisis revealed that financial crises in this region can originate from two distinct sources. On the one hand, East Asian economies are vulnerable to external shocks such as changes in exchange rates and interest rates of major international currencies, fluctuations of international commodity prices and reversions in international short-term capital flow. On the other hand, East Asian economies are also plagued by undeveloped and fragile domestic financial systems and misalignments of their own exchange rates. Ideally, both the external vulnerability and internal fragility should be addressed simultaneously to avoid future crises, however, domestic reform potentially takes a great deal of time and may encounter political resistance. Regional monetary cooperation, however, can be effective not only in safeguarding against the contagion of financial crisis but also in fostering consensus among policy makers and stimulating domestic reforms in individual countries.

East Asian economies have traditionally adopted an export-led strategy which leads to a heavy dependence on external markets like the US. They are small economies in the sense that they are price-takers in the global market. Their currencies are not international currencies and because they cannot borrow and lend freely in their own currencies within international financial markets, they are plagued by the problem of 'currency mismatch' and 'maturity mismatch'. Most of the Asian economies have few natural resources such as crude oil, and therefore their economic growth is sensitive to price fluctuations in the international commodity markets. Typically, East Asian economies have already liberalised their capital account and financial sectors. This exposes them to both international short-term capital reversion and means that they can easily be attacked by speculative capital outflows. Furthermore, most Asian economies have comparatively small domestic markets which limit their maneuverability when facing external shocks. Often they find it difficult to offset these negative impacts by making adjustments within their domestic economies.

In the past 20 years, East Asia has accelerated its pace of trade integration. Intra-regional trade accounted for 55% of total trade values in 2003 compared to 34% in 1980. Although this ratio is still lower than that of the EU (62% in 2001), it is higher than that of the NAFTA countries (46% in 2001). In the past 20 years, the relaxation of financial regulations and liberalisation of capital accounts have promoted financial integration in East Asia. Regional integration not only ties the East Asian economies together more closely, but it also facilitates contagion through both trade and financial channels. East Asian economies are confronted with similar and synchronised external risks which have in turn increased potential benefits from collective action on building regional early-warning systems, policy coordination mechanisms and common exchange rate regimes.

2.1. New external risks

2.1.1. Global imbalance and the depreciation of the US Dollar

At a time when East Asian economies are building up large volumes of foreign exchange reserves, the U.S is accumulating a substantial current account deficit. In 2005, the current account deficit in the U.S reached an historic high of US$804.9 billion, up from US$668.1 billion in 2004. It is therefore necessary to substantially depreciate the US dollar in order to correct the imbalance in the US current account (Roubini and Setser, 2005; Blanchard, Giavazzi and Sa, 2005). However, this potential sharp decline in the value of the US dollar would have significant negative impacts on the Asian economy. The sudden depreciation of the dollar would reduce East Asian economies' dollar denominated foreign reserves and cause huge losses. At the same time, the majority of these economies are also burdened with Yen or Euro denominated debt, and the depreciation of the US Dollar to the Yen and Euro would exacerbate their debt burdens and may even lead to a debt crisis. After the Asian financial crisis, many East Asian economies adopted a *de facto* peg-to-dollar exchange rate regime (McKinnon and Schnabl, 2003). This arrangement puts Asian economies in a dilemma. If they stop pegging to the dollar, their currencies will appreciate, and their export competitive edge will be impaired. This would lead to a deterioration of their current account, or at worst to an international payment crisis. If these countries choose to continue pegging to the dollar, it may introduce speculative capital inflows, which are based on the hypothesis that the fixed exchange rate regime is unsustainable.

2.1.2. US interest rate hike and the reversion of international capital flows

Since June 2004, the US Federal Reserve has successively lifted its benchmark interest rate from 1% to 5% and it is quite possible that the Federal Open Market Committee (FOMC) will consider further increases. This ended a long period of extraordinarily low interest rates. We can see from Table 1 that the interest rates of the East Asian

Table 1. Correlation between the East Asian and U.S. Interest Rate

	Japan	China	South Korea	Indonesia	Malaysia	Thailand	Philippines	Singapore
US	0.599	0.826	0.445	0.431	0.377	0.385	0.847	0.731

Note: Interest rate used for the U.S. is the benchmark interest rate; Interest rates used for Asian countries (except China) are money market rates; Interest rate used for China is the interest rate on loans.
Source: IMF database, from 1998 to 2003.

economies are closely correlated with the US interest rate. Following this substantial increase in the US interest rate, East Asian countries face a difficult choice. A number of East Asian economies are concerned that a sudden increase in interest rates may slow an already tentative economic recovery, however, they are also aware that keeping their interest rates unchanged may dampen or even reverse capital inflows. More capital will flow to the US, which may cause short-term liquidity shortages.

2.1.3. A surge in the price of oil

Since 2002, international crude oil prices have been on the increase, rising from $24 per barrel in November 2002 to $70 per barrel in 2005. For oil-importing East Asian countries, oil price surges are an impending threat to their growth and to their macroeconomic stability. High oil prices negatively affect the profits of manufacturing enterprises and reduce the consumption of households in these countries. Oil price increases can also lead to cost-pull inflation. Asian economies have to pay more for their imports, which may reduce their current account surpluses or even cause current account deficits.

2.2. Asymmetry of external impacts on East Asian economies

Although East Asian economies have some common external risk exposure, the impact of these external risks on individual economies are not symmetric. The most fundamental reason for this lies in the significant differences between Japan, China and the ASEAN members in terms of their position in their business cycle and their economic structure. This is both bad news and good news for Asian monetary cooperation. On the one hand, it is evident that the countries of East Asia do not fulfill the standard criteria for optimal currency area. On the other hand, the asymmetric impact and responses associated with external risks implies East Asian economies are unlikely to suffer crises simultaneously. It would therefore be reasonable and desirable to expect certain countries to provide aid if and when other countries were hit by economic crisis.

We use a structured VAR method to analyse external impacts on East Asian economies[2]. We divide external impacts into demand impact and

Table 2. Correlation of External Demand Impacts between Asian Economies

	China	Japan	South Korea	Indonesia	Malaysia	Philippines	Singapore	Thailand
China	1.00							
Japan	0.04	1.00						
South Korea	0.38	0.19	1.00					
Indonesia	0.04	0.25	0.48	1.00				
Malaysia	0.00	0.28	0.10	0.40	1.00			
Philippines	0.18	0.25	-0.27	-0.03	-0.22	1.00		
Singapore	-0.05	-0.23	0.30	-0.14	-0.32	-0.31	1.00	
Thailand	0.18	0.09	-0.36	-0.32	-0.28	0.52	-0.38	1.00

Source: IMF database, from 1978 to 2002.

Table 3. Correlation of External Supply Impacts between Asian Economies

	China	Japan	South Korea	Indonesia	Malaysia	Philippines	Singapore	Thailand
China	1.00							
Japan	0.12	1.00						
South Korea	0.15	0.59	1.00					
Indonesia	-0.01	-0.42	-0.83	1.00				
Malaysia	0.03	0.45	0.64	-0.80	1.00			
Philippines	0.38	0.08	-0.08	0.19	-0.08	1.00		
Singapore	-0.26	0.34	0.50	-0.59	0.70	-0.32	1.00	
Thailand	0.25	0.19	0.16	0.15	0.08	-0.02	0.16	1.00

Source: IMF database, from 1978 to 2002.

---

[2] For more technical explanation please refer to the Appendix.

supply impact and analyse their different effects on production and price fluctuations.

From the above analysis we can derive the following conclusions:

(1) Nearly all countries involved show weak correlation on demand impact, which demonstrates that demand impact is asymmetric. The only exception is the Thailand-Philippines' correlation which is above 0.5. The reason for weak demand correlation is that economies in East Asia lack coordination in macroeconomic policy. In the Structured VAR model, the more they coordinate their macroeconomic policies, the higher the correlation;

(2) Supply impact correlation is generally higher than that of the demand impact; and

(3) China has both weak demand and supply impact correlation with the ASEAN members. This demonstrates that China could act as a stabiliser within the East Asian economy.

3. Exploring Ways to Enhance the Functions of the CMI

In May 2000, Finance Ministers from the ASEAN plus China, Japan and South Korea signed the Chiang Mai Initiative (CMI). The CMI has two components. Firstly, the expansion in numbers and volume of the ASEAN Swap Agreements (ASAs) and secondly the establishment of bilateral swap agreements between the ASEAN and China, Japan, and South Korea. At the annual meeting of the Asian Development Bank (ADB) in April 2004, finance ministers of ASEAN+3 agreed to undertake a further review of the CMI, which aimed to explore new ways to enhance its functions. A working group was created to conduct the review and this group presented a report on some of the major issues relating to the enlargement and consolidation of the CMI to the ASEAN+3 Finance Ministers' Meeting (AFMM+3) in May 2005 in Istanbul (ASEAN+3, 2005). The ASEAN+3 finance ministers approved its proposal to double the size of the existing bilateral swap arrangements

(BSAs) and enlarge the International Monetary Fund (IMF) non-linked portion from 10 percent to 20 percent.

Table 4. Bilateral Swap Agreements under the CMI (by April 2005)

BSA	Currencies	Size (US$, bn)	Total Size (US$, bn)
Japan-Korea	US$/Won (one way)	2.0	2.0
Japan-Thailand	US$/Baht (one way)	3.0	
Japan-Philippines	US$/Peso (one way)	3.0	3.0
Japan-Malaysia	US$/Ringgit (one way)	1.0	1.0
China-Thailand	US$/Baht (one way)	2.0	
Japan-China	Yen/RMB, RMB/Yen (two way)	3.0	6.0
China-Korea	RMB/Won, Won/RMB (two way)	2.0	4.0
Korea-Thailand	US$/Baht, US$/Won (two way)	1.0	2.0
Korea-Malaysia	US$/Ringgit, US$/Won (two way)	1.0	2.0
Korea-Philippines	US$/Peso, US$/Won (two way)	1.0	2.0
China-Malaysia	US$/Ringgit (one way)	1.5	1.5
Japan-Indonesia	US$/Rupiah (one way)	3.0	3.0
China-Philippines	Peso/RMB (one way)	1.0	1.0
Japan-Singapore	US$/SG$(one way)	1.0	1.0
Korea-Indonesia	US$/Rupiah, US$/Won(two way)	1.0	2.0
China-Indonesia	US$/Rupiah(one way)	1.0	1.0
Japan-Thailand	US$/Baht, US$/Yen (two way)	3.0	6.0

Source: ASEAN+3 (2005).

3.1. Inherent drawbacks of the CMI

However, the CMI still has some inherent drawbacks and without reform, it cannot provide a meaningful regional mechanism. All the CMI participating countries have now reached a consensus to enhance the effectiveness of the CMI. In this section, we will outline the frequently reported shortcomings of its current structure.

3.1.1. Lack of a central body

The CMI is composed of a set of bilateral swap agreements (BSAs) with a maximum amount that can be drawn under each BSA determined by each pair of contracting countries. There is no coordinating institution. Agreements have a great deal of flexibility and are tailor-made to suit each individual country's requirements. This arrangement is positive in that creditors have discretion over the activation of the swap. However, the individual decision-making and activation process brings about uncertainty for the swap receiving countries and induces the problem of free riding. It therefore discourages the swap providing countries from agreeing on the activation action. In order to address this problem the member countries decided to take the concrete step of initiating a change to its mechanisms. It agreed to transform current individual decision-making mechanisms into a collective one and the current individual activation of swaps into a joint activation process.

3.1.2. Shortage of available funds

The size of the CMI already exceeds other similar swap agreements such as the G10 ($38.4 billion), the European Monetary System (EMS) financing facilities and the North American Framework ($8.6 billion). However, the current maximum amount that can be provided is still a drop in the ocean compared with the size of global financial markets. It is also much smaller than the past financial rescue packages for the East Asian crisis-hit countries. Taking an example, imagine that in 2005 Thailand was struck by another financial crisis similar to that which occurred in 1997, and that other East Asian countries that had not been affected were willing to provide financial assistance. At this time Thailand had signed 3 currency-swap agreements with Japan, China and South Korea, with a total value of $6 billion. However, with 90% of the swap capital linked to IMF credit, Thailand could only achieve an immediate credit of $600 million. This is much smaller amount than the $17.2 billion credit that Thailand borrowed from the IMF in August 1997.

Member countries have agreed on an enhancement of up to a 100% increase of the existing BSAs (ASEAN+3, 2005). Transforming all the existing one-way swaps into two-way swaps would also enlarge the financing amount. All participating countries would have access to commonly shared resources. The advantage of increasing financing capacity can be enhanced if it can be supported by other reforms such as a prompt joint activation process and even a standardised single agreement for all BSAs. In addition to regional sources under the CMI, the huge accumulated volume of foreign exchange reserves is another resource for East Asian countries to draw upon when needed. Thus we should also think of alternative options beyond the CMI, such as earmarking or reserve pooling. In turn, these may result in more radical reform of the CMI.

3.1.3. Linkage with the IMF

The CMI previously allowed a 10% automatic draw in case of emergencies; however, the remaining 90% was linked with an IMF rescue plan. This practice helps to safeguard the funding provided by IMF member countries. The conditionality of the IMF funding is to encourage macroeconomic stability and structural reform, and to discourage negative outcomes that may be associated with moral hazard. However, this linkage reduced the extent of the available funding and the conditions imposed by the IMF were not always able to be flexibly adapted to local circumstances. In 2005, member countries agreed to significantly enlarge the available portion of funds not linked to the IMF from 10 percent to 20 percent. However, until the ASEAN+3 countries have their own regional independent and credible economic surveillance mechanism, this linkage of BSAs' activation to the IMF has to be maintained.

3.2. A road map for CMI multilateralisation

Most member countries agree on the desirability of enhancing and consolidating the CMI within a regional financial institution. However, no individual country is currently prepared to give up autonomy over its domestic policy-making. This collective-action dilemma impedes real progress in regional monetary cooperation and may eventually lead to members becoming frustrated and disappointed. To ensure that this does not happen, a road map is required to show future goals, as well as a feasible path to achieve these goals.

Learning from experience, we have to bear in mind that successful institutions are seldom the product of a grand design, but rather the result of endless bargaining, compromise, and accommodation. Perhaps the most realistic scenario for the development of Asian monetary cooperation is that member countries will continue to exchange information, discuss the modalities, propose new plans while gradually building a consensus. A road map, however, can give a sense of direction and provide greater assurance in the process.

3.2.1. The first step

Currently, individual swap providing countries have the right to opt-out of the BSA activation process. Therefore there is no guarantee that the BSAs will be activated. What is needed is to transform the individual decision-making and individual activation processes into a collective format. At the Istanbul meeting, the financial ministers of ASEAN+3 agreed to adopt in principle a collective decision making mechanism, but the operational details have yet to be worked out. Another process that needs to be established at this stage is the creation of an informal coordination meeting (C/M), to implement the activation process and surveillance system. This group would act as the virtual surveillance body and would consist of experts both from within the region and outside the region. Their remit would be to follow trends in the world and regional economy and to identify the potential external risks to each of its members. They would also provide up-to-date reports and work on specific rescue projects with the C/M or the secretariat. It is essential that the CMI develop a robust early warning capability and in effect this proposed monitoring system would identify sources of instability and determine whether the instability is exogenous or internally generated. It also needs to distinguish between short-term portfolio capital flows and long-term capital flows. To help the group of experts monitoring short-term capital movements, a legal framework of capital markets registration and reporting should be established. For example, it may involve the imposition of limitations on residents' holding of financial assets and liabilities denominated in foreign currencies, and non-residents' holding of similar instruments denominated in local currencies.

At this stage of development, financial schemes under the CMI can either remain unchanged or increased by expanding the BSAs. Another suggestion is to earmark a certain percentage of each country's reserves as an additional resource to support the CMI. For this plan to be successful, the pool needs to at least exceed the current CMI size. For example, it may require the region to put aside 5% of the total accumulated foreign exchange reserves. To achieve credibility for using this pooling reserve, the scale of drawing down from this pool could be linked to a country's exchange rate movement against the newly created synthetic Asian Currency Unit (ACU). If a country's exchange rate deviates from the ACU beyond a certain band, then it signals a country's poor performance in maintaining macroeconomic stability, and as a consequence its right to borrow money from this pool could be automatically restrained. This mechanism is desirable because it allows flexibility in an individual country's choice of exchange rate regime and at the same time creates a set of incentives to enhance exchange rate cooperation.

3.2.2. The second step

At this stage, a collective decision-making process and a prompt activation process would have been implemented. Linkage to the IMF would remain an issue; however, this may be changed if all the participating countries see it as appropriate. The group of experts would now be transformed to a permanent surveillance unit and a central body called either the Secretariat or the Committee, would be established. The functions of this central body would include: organising and supervising a 10+3 monitoring unit; responsibility for the disbursement of the fund and setting up the terms and conditions for the swaps; and performing secretariat functions for policy dialogue and coordination amongst the members. Although this central body would not have the same formal institutions as could be found within a regional monetary fund, a number of operational details would need to be discussed at this stage. It is necessary to decide, for example, who should be responsible for setting the agenda, the details of the voting rules and the impact of one country holding the majority voting weight or veto.

To move on from joint decision making and joint activation mechanisms, the next step forward should be to create an umbrella organisation to both shift one-way swaps into two-way swaps and to nest all the two-way swaps and ASA. Bilateral agreements would still exist; however, they would have to abide by a set of common rules. This implies that there would be an agreement containing binding rules which would govern all the lower level agreements. Another more aggressive proposal is the standard contract which means all agreements should be subject to a uniformed format which ensures that no country can apply for an exception or an opt-out.

3.2.3. The third step

At this stage, the emphasis on Asian monetary cooperation would be guided by a greater degree of policy coordination and institutional building. The CMI's function as liquidity provider would already have been greatly enhanced and more importantly, a well functioning early warning system would be working efficiently thereby averting the potential danger of another currency crisis.

With a growth in mutual understanding and co-operation, member countries would by now have worked out the organisational structure, the location, and the voting rules of the central body. The establishment of this central body would now makes it realistic to forge all the components of Asian monetary cooperation, for example a surveillance system, a lender of last resort, exchange rate coordination, and a regional bond market.

The linkage to the IMF would be substantially reduced or even de-linked completely. The institutionalisation of Asian monetary cooperation would also have a significant impact on the reform of international financial architecture. The progress of Asian monetary co-operation is to some extent the result of the limited and slow reform of the international financial system. Due to the previously mentioned potential external risks Asian economies are facing, they will remain in a vulnerable situation. Having lost patience waiting for the G-7 to reform the current Bretton Woods institutions, Asian countries would take the initiative to work together and build their own defence mechanism. A fortified Asian monetary union may force the G-7 to launch serious reform of their international financial architecture. Ironically, given that most Asian economies are in favour of multilateral integration, if there can be real progress on the reform of the international financial system, enthusiasm among Asian economies toward regional integration may be reduced.

4. Sequencing of East Asian Exchange Rate Coordination

Since the Asian financial crisis, exchange rate coordination has become a hotly debated topic. Without exchange rate coordination, the region will continue to be vulnerable to further contagion simply by the correlated nature of both capital flows and structural shocks. Contagion exacerbates liquidity risk because it complicates the timing (herd-like flows) and magnifies the volume needed to stem the parallel action of market traders. On the other hand, exchange rate stability could bring potential benefits for inter-regional trade and investment. Following the CMI, exchange rate co-ordination should be put on the agenda of Asian monetary cooperation. This section will review several of the most significant proposals on Asian exchange rate coordination and explain why they have failed to materialise. The sequencing of exchange rate co-ordination is missing in all these proposals. In other words, a blueprint without a manual for operation is meaningless for practitioners.

There have been several proposals on East Asian exchange rate coordination mechanisms. Williamson (1999), Ogawa and Ito (2000), Kawai and Takagi (2001) suggest that East Asia countries should peg to a G-3 currency common basket. Wyplosz (2002) propose that an Asia Exchange Rate Mechanism may be the most feasible option for East Asia exchange rate coordination while Dornbush and Park (1999) and Kwan (2001) advocate a "Yen Bloc" in East Asia. McKinnon (2002) believes that a "Dollar Zone" is still the most reasonable and feasible solution. It should be noted that the economic structures of individual Asian countries differ significantly, and as such different countries have different attitudes towards each of these proposals. Some countries may be ready for a close exchange rate coordination arrangement in East Asia, such as a common basket peg, while others need more time to prepare. Currently there is no exchange rate coordination scheme that is acceptable to all economies

4.1. Common basket peg

The main features of a common basket peg include[3]: targeting a common basket of currencies (US Dollar, Japanese Yen and the European Union Euro); attaching a common set of weights to these currencies based on regional (rather than country) trade share implying that both explicit and implicit idiosyncratic trade-based weights currently used need to be removed; the pledging by each participating member to maintain a central parity vis-à-vis the basket and to keep within this unilaterally chosen band; allowing a range of formal exchange rate regimes such as the currency boarding in Hong Kong or the fixed parity in China and Malaysia or various types of managed floating in Korea and Singapore; adopting McKinnon's "restoration rule" which states that national authorities, when confronted with speculative attack, be allowed temporarily to suspend the peg on the provision that a pledge to return to the original arrangement is credibly made; since changes in economic fundamentals and basket currency misalignment are a fact of life, member countries may allow central parity and the band to crawl as a response to these fundamental changes; safeguarding member currencies under attach from speculators, with financing arrangement analogous to the European VSTFF (Very Short Term Financing Facility).

There are a number of benefits of a common currency basket. Firstly, there would be a reduction in the intra-regional nominal effective

---

[3] The features of different schemes are summarised by Fabella (2002).

exchange volatility. Compared to the existing peg-to-dollar system, incorporating Japanese Yen and the Euro into the peg could help East Asia economies keep more stable bilateral nominal exchange rates between Japan and the Euro region. This will help to stabilise East Asian economies' intra-regional exchange rate (by pegging the Yen) and even their nominal and real effective exchange rates (by pegging both the Yen and Euro). All those improvements will help to promote intra-regional trade and macroeconomic stability in East Asia. Secondly, the mechanism does not have binding rules for policy coordination and surveillance (Kawai and Takagi, 2001). All participants in a common basket peg regime could keep their existing exchange rate regime; only changing their US dollar peg to G-3 currency peg.

Although a common basket peg scheme has a number of advantages, it is not infallible. Firstly, a common basket peg scheme could bring significant exchange risks and transaction costs to those East Asia economies that do not already have developed bond markets and forward foreign exchange markets. Under the dollar peg exchange rate regime, merchants and investors do not need to worry about exchange rate risk because most of their trade is invoiced in US dollars and most of their foreign assets are also US dollar denominated assets. Once their currency is pegged to the US dollar, the exchange rate risk between local currency and the US dollar is also hedged by their monetary authority. By credibly pegging to the US dollar, the monetary authority in East Asia economies optimally reduce the exchange rate risks that may occur in the international economic arena. When East Asian economies switch from a US dollar peg to a common basket peg, it means that the bilateral nominal exchange rate between local currencies and the US dollar will be adjusted with high frequency. If there is support from the foreign exchange markets to hedge the exchange rate risks, this will not be a problem. However, due to under-development of domestic financial markets, many East Asian economies do not have a well functioning foreign exchange market. Excessive fluctuations between the US dollar and local currencies will bring merchants and investors unbearable exchange rate risks and transaction costs.

Secondly, a common basket peg scheme cannot survive without the strong commitment of member countries and an efficient institutional framework. To implement a common peg, member countries must be ready to protect the peg at the expense of national sovereignty. Moreover, when a weak currency is under speculation, there must be an efficient institutional framework to facilitate policy coordination among member countries and to provide unlimited financial help.

Thirdly, the choosing of a common set of weights is also questionable. A common basket for all member countries neglects the fact that different economies have different trade structures. If a member country trades mostly with the United States, a common basket peg cannot stabilise its nominal effective exchange rate (NEER). Moreover, even if all East Asian economies had similar trade structures, a simple trade-weighted basket is also controversial. Theoretically, under different policy objectives, there should be a different calculation of weights for each currency in the basket. If the policy objective is to minimise the fluctuation of trade balance, a simple trade-weighted basket is suitable. If there are two or even more policy objectives, such as minimising the fluctuation of domestic price or foreign debt, the weight for each currency in the basket will be quite different.

4.2. East Asia Exchange Rate Mechanism

An East Asian Exchange Rate Mechanism may appeal to many policymakers because of the successful precedent of the European Monetary System (EMS). The main features of an East Asian Exchange Rate Mechanism would include an Asia Currency Unit (ACU) designed on the same principle as the European Currency Unit under EMS. ACU would be a basket of East Asia member country currencies, which would serve as a single basket currency target with the weights assigned to each country equivalent to the trade share of the country as a proportion of the total trade of the region. The exchange rates of member countries would float within a band of 15 percent plus or minus the central parity in a similar way to the post-1993 "soft" EMS, where the central parities are not unilaterally determined and there would be a lender of last resort in the form of a quick disbursing loan facility akin to the EMS 'Very Short Term Financing Facility' to weather speculative attacks. An authority, the Asian Monetary Institute, which would be similar to the European Monetary Institute, would approve the central parity and which would also manage the East Asia Exchange Rate Mechanism and implement agreed coordination and surveillance policies. Finally, the target zone exchange rate regime would be obligatory for each country.

There would be benefits from the implementation of the East Asia Exchange Rate Mechanism. There would be a greater degree of co-movement of the regional intra-exchange rate, and therefore more stable nominal effective exchange rate within the region. Wyplosz (2002) shows that an Asian Monetary System would be as effective as pegging to a common basket in stabilising the bilateral exchange rate of the regional currencies.

In addition, an East Asia Exchange Rate Mechanism would increase the influence of the Yen, the RMB, and other major currencies within the region. The main difference between a common basket peg scheme and an East Asia Exchange Rate Mechanism is that the former pegs to the US dollar, the Euro and the Yen while the later pegs to regional currencies. To keep the peg, East Asia economies would tend to hold more regional currencies, such as the Yen or the RMB or other major currencies in the region. The increased use of local currencies would also help the development of regional currency denominated bond markets. Finally, an East Asia Exchange Rate Mechanism could reduce the possibility of beggar-thy-neighbor devaluation and would strengthen East Asia's voice in international finance arena.

An East Asia Exchange Rate Mechanism also has its defects. Similar to a common basket peg scheme, an East Asia Exchange Rate Mechanism would bring higher frequency fluctuations between local currencies and the US dollar, thereby creating unbearable exchange risks for those economies that do not possess developed financial markets. On the one hand, an East Asia Exchange Rate Mechanism could not reflect the changes in the alignment between major currencies, such as fluctuations between the US dollar and the Euro and on the other hand, it is highly likely that it would be prone to currency crises especially when demand and supply shocks were asymmetric. The experience of EMS shows that weaker currencies in the system are always vulnerable to currency speculation. In addition an East Asia Exchange Rate Mechanism needs strong political commitment and the support of institutional arrangements. Without a widely accepted political consensus and strong commitment, it would be impossible for member countries to sacrifice national sovereignty to defend the ACU. Moreover, an East Asia Exchange Rate Mechanism would rely on institutional arrangements to provide unlimited financial help to those weaker currencies under speculation.

4.3. Yen Bloc and Dollar Zone

The main feature of Yen Bloc is that East Asia economies would target the Japanese Yen as a nominal anchor. The main feature of the Dollar Zone is that East Asia economies would target the US dollar as a nominal anchor. Since the US dollar is already an important nominal anchor for most East Asian economies, with the exception of Japan, the Dollar Zone proposal requires that Japan keep a more stable bilateral exchange rate with the United States.

If the Yen Bloc scheme were to be adopted in East Asia, the main advantages are as follows. Firstly, given that Japan is the main capital and technology supplier for other East Asia economies, a Yen Bloc would increase Japanese investment in this region, thereby enhancing the technology transfer from Japan to other Asian economies. However, the actual benefits of a Yen Bloc depend on the reliability of the Japanese Yen as a nominal anchor. The desirability of a Yen Bloc is dependent on the performance of the Japanese economy and the stability of the overall price level in Japan. If the Dollar Zone scheme were to be adopted in East Asia, the main benefits are twofold. First, due to the prevalence of the use of US dollar in East Asia and the rest of the world, a Dollar Zone would be helpful in reducing the region's exchange rate risks as a whole. When East Asian economies trade with the US or other economies that use the dollar as their main trading currency, exchange rate risk can be ruled out. Even when East Asian economies trade with the Euro area or other economies that use the Euro as their main trading currency, the exchange rate could also be easily hedged through forward foreign exchange markets. Secondly, the US economy has performed very well in the last ten years, with overall stable price levels. Therefore, the US dollar could be seen as a reliable nominal anchor for the East Asia economies.

There are potentially two main costs associated with adoption of the Yen Bloc. Firstly, any fluctuation between the Yen and other world major currencies could destabilise the competitiveness of the East Asia economies. If the Yen were to appreciate against the US dollar, other economies would lose their competitiveness. If those economies in the Yen Bloc compete heavily with Japan in a third market, the negative effects would be less than would otherwise be the case because both Japan and those economies' prices would all rise in the third market. If the economies in Yen Bloc compete heavily with economies in the Dollar Bloc in the third market, the negative effects will be much more significant. Secondly, for those economies that do not own developed forward foreign exchange markets, switching from a US dollar peg to the Yen Bloc will bring unbearable exchange rate risks and transaction costs in the transitional period.

In the Dollar Zone, the main costs are that the fluctuation between US dollar and other world major currencies will destabilise the competitiveness of East Asia economies. The mechanism is similar to that of Yen Bloc.

4.4. A timeframe for East Asia exchange rate coordination

However attractive the two options outlined above may seem, neither of these coordination schemes has won the approval of all member countries. Certain countries, such as Japan, prefer a common basket peg, while other countries, such as China, cannot afford to accept either of these options in the near future[4]. If major participants cannot agree on a solution, exchange rate coordination may not see any meaningful progress.

Different countries need to be given more autonomy over their own involvement. They should be permitted to participate when they feel confident and comfortable with the circumstances. If simultaneous policy change by all member countries is impossible, then it is necessary to seek the sub-optimal choice of progressing step by step. We believe the timeframe towards Asian exchange rate coordination is very important and should allow Asian economies to start from a very limited consensus and proceed in a gradual way. A formal and obligatory exchange rate coordination scheme can only be introduced when the majority of potential participants are prepared for it.

To promote Asian exchange rate coordination, we have considered the following steps. First, facing common external risks may help to foster friendship and coalition. Current risks include a growing trade imbalance between the U.S and East Asia; increasing pressure from US politicians for an appreciation of Asian currencies (mainly the RMB and Yen); and an increasing foreign exchange reserve. Asian economies need to work out a common policy to deal with these risks at the same time as avoiding non-cooperative action that may jeopordise regional coordination. If member countries need to revalue their currencies, it is better to undertake this in a cooperative way. Thus the burden for individual countries can be substantially reduced.

Secondly, we suggest that a joint announcement should be made by all member countries stating that regional exchange rate stability is regarded

---

[4] There are at least three considerations in the adjustment of RMB exchange rate: stable bilateral nominal exchange rate between RMB and US dollar; comparatively stable nominal effective exchange rate (NEER); and moving toward fundamental equilibrium exchange rate(FEER). A common basket may help in stabilising RMB's NEER, but this is not the only target. Without the support of sophisticated foreign exchange market, a stable bilateral nominal exchange rate between RMB and US dollar is more important than a stable NEER.

as a key policy objective. In addition, Japan should be encouraged to maintain a more stable exchange rate between the Yen and the US Dollar, while other Asian countries should be encouraged to maintain more stable exchange rates between their own currencies and the US Dollar and the Yen. These policy adjustments, if made by individual countries in a joint way, could help to manage intra-regional exchange rate stability.

Thirdly, member countries should cooperate with each other to reform their domestic financial systems, at the same time as working towards enhancing intra-regional financial integration arrangements. This may include: developing domestic and regional bond markets; introducing an intra-regional banking sector supervision system; establishing an intra-regional capital flow monitoring system, and setting up a regional infrastructure (settlement, clearance and depository, etc) to encourage the use of local currencies. These arrangements are fundamental to further monetary integration in East Asia. In addition, these arrangements would reduce the potential switch costs to any country entering into a new exchange rate regime.

5. China's Role in Asian Monetary Cooperation

China has emerged as a key player in both the international and regional arenas. China has become a formal member of all the important multilateral organisations, and has, since the mid 1990s played a positive role in regional economic cooperation while expanding the number and depth of its bilateral relationships.

Worried about the slow progress on international financial reform and troubled multilateral trade negotiations, China has become more and more interested in regional economic cooperation. This change also reflects the existence of broader economic ties amongst China and East Asia. China's strategy can be seen quite clearly from the fact that it courted ASEAN for a free trade agreement and in November 2001 joined the Bangkok agreement on a free trade area that includes Korea and other South Asian countries (Bangladesh, India, Laos and Sri Lanka). In the

China-ASEAN FTA negotiation, China took the unprecedented step of including an 'early harvest' programme which offered ASEAN early access to its agriculture sector. This is in sharp contrast to Japan's insistence on protecting its own agriculture sector. Looking to the future, we expect to see more intra-industry trade in East Asia, and China will increase its imports from and investment to neighboring economies. From bilateral FTAs, China should move a step forward and encourage the formation of a region-wide free trade area.

The potential benefits to China from Asian monetary cooperation are difficult to comprehend, especially when Asian monetary cooperation still remains principally a liquidity providing function. If China undergoes a financial crisis, it is unlikely that either a financial support package from the CMI, or a loan from the IMF would be of any help. Despite the fact that China still has a fragile financial system, the prediction that China will encounter a financial crisis has always been proven wrong. The fast growing economy and the potentially huge domestic market makes China fairly resilient and thus far China has shown no ambitions of becoming an international or even a regional centre. China still maintains capital control as a "China Wall" to offset external shocks and while China's current account has been liberalised there is no timetable for a rapid liberalisation of its capital account. Although China is growing rapidly, it still has a huge gap in terms of industrial and financial sophistication *vis-à-vis* Japan.

Leadership in Asian monetary cooperation is a crucial issue. Both China and Japan play very important roles but neither country can fulfill the leadership role alone. Other countries will be suspicious of and unwilling to join any regional financial arrangement in which only one of these two regional powers takes the lead. China alone cannot be the leader because the RMB is not convertible, and at the same time cannot provide a commitment to finance the balance of payments deficits of all ASEAN member states. Japan is the largest contributor to Asian monetary cooperation but it has disputes on historical claims with many neighboring countries and its strategy toward Asian economic cooperation is often seen to be inconsistent.

The key to the success of Asian monetary cooperation depends on the relationship between Japan and China. As Sakakibara (2003) argued: "It is essential for Japan-China cooperation, as a core in East Asia, to lead the process of economic and financial integration, as the France-Germany alliance played a central role in the integration and cooperation process in Europe." China and Japan share some common interests on Asian monetary cooperation. Both countries contribute a great deal to the CMI, however, only an efficient surveillance system would make these two countries confident with their financial input and willing to increase financial assistance. There are further difficulties in the two countries working together. Not only are there unsettled historical issues, but more practically, China may have concerns that that Japan, as the largest contributor, would have de facto control over Asian monetary cooperation.

What should China's strategy be toward the multilateralisation of the CMI? Generally speaking, Asian monetary cooperation can ensure financial stability in the East Asian region, creating a positive environment for China's economic development while facilitating China's trade and investment with neighboring countries. It may also help to increase China's influence on international financial issues. The benefits are certainly great, while the costs to China are manageable. It is important that China maintains certain controlling rights, especially the right to veto those bills conflicting with China's own interests. It is also essential that the cost of multilateralisation and institutionalisation of the CMI be reduced to the lowest levels. Furthermore during the polling process, China could strengthen its cooperation with other countries by collectively objecting to those bills that might injure mutual interests.

References

1. ASEAN+3, *Report of the Review of the Chiang Mai Initiative: Ways of Enhancing Its Effectiveness*, ASEAN+3 Finance Ministers Meeting, 4 May, Istanbul, Turkey (2005).
2. Blanchard, O., F. Giavazzi and F. Sa, "The U.S. Current Account and the Dollar", mimeo, (MIT, Massachusetts, 2005).

3. Dornbusch, R. and Y. C. Park, "Flexibility or Nominal Anchors?" in S. Collignon, J. Pisani-Ferry and Y.C. Park, eds., *Exchange Rate Policies in Emerging Asian Economies*, (Routledge, New York, 1999).
4. Fabella, R., "Monetary Cooperation in East Asia: A Survey", ERD Working Paper No.13, (Economics and Research Department, 2002).
5. Kawai, M., "Regional Economic Integration and Cooperation in East Asia", paper presented to the experts, Seminar on the Impact and Coherence of OECD Country Policies on Asian Developing Economies, (Policy Research Institute of the Japanese Ministry of Finance and the OECD Secretariat, Paris, 2004).
6. Kawai, M. and S. Takagi, "Proposed Strategy for a Regional Exchange Rate Arrangement in Post-crisis East Asia", World Bank Working Paper, (World Bank, Washington, 2001).
7. Kwan, C. H., *Yen Bloc*, (Brookings Institution Press, 2001).
8. McKinnon, R., "The East Asian Exchange Rate Dilemma and the World Dollar Standard", (Asian Development Bank, 2001).
9. McKinnon, R. and G. Schnabl, "The East Asian Dollar Standard, Fear of Floating, and Original Sin", (2004).
10. Ogawa, E. and T. Ito, "On the Desirability of A Regional Basket Currency Arrangement", NBER Working Paper 8002, (National Bureau of Economic Research, Washington, 2000).
11. Park, Y. C., "Whither Regional Financial and Monetary Integration in East Asia?", paper presented at the Conference on East Asian Economic Integration: Reality and Vision, (Seoul, 2005).
12. Roubini, N. and B. Setser, "Will the Bretton Woods 2 regime unravel soon? The risk of a hard landing in 2005-2006", mimeo, (New York University, New York, 2005).
13. Sakakibara, E., "Asian Cooperation and the End of Pax Americana", in J. J. Teunissen and M. Teunissen, eds., *Financial Stability and Growth in Emerging Economies: The Role of the Financial Sector*, (FONDAD, The Hague, 2003).
14. Sangsubhan, K., "Exploring Ways to Enhance the Functions of the CMI in the Medium Term", (ASEAN, 2005).
15. Williamson, O., "The Case for a Common Basket Peg for East Asian Currencies", in S. Collignon, J. Pisani-Ferry and Y. C. Park, eds., *Exchange Rate Policies in Emerging Asian Countries*, (Routledge, New York, 1999).
16. Wyplosz, C., "Regional Exchange Rate Arrangements: Lessons from Europe for East Asia", in Asian Development Bank, ed., *Monetary and Financial Integration in East Asia: The Way Ahead*, Volume 2, (Palgrave Macmillan, 2004).

Appendix: The Structured VAR to Analyse the Symmetry of Macro Impact

According to the basic idea of

VAR $X(t) = B_1 X_{t-1} + B_2 X_{t-2} + \cdots + B_n X_{t-n} + e_t$, we establish a structured VAR model which includes two endogenous variables – the output fluctuation y(t) and the price fluctuation p(t) to represent the dynamic economic system. The y(t) and p(t) variables can be illustrated as the unlimited summation of supply impacts and demand impacts:

$$\begin{bmatrix} y(t) \\ p(t) \end{bmatrix} = \sum_{i=0}^{\infty} L_i \begin{pmatrix} a_{11i} & a_{12i} \\ a_{21i} & a_{22i} \end{pmatrix} \begin{bmatrix} \varepsilon d(t) \\ \varepsilon s(t) \end{bmatrix}$$

L is the lagged operator while the $\varepsilon d(t)$ and $\varepsilon s(t)$ are the demand impact and supply impact respectively. In the above model, y(t) and p(t) are both stationary stochastic process; $\varepsilon s(t)$ and $\varepsilon d(t)$ are white noises, which are vertical vectors and their covariance is 0. The structured VAR model introduces the interactions and feedback interactions between variables. Although $\varepsilon s(t)$ and $\varepsilon d(t)$ are stochastic impacts which could only influence y(t) and p(t) respectively, however, the influence which $\varepsilon s(t)$ applies on y(t) could be transmitted to p(t). On the other hand, $\varepsilon d(t)$ could also indirectly influence on y(t). The interaction of two impacts demonstrates the two-way and feedback relationship of variables' actions.

We could illustrate the n period lagged VAR as the unlimited moving average process of residuals:

$$\begin{bmatrix} y(t) \\ p(t) \end{bmatrix} = e_t + D_1 e_{t-1} + D_2 e_{t-2} + \cdots ,$$

$$e_t = \begin{bmatrix} e_{yt} \\ e_{pt} \end{bmatrix} e_t = \begin{bmatrix} e_{yt} \\ e_{pt} \end{bmatrix}$$ is the residual of VAR process. The relationship

between this residual and the impact of the structured formula is $e_t = C\varepsilon_t$, which is also the relationship between supply and demand. Therefore, so long as we estimate the transformation matrix $C = \begin{pmatrix} c_{11} & c_{12} \\ c_{21} & c_{22} \end{pmatrix}$, we could find the $\varepsilon d(t)$ and $\varepsilon s(t)$.

In order to get C, we should apply some constraint qualifications: (1) the covariance matrix of $\varepsilon_d(t)$ and $\varepsilon_s(t)$ are standardised, i.e. all their variances equal to 1; (2) $\varepsilon_d(t)$ and $\varepsilon_s(t)$ are vertical vectors, which means their covariance is 0; (3) the demand impact do not have long-term influence over output.

From (1) and (2) we know:

$\Sigma_e = C \times \Sigma_\varepsilon \times C^T = C \times C^T$, included Σ_e is the covariance matrix of $e_y(t)$ and $e_p(t)$, and $\Sigma_\varepsilon = I$ is the covariance matrix of $\varepsilon_d(t)$ and $\varepsilon_s(t)$.

According to macroeconomic theory, the positive demand impact will increase output in the short term. However, in the long term, the output will revert to the long-term trend. Therefore, we could assume that the demand impact do not have influence over output in the long term, so the $\sum_{i=0}^{\infty} a_{11i}$ in (2) equals to 0, which is exactly the long-term constraint introduced by Blanchard and Quah (1989).

Because

$$X(t) = e(t) + D_1 e(t-1) + D_2 e(t-2) + \ldots$$
$$= [I - B(L)]^{-1} e(t)$$

$$= \sum_{i=0}^{\infty} D_i e(t)$$

$$= \sum_{i=0}^{\infty} D_i C \varepsilon(t)$$

$$= \sum_{i=0}^{\infty} L_i A_i \varepsilon(t)$$

Therefore: $\displaystyle\sum_{i=0}^{\infty} D_i = \sum_{i=0}^{\infty} A_i$, i.e.

$$\sum_{i=0}^{\infty} \begin{pmatrix} d_{11i} & d_{12i} \\ d_{21i} & d_{22i} \end{pmatrix} \begin{pmatrix} c_{11} & c_{12} \\ c_{21} & c_{22} \end{pmatrix} = \begin{pmatrix} 0 & . \\ . & . \end{pmatrix}$$

$$\sum_{i=0}^{\infty} (d_{11i}c_{11} + d_{12i}c_{12}) = 0$$

As in the equilibrium,

$$X(t) = X(t-1)$$

In this point

$$\sum_{i=0}^{\infty} D_i = [I - B(L)]^{-1} = (I - B_1 - B_2 - \cdots B_n)^{-1},$$

So we could get $\sum D_i$ according to the above formula, then we could achieve the transformation matrix C. Therefore, we could estimate the supply impact vector and demand impact vector though the residuals in the simplified VAR model, then we could analyse their correlation.

When we calculate the transformation matrix, we get the following 4 formulae:

$$d_{11} \cdot C_{11} + d_{12} \cdot C_{21} = 0$$
$$C_{11}^2 + C_{12}^2 = \Sigma_{11}$$
$$C_{11} C_{21} + C_{12} C_{22} = \Sigma_{12}$$
$$C_{21}^2 + C_{22}^2 = \Sigma_{22}$$

Included Σ represents the covariance matrix

$$\Sigma = \begin{bmatrix} \mathrm{var}(e_y(t)) & \mathrm{cov}(e_y(t), e_p(t)) \\ \mathrm{cov}(e_y(t), e_p(t)) & \mathrm{var}(e_p(t)) \end{bmatrix}$$

After the calculation, we get the following formula:

$$\left[\frac{\Sigma_{12} + \dfrac{d_{12}}{d_{11}} \Sigma_{22}}{C_{22}} \right]^2 - 2\left[\frac{d_{12}}{d_{11}} \Sigma_{12} + \left(\frac{d_{12}}{d_{11}} \right)^2 \Sigma_{22} \right] = \Sigma_{11} - \frac{\Sigma_{22}}{\left(\dfrac{d_{11}}{d_{12}} \right)^2}$$

Then we get the following formula:

$$C_{22} = -\sqrt{\frac{A_3}{A_1 + A_2}}$$

Included A_1, A_2, A_3 are simplified parameters. Also

$$C_{12} = \frac{(\Sigma_{12} + \dfrac{d_{12}}{d_{11}} \Sigma_{22}) - \dfrac{d_{12}}{d_{11}} C_{22}^2}{C_{22}}$$

$$C_{21} = \sqrt{\Sigma_{22} - C_{22}^2}$$

And because

$$
\begin{bmatrix} e_y(t) \\ e_p(t) \end{bmatrix} = C^{2\times 2} \bullet \begin{bmatrix} \varepsilon_d(t) \\ \varepsilon_s(t) \end{bmatrix},
$$

We get

$$
\begin{bmatrix} \varepsilon_d(t) \\ \varepsilon_s(t) \end{bmatrix} = C^{-1} \bullet \begin{bmatrix} e_y(t) \\ e_p(t) \end{bmatrix}.
$$

PART III

CONCLUSIONS AND IMPLICATIONS

CHAPTER 10

CHINA'S ECONOMIC REFORMS IN THE GLOBALISATION ERA

Justin Yifu Lin*, Yang Yao* & Linda Yueh**[1]

*China Center for Economic Research, Beijing University

**Pembroke College, University of Oxford, and the Centre for Economic Performance, London School of Economics and Political Science

Abstract: This paper assesses China's economic reforms in the context of globalisation. We argue that the economic reforms undertaken in China must be consistent with its gradualist approach to transition, and that given its status as a developing country, a slower pace of liberalisation is required. We analyse the effects of globalisation on major aspects of economic reforms in China, such as on trade and financial liberalisation, and on privatisation. The Chinese exchange rate is then presented as a primary example for understanding the interplay of globalisation and economic reforms. This is followed by an analysis of China's wider economic impact, where we reflect on the ways in which China's growth has affected both the global economy and the globalisation process in other countries. We conclude that China has been affected by, and benefited from, globalisation and that this process has changed the global economy in terms of trade, capital flows, global commodities markets, and influenced global incremental growth. We also find that given China's wider impact, its slower pace of reform will likely come under increasing scrutiny. Globalisation, though beneficial, is another factor that will challenge the pace of China's preferred gradual approach to economic growth.

---

[1] We wish to thank Peihe Bao for his research assistance.

1. China's Approach to Reforms

The past 27 years has seen China achieve a remarkable rate of economic growth standing at over 9% per annum. This growth has been fuelled both by domestic reforms that have instilled market-oriented incentives and by external reforms, which have gradually opened up the economy. Its external reforms have been characterised by China's "open door" policy, which started in 1979 with market-oriented reforms, sped up in the early 1990s, and culminated in accession to the World Trade Organisation (WTO) in 2001. With WTO membership, China has joined the world's trading club, which accounts for 95% of global trade.

We argue that opening to the global economy offers potential benefits for China, but globalisation also poses challenges to China's reform path. Opening allows China to increasingly utilise exports as a source of GDP growth, allowing more time to reorient away from investment and toward aggregate consumption. WTO membership also makes China a member of an international rules-based organisation where trade is governed and disputes can be resolved by reference to agreed articles. The anticipated opening of China's markets under the WTO timeline also generates a pace of reform that can be followed and anticipated by foreign investors. Recent years of rapidly growing foreign direct investment (FDI) in the vicinity of $50-60 billion per annum are examples.

The same opening, however, brings about challenges to China's reform path. Although opening is paced, the speed at which China has adopted agreed reforms has been challenged. The trade disputes between China and the EU, U.S., as well as the valuation of the Chinese currency (RMB) are some examples. Moreover, WTO obligations reach not only the external sector, but also internal reforms, such as the opening of banking and services sector. Using banking as an example, China has agreed to open the sector to foreign banks to transact in RMB business at the end of 2006. The banking sector in China, though, is not simply underdeveloped, it is also plagued with legacy issues from central planning, namely, non-performing loans due to decades of policy-directed lending. Reform of the sector is multi-faceted, involving making them independent, profit-oriented, and redefining the relationship of state-owned enterprises to the state and the banks. This will further involve resolving the multiple objectives of state-owned entities in providing social securities and helping the government fulfil the objective of full employment (Bai *et al.*, 2000). Privatisation of the state-owned enterprises in China is therefore an area where the potential challenges of opening can be felt. Finally, one of the most worrying risks from globalisation is the possibility of an external currency/financial crisis (Sachs and Woo, 2003). With underdeveloped financial markets in an era of large-scale, rapid short-term capital flows, China would be susceptible to a crisis similar to that which plagued Asia in the late 1990s. It further raises the debate surrounding how quickly financial liberalisation should be undertaken. Therefore, we argue in this paper that China's reforms in an era of globalisation must be consistent with its gradualist approach to transition and a slower pace of liberalisation due as well to its developing country status. With China's growing impact on the global economy, however, it is likely that China's economic policies will come under increasing international scrutiny and their external impact will make the process more complex.

The rest of the chapter is organised as follows. The first part of the paper analyses the effects of globalisation on China's economic reforms. We analyse major aspects of external reforms in China related to the pillars of development: trade and financial liberalisation, and privatisation. The Chinese exchange rate regime is presented as the primary example of the argument of the paper. The final section investigates how China's growth in turn affects the global economy. We conclude with a view on how China has been affected by and benefited from globalisation, but also how it has changed the global economy in terms of trade, capital flows, global commodities markets, and influenced global incremental growth.

2. Trade and Financial Liberalisation

China's approach to trade and financial liberalisation has been consistent with its gradual transition approach from a centrally planned to a more market-oriented economy. The "open door" policy which began to open China to international trade and corresponding capital account liberalisation took over 12 years to become more fully implemented from when it began at the end of 1978. In 1982, China accounted for only just over 1% of global markets in manufactured exports, but two decades later, it holds a market share of 6% that rivals the fast growing export-oriented economies of East Asia. Moreover, as a proportion of GDP, exports increased from 15% in 1990 to 30% in 2000, which marks China as one of the most open economies in the world. When imports are added to exports, the proportion of trade to GDP places China well ahead of comparable economies in terms of openness.

A similar argument can be made for foreign direct investment. China has enjoyed an explosive rate of growth of FDI since the "open door" policy geared up in the mid 1980s. Figure 1 shows the amount of FDI in China. These figures are particularly notable in contrast to the early part of the reform period. From 1979 to 1982, China received FDI of only $1.17 billion from just 922 FDI projects. The contrast with the period beginning in 1983 is remarkable. In 1984 alone, the number of FDI projects exceeded the prior period since 1979. The peak in 1992 can be seen clearly in Figure 1. By 2003, FDI reached $53.50 billion.

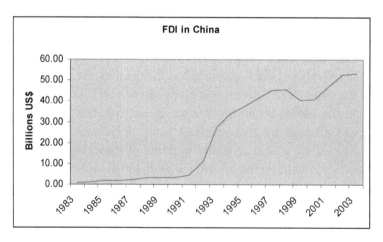

Figure 1. Foreign Direct Investment in China, 1983-2004
Source: *China Statistical Yearbook*, various years.

By this date, China was the leading destination for inward FDI among developing countries, and in addition, was one of the top three destinations for global FDI, often ranking just behind the US.

China undertook trade and financial liberalisation at a pace that suited its general approach to transition, which might be described as a gradual or incremental path of reform (Murphy *et al.*, 1992; Young, 2000). The "dual track" transition (Fan, 1994) is characterised by partially liberalizing some sectors of the economy, while allowing for transfers to fuel the lagging state sector. This approach was found in nearly every aspect of the economy (Lin 1992; Lau *et al.*, 2000). The pace of reform, however, has been gradual.

China undertook trade liberalisation for 15 years before joining the WTO. Liberalisation also induced an accompanying improvement in the overall business climate, which makes China an increasingly attractive location for FDI. China reduced the number of products subject to non-tariff barriers (*i.e.*, quotas and licenses) from an estimated 1,200 in the early 1990s to approximately 200 by the time of accession (Lardy, 1998). The pace of tariff reform has also been rapid following a significant tariff reform in 1997, with rates approximating 20% across all sectors. China is now expected to move toward a regime based on tariffs to ensure that quotas, licenses and designated trading can be phased out. State trade of commodities is still permitted but is subject to WTO rules and China has agreed to reduce the average tariff on manufacturing goods to 6.95% and on agricultural goods to 17%.

Financial liberalisation has seen both reform in the domestic financial sector and increased openness in the capital account. With greater trade liberalisation, it is increasingly difficult to control capital movements and therefore China has also gradually increased the convertibility of limited amounts of currency holdings for households and firms. In other words, China is moving toward a much greater degree of financial liberalisation.

China has seen substantial benefits from both trade and financial liberalisation and accession to the WTO has helped fuel exports, imports, and foreign direct investment. At a time when China reorients its economy towards greater consumption, the increased volume of exports also provided a source of growth. The push for greater consumption to fuel economic expansion is intended to reduce the high saving rate and induce spending. The contribution to GDP of consumption remains less than 50% in China, which is below the levels seen in many of developed economies. Moreover, the inefficiency of investment is another reason to reorient the economy toward consumption. In a dual track transition, having a fast growing sector to support this type of economic reform is beneficial, and trade liberalisation has served this purpose in China. The other major benefit is indeed the improvement in investment climate and the possibility of adopting international best practice, particularly in terms of regulatory standards in China. With an incomplete legal system, these measures are intended to reduce some of the uncertainty associated with investing in China, which in turn can help with the reorientation of investment toward more productive sectors.

However, there are also challenges that have arisen from trade and financial liberalisation. Firstly, there has been the disagreement over the pace of reform and secondly, there has been debate surrounding the nature of the accompanying reform in the domestic economy. The legacy issues surrounding the reform of state-owned enterprises, state-owned banks and the opening of China's domestic markets are complex and intertwined. Challenges are also posed by China's position as a developing country. The progress of reform is driven by an agenda that has to contend with both the impact of transition and the effects of globalisation. For example, China's banking sector, which is already in much need of reform, will shortly be affected by the entry of foreign banks into the sector. Moreover, there are also concerns about the speed and the spread of financial liberalisation. The Asian financial crisis showed how otherwise strongly performing economies can be susceptible to a currency crisis which in turn may be transformed into a full-scale financial crisis and economic downturn. The features of these crises include "thin" financial markets that allow for unregulated lending and vast amounts of short-term capital flows. China was not affected by the Asian financial crises in the late 1990s; however, its increased openness means that it is more susceptible to this form of instability than in the past. Therefore, globalisation, and more specifically trade and financial liberalisation, can benefit China's economic growth, whilst also raising significant concerns. A similar scenario can be seen when we examine the impact of privatisation, the third major aspect of economic development.

3. Privatisation

During the past decade, there has been privatisation on a mass scale of Chinese state owned enterprises (SOEs). During the period from 1996 to 2003, about 60% of industrial SOEs were fully or partially privatised (Garnaut *et al.*, 2005). Globalisation has driven privatisation by increasing competition, bringing in capital, and enhancing domestic human capital (Su, 2004).

The influx of FDI into China intensifies domestic competition on two fronts with international companies entering China either to seek markets inside China or to use China's labour and land resources to produce exports more cost effectively. Either way, these companies compete with domestic firms and as a result, traditionally SOE dominated industries, such as those involved in the production of machinery and heavy equipment, have been penetrated by large multinational companies. This has forced many large SOEs to the verge of bankruptcy. In the past, failing SOEs were frequently rescued by the government using soft bank loans; however, competition from foreign banks has forced domestic banks to adopt more commercially viable policies, which has in turn hardened the budget constraints faced by SOEs, causing many loss-making SOEs to privatise (Guo and Yao, 2005). On the other hand, as China becomes more deeply integrated into the international market, the quality of the exporting firms, many of which are privately run, has also improved. This has resulted in private firms gaining a better competitive position in the domestic market. The emergence of a large private sector, together with the influx of foreign firms, has gradually eroded many government restrictions and regulations that were aimed at protecting the privileges enjoyed by the SOEs. The playing field in the market has been gradually levelled out, revealing that China's privatisation has largely followed its pace of market building (Cao *et al.*, 1999; Guo and Yao, 2005).

Many foreign companies, especially those aimed at tapping into China's domestic markets, form joint ventures with local Chinese firms. In many cases, these joint ventures serve as a catalyst for privatisation. The local partner learns from the foreign partner that private ownership has advantages. Su (2004) provides evidence that SOEs in a joint venture with a foreign firm are more likely to privatise.

Finally, while privatisation has significantly improved firm performance in China (Garnaut *et al.*, 2006; Song and Yao, this volume), there have also been accusations regarding its part in causing massive unemployment in the past decade. In the period between 1995 and 2003, employment in the SOE sector fell from 112.6 million to 68.8 million (Garnaut *et al.*, 2005). However, a careful study by Huang and Yao (2006), using firm level data collected from 11 cities for the period 1995-2001, find that this attribution is not well founded. Both traditional SOEs and privatised SOEs saw a fall in the numbers employed; however, it was evident that privatised SOEs actually shed labour at a slower rate. When controls in the data were made for time trends, firm performance, and financial and employment conditions, it is found that privatised firms make 11% fewer workers unemployed when compared with traditional SOEs.

We do not deny that there are negative aspects associated with privatisation. However, globalisation is an opportunity for China, and also a necessary step for China to take. The challenges from globalisation have brought about gains to the development China's corporate sector, but they have also highlighted the negative aspects of privatisation in a transition context. Judging by the efficiency improvements and slower workforce reduction associated with privatisation, we contend that the overall benefits of privatisation outweigh the costs.

4. Exchange Rate Reform

We now turn to the Chinese exchange rate as an illustration of the complexity of managing domestic reforms while addressing the effects of globalisation.

China implemented a new exchange rate policy in July 2005. On the one hand, China allowed the RMB to appreciate by 2 percent against the US dollar (from 8.27 to 8.11), while; on the other hand, China "resumed" the controlled float foreign exchange regime where the exchange rate is linked to a basket of foreign currencies. The Chinese government implemented these reforms with the aim of ensuring that the RMB exchange rate was no longer controversial within the global arena. However, the success of this reform greatly depends on the external response and the interplay between China's internal needs and the forces of globalisation.

China's aim was to gradually adjust its exchange rate within a narrow range, as it did between 1994 and 1997. The success of this approach depends on whether China can successfully dispel the expectation of RMB appreciation in international financial markets. If China can reduce the speculation on RMB appreciation, and instead establish a long-term controlled exchange rate adjustment in a narrow range that is consistent with its economic fundamentals, then the exchange rate regime reform will be considered successful.

Since 1994, China has maintained a controlled float exchange rate regime. The exchange rate at that time was set at RMB 8.7 per US Dollar. From 1994 to 1997, the exchange rate appreciated by 5 percent to RMB 8.29 against the US Dollar. After the 2005 reform of the exchange rate regime, the question remains as to whether China can continue this kind of gradual approach to exchange rate adjustment, driven by economic fundamentals such as trade, prices and productivity? In order to answer this question, we need to explain why the RMB exchange rate has become a significant issue capable of creating international concern.

There are two different issues here: one relates to the exchange rate regime, and the other is the exchange rate level. In terms of the exchange rate regime, it is thought that the preferred exchange rate system in developing countries is a controlled float, the type of regime that has been implemented in China since 1994. However, during the period of the Asian financial crisis in 1997, most Asian countries and regions faced currency devaluations, and as such international financial markets expected that the RMB would also be devalued. However, China did not devalue the RMB to the floor of the controlled float exchange rate band. After 2000, in contrast, international financial markets expected that the RMB would appreciate. However, the Chinese government again did not act as expected and the exchange rate was fixed to the ceiling of controlled float band. As long as the pressures of speculation on RMB devaluation or revaluation do not exist, the exchange rate should gradually adjust according to economic fundamentals.

China's trade surpluses in recent years can be found in Table 1.

Table 1. China's Trade Surplus in US$ billion, 1996-2004

Year	1996	1997	1998	1999	2000	2001	2002	2003	2004
Trade Surplus	$12.2	$40.4	$43.5	$29.2	$24.2	$22.6	$30.5	$25.5	$31.9

Source: *China Statistical Yearbook*, various years.

Therefore, against the predictions of economic theory, it seems that international capital markets were speculating on RMB depreciation when the Chinese trade surplus was relatively large, and speculating on an appreciation of the RMB when the Chinese trade surplus was comparatively small. If this behaviour was based on an estimated departure from the equilibrium exchange rate value of the RMB, then it can be reasoned that they should have gambled on an appreciation of the RMB in 1997 and 1998, and depreciation in 2000 and 2001. However, the statistics suggest that for the past few years, the pressure of either an RMB appreciation or depreciation is not directly related to departures from the equilibrium exchange rate of the RMB when considered in light of the relative proportion of trade surplus to China's GDP or total volume of trade. However, we would not claim that the recent RMB exchange rate represents the long-run equilibrium exchange rate, but since the trade surplus is a small proportion of GDP, we would estimate that the gap between these rates is not large.

There are several reasons why international financiers speculate on the potential appreciation of the RMB. The external reason is that there is a large amount of "hot money" in the international capital markets. Before the Asian financial crisis, it flowed into East Asia and caused stock market and real estate market bubbles. After the crisis, the "hot money" returned to the U.S. and contributed to the dot.com bubble. After that bubble burst, the excess liquidity needed a new outlet and in recent years, China's economic growth has been so remarkable that it has become attractive to short-term capital flows. Perhaps more importantly, while the US government exerts pressure on a particular country, the exchange rate of this country will likely appreciate greatly within a short period of time, such as Japan during 1985 after the Plaza agreement.

If the current rate of exchange of the RMB is undervalued by between 20% and 30%, China's economy will eventually benefit from large-scale RMB appreciation to help it return to the long-run equilibrium exchange rate. However, if the exchange rate is undervalued between 2% and 5%, then an appreciation beyond this range, as has been demanded in global markets, will not benefit either the US or China. This is because the economic situation in China is quite different from that of Japan in the 1980s. At that time, the level of development of Japan approached that of the US. The appreciation of the Japanese yen reduced the competitiveness of Japanese goods, which benefited industrial development and reduced the trade deficit with the US. However, China's economic structures are currently very different. Chinese per capita national income is $1,600, compared to a per capita income of approximately $36,000 in the US. China's trade surplus with US derives largely from goods that are now produced in China, but had been from other East Asian countries and regions. "Made in China" is not a substitute for "Made in America". If China were to undertake a substantial appreciation of the RMB, the US would either continue to import from China at higher prices, or would import the same goods from other countries, also at higher prices in all probability. Therefore, RMB appreciation would not solve the problem of unemployment in US, but may actually increase the US trade deficit. In fact, after the reform of the RMB exchange rate regime, the value of the US dollar fell and the ten-year US bonds yield rose, suggesting that the devaluation of the RMB was not viewed favourably vis-à-vis the US economy.

Since the speculation on the appreciation of the RMB is not clearly related to economic fundamentals, there would not be such an expectation of a significant RMB appreciation in a short term in global markets, so long as international pressures ease. When there is no longer speculative pressure on the RMB, China would be in a position to resume the controlled float exchange rate regime that was first undertaken in 1994. Using a trade-weighted basket of currencies and allowing the RMB to fluctuate in line with economic fundamentals such as external trade and internal growth, China's exchange rate could be more sensibly reformed. In this way, reforms in China could remain consistent with its transition path; even where global pressures and globalisation in the form of international currency traders pose significant challenges. Balancing the domestic objectives with the international factors is nowhere seen more clearly than in the issue of the Chinese currency.

5. China's Impact on the Global Economy

This final section of the article focuses on the impact of greater openness in China on the global economy. We have covered the interplay between China's economic reforms and the forces of globalisation. China is itself a growing power in the global economy, and we turn to analyse China's impact on international trade, global markets (particularly commodities), international capital flows, and finally its contribution to global incremental growth.

In terms of international trade, in the span of a decade China has become the world's third largest exporter and importer. Perhaps more significantly, China has produced low priced manufactured goods, which in turns lowers import prices for consuming nations around the world. The low inflation, low interest rate environment in many developed countries, particularly in the relatively open economies of the UK and other European countries, is at least partly attributable to the low level of world prices and correspondingly cheap imports. The evidence since WTO accession suggests an additional phenomenon. Since the lifting of a number of import restrictions, the growth rate of imports has exceeded that of exports. Although in 2005, China had a stronger than expected trade surplus of $101.9 billion, there is evidence that imports and their effects on domestic consumption are an increasingly important policy focus. China's growth in imports, split between 80% intermediate goods and 20% consumer goods, has already been felt in the global raw materials and commodities market as well as in the market for food where China recently became a net importer (Zebregs, 2004). With a push toward greater consumption alongside falling trade barriers, imports are likely to continue to grow. China could well become positioned as the consumer market in Asia.

Accordingly, China's impact on several global markets, including, oil, copper, iron ore, aluminium and steel, is considerable. China is a leading consumer of major commodities, behind only the US in its consumption of oil. Although some of the demand is driven by exports, the bulk is attributed to China's continuing industrialisation, particularly notable in its energy demands. During the period of central planning, China's industrialisation concentrated to a large extent on heavy industry. However, the reforms of the past 27 years have been geared at moving into the production of high tech and consumer goods. The transformation of an already industrialised economy is a difficult task; however, China's continuing industrial upgrading and urbanisation with more people leaving the agrarian sector suggest that it will likely continue to affect world markets in raw materials and commodities for some time.

China's influence can also be felt in terms of the capital account. China impressively holds the third largest stock of FDI globally, behind only the US and the UK. Joining the WTO in 2001 has resulted in greater trade and financial liberalisation, which is reflected in China becoming a leading destination for inward FDI in recent years. Another development is China's outward investment. Since the mid 1990s, China has permitted outward FDI. These amounts were small relative to the inflow of FDI. However, since WTO accession, China has increased the amount of overseas investment in both commercial and strategic sectors – China's so-called "going out" policy for its enterprises. Chinese TCL's deal with Thomson in 2003 and Lenovo's purchase of IBM's PC business in 2004 are examples of China's "national champions" policy going global. China has also actively promoted investment in energy sectors, notably oil and natural gas, in countries ranging from Nigeria to Kazakhstan. Both types of outward FDI have affected the global economy, but the investment in energy especially holds geo-political implications. Short-term portfolio flows and the Chinese currency have been discussed earlier, which have certainly had a wide impact.

China's influence extends beyond balance of payments, though. Its fast growing economy has also been a factor in global incremental growth and global economic cycles. Although China accounted for less than 5% of world GDP in 2005, compared to a US share of 28%, its contribution to global incremental growth is substantially greater than its weight in the global economy. Between 1980 and 2000, using measurements calculated on the basis of purchasing power parity (PPP), China's contribution to world economic growth accounted for approximately 14% of the total, second only to the US, which contributed to approximately 20% of global growth. In the past five years, China's contribution to global growth in PPP terms was approximately 30%. When calculated at market exchange rates, its contribution to global growth averaged 13% between 2000 and 2004, rising to 14% in 2005. These figures illustrate why attention is increasingly paid to China as one of the so-called twin engines of growth in the global economy.

The implications extend further to the correlation between China's economic cycle and the global cycle. During the reform period of 1979 to the present, China's economic cycles ranged from peak GDP growth exceeding 14% per annum to lows of around 4% per annum. However, these cycles were not driven by market economy forces, but by the features of a planned economy that included soft budget constraints and decentralisation. Added to this is the fact that, until 2004, China's main trading partners were Japan and other Asian economies. Thus, its economy was more closely aligned with the Asian region than the West.

China's economy was therefore somewhat counter-cyclical to the global slowdown at the start of the 2000s. However, since WTO accession, its economic cycles are increasingly driven by market forces, including those of the global economy. Further, as of 2004, the EU became China's largest trading partner, closely followed by the US and then Japan. China's growing trade with the EU and the US suggests that their economic cycles could become more closely aligned. Coupled with the growing view that the US and China are the twin engines of growth in the global economy, these changes imply that a slowdown in China could well be aligned with a global slowdown.

Doubtless there are numerous other areas where China's economic rise will be felt. We have highlighted the economic interactions based on the balance of payments and also identified the role China plays in the global economic cycle. With China's move toward greater global integration, these effects should become more and not less pronounced. With the influence of globalisation on China's economic path, China's development will undoubtedly become increasingly intertwined with that of the global economy.

6. Conclusions

This article has argued that China's economic reforms are more difficult to manage in an increasingly globalised era. The pace of reform is likely to be challenged, and the adoption of economic reforms will be increasingly scrutinised. However, there are benefits from globalisation.

Increased openness has allowed China to gain from integration into global markets, giving it an external source of growth, which has aided its domestic reform process. While China aims to undertake reforms of domestic investment and increase consumption, exports can help in these aims, as well as providing pro-competitive effects in the economy through making state-owned firms more profit-orientated.

Secondly, increased openness has given China the potential to adopt international best practice in respect to specific legal and regulatory processes, which in turn bolsters investor confidence. With an incomplete legal system, the potential to quickly upgrade the existing commercial institutional framework would be valuable.

However, globalisation also poses substantial risks for China's economic reforms. The pace of increasing openness is a subject of contention, as seen in its trade disputes and the accessibility of China's markets. For China's domestic markets, the presence of foreign companies can stimulate competitiveness but large multinational corporations also carry the potential to dominate markets. Moreover, openness with weak institutional foundations, particularly in the financial markets, makes China susceptible to an externally driven macroeconomic crisis. Liberalisation that is too rapid may be destabilising if sound institutional foundations do not support it.

We then examined the issue of the Chinese exchange rate as an example of the complex nature of reform in an era of globalisation. The difficulty of assessing the value of the equilibrium exchange rate and the political importance of this issue among key trading partners make it a good example of how reforms in China are increasingly challenging to implement. The role of currency traders and expectations in international financial markets increase the challenge facing China; however, it also points to why it is essential for China to undertake exchange rate reform in a manner that is consistent with its domestic transition to a more market-oriented economy.

Having examined the influence of globalisation on China's reforms, we analyse the various ways in which China in turn affects the global economy. China's influence can be felt in terms of international trade, particularly in contributing to low worldwide prices that have helped keep inflation low, especially in the more open economies of Europe. China's demand for imports has also been growing at a faster rate than exports, and this has been especially felt in global commodities markets. China's demand and economic cycle will have a significant impact in a range of markets, affecting these markets already mentioned and those countries that specialise in the production and sale of such goods.

China "going out" strategy is another factor affecting the global economy, as capital begins to flow out of China. The issue of capital account liberalisation in China will become an increasing factor in international capital markets.

Finally, we analysed the extent of China's contribution to global incremental growth and found that China is rapidly becoming one of the two engines of growth in the global economy, alongside the US. The issue of economic cycles, moreover, was raised as China's trade integration moves increasingly west. Together, China's wider impact on the world economy adds a further dimension to the challenge of undertaking economic reforms in the context of globalisation.

In this paper, we have touched on numerous facets of economic reform in China and the phenomenon of globalisation. There are doubtless many others. We hope to have begun exploring this question, which is important not only for China, but can also inform the liberalisation debate for other developing countries. We have also posited several ways in which China will affect the global economy. We expect that so long as the reforms discussed in this paper and in this volume are managed, then China's impact on the global economy and the effect of the globalisation process on China will become not less, but more, significant in the years to come.

References

1. Bai, C., D. Li, Z. Tao and Y. Wang, "A Multitask Theory of Enterprise Reform," *The Journal of Comparative Economics*, 28(4), 716-738, (2000).
2. Cao, Y., Q. Yingyi and B. Weingast, "From Federalism, Chinese Style to Privatisation, Chinese Style," *Economics of Transition*, 7, 103-131, (1999).
3. Fan, G., "Incremental Change and Dual-Tack Transition: Understanding the Case of China," *Economic Policy*, 19(Supp.), 99-122, (1994).
4. Garnaut, R., S. Ligang, T. Stoyan and Y. Yang, *Ownership Transformation in China*, (The World Bank, Washington DC, 2005).
5. Garnaut, R., S. Ligang and Y. Yang, "Impact and Significance of State-Owned Enterprise Restructuring in China," *China Journal*, 55, 35-66, (2006).
6. Guo, K. and Y. Yang, "Causes of Privatisation in China: Testing Several Hypotheses," *Economics of Transition*, 13(2), 211-238, (2005).
7. Huang, L. and Y. Yang, "Impacts of Privatisation on Employment: Evidence from China," CCER Working Paper, (China Center for Economic Research, Beijing University, Beijing, 2006).
8. Lardy, Nicholas R., *China's Unfinished Economic Revolution*, (The Brookings Institution, Washington DC, 1998).
9. Lau, L., Y. Qian and G. Roland, "Reform without Losers: An Interpretation to China's Dual-Track Approach to Transition," *The Journal of Political Economy*, 108(1), 120-143, (2000).
10. Lin, J. Y., "Rural Reforms and Agricultural Growth in China," *The American Economic Review*, 82(1), 422-427, (1992).
11. Murphy, K. M., A. Schleifer and R. W. Vishny, "The Transition to a Market Economy: Pitfalls of Partial Reform," *Quarterly Journal of Economics*, 107(3), 889-906, (1992).
12. Sachs, J. and W.T. Woo, "China's Growth after WTO Membership," *Journal of Chinese Economics and Business Studies*, 1(1), 1-31, (2003).
13. Su, J., "Globalisation and Privatisation: Evidence from China," Chapter 5, Ph.D. thesis, (Department of Economics, Brandeis University, 2004).
14. Young, A., "The Razor's Edge: Distortions and Incremental Reform in the People's Republic of China," *Quarterly Journal of Economics*, 115(4), 1091-1135, (2000).
15. Zebregs, H., "Intraregional Trade in Emerging Asia," IMF Policy Discussion Paper No. PDP/01/1, pp. 1-23, (2004).

INDEX

Printed in the United States
By Bookmasters